FEARLESS
SPEECH

Also by Mary Anne Franks

The Cult of the Constitution

FEARLESS SPEECH

BREAKING FREE FROM
THE FIRST AMENDMENT

MARY ANNE FRANKS

 BOLD TYPE BOOKS

New York

Bold Type Books
Hachette Book Group
1290 Avenue of the Americas, New York, NY 10104
www.boldtypebooks.org
@BoldTypeBooks

Printed in the United States of America
First Edition: October 2024

Published by Bold Type Books, an imprint of Hachette Book Group, Inc. Bold Type Books is a copublishing venture of the Type Media Center and Perseus Books.

The Hachette Speakers Bureau provides a wide range of authors for speaking events. To find out more, go to hachettespeakersbureau.com or email HachetteSpeakers@hbgusa.com.

Bold Type books may be purchased in bulk for business, educational, or promotional use. For more information, please contact your local bookseller or the Hachette Book Group Special Markets Department at special.markets@hbgusa.com.

The publisher is not responsible for websites (or their content) that are not owned by the publisher.

Print book interior design by Amnet Contentsource

Library of Congress Cataloging-in-Publication Data

Names: Franks, Mary Anne, 1977- author.
Title: Fearless speech : breaking free from the First Amendment / Mary Anne Franks.
Description: First edition. | New York : Bold Type Books, 2024. | Includes bibliographical references and index.
Identifiers: LCCN 2024013503 (print) | LCCN 2024013504 (ebook) | ISBN 9781645030539 (hardcover) | ISBN 9781645030553 | ISBN 9781645030553 (ebook)
Subjects: LCSH: Freedom of speech–United States. | Freedom of speech–Political aspects–United States. | United States. Constitution. 1st Amendment.
Classification: LCC KF4772 .F733 2024 (print) | LCC KF4772 (ebook) | DDC 342.7308/53–dc23/eng/20240509
LC record available at https://lccn.loc.gov/2024013503
LC ebook record available at https://lccn.loc.gov/2024013504

ISBNs: 9781645030539 (hardcover), 9781645030553 (ebook)
LSC-C
Printing 1, 2024

For my mother, Kang Tu-Kuei

Here is the time for the *sayable*, *here* is its homeland.
Speak and bear witness. More than ever
the Things that we might experience are vanishing, for
what crowds them out and replaces them is an imageless act.

—Rainer Maria Rilke, *The Ninth Duino Elegy*
(Stephen Mitchell translation)

Contents

Prologue

What are the bravest words you have ever heard? What are the words that have changed your mind, or made you feel something you had never felt before, or imagine something you had never thought was possible? What are the words that are burned in your memory because they are so powerful, so true, so revolutionary?

I could fill every page in this book and many pages more with the extraordinary words I have been fortunate enough to encounter in my life. Some have been spoken by people I see every day, some by people I have never met, some by people who have long since passed from this Earth. The speakers I am most fascinated by are the ones who know that their words put them in peril but who are moved—by love, by justice, by truth—to speak despite the danger.

I will never forget the first time I attempted to recount, in a public lecture, the story of Sophie Scholl and the White Rose student resistance group. In 1943, twenty-one-year-old Scholl was beheaded by the Nazis for distributing pamphlets that exposed Nazi atrocities. When I tried to read Scholl's last words out loud— "Such a fine, sunny day, and I have to go, but what does my death matter, if through us, thousands of people are awakened and stirred to action?"[1]—I suddenly had to stop, overwhelmed by unexpected tears. Even now, having repeated those words many times in many settings, I cannot get all the way through them without having to pause and gather myself. I think her words will always halt and haunt me, and that I will always be struck by their almost unbearable poignancy.

Scholl's is one of many stories told in this book, and these stories are the reason I wrote this book. She and the other speakers highlighted in these pages exemplify what the ancient Greeks called *parrhesia*, a concept often translated as "free speech" but more accurately rendered as "fearless speech." This is not speech for speech's sake, or for self-interest, or performance, or exploitation, but rather speech that seeks to communicate truth no matter what it might cost the speaker. It is speech not as a legalistic or abstract exercise but as a flesh-and-blood practice.

This is a book that takes speech seriously, and as such, it is about speech first and the First Amendment second. The dysfunction of current American free speech discourse can largely be attributed to the inversion of that order. For far too long, the First Amendment has been treated as the measure and the model of expressive freedom, as if the vast potential and the power of speech could be contained within a narrow legal doctrine. But it was not the First Amendment that abolished slavery, or exposed the horrors of lynching, or fought for women's equal rights. Fearless speakers accomplished those things. Most of the time they did it without the shield of the First Amendment, even as their persecutors wielded the First Amendment as a sword.

This book, accordingly, is partly a critique of First Amendment doctrine and how it has stifled and domesticated the possibilities of free speech. Even more importantly, it is an introduction to and a celebration of speakers whose expression has sparked revolutions, protected the vulnerable, and held the powerful accountable— without, despite, or beyond the First Amendment.

FEARLESS
SPEECH

INTRODUCTION

When Free Speech Burned

WHEN THE MAY 21, 1892, EDITION OF THE MEMPHIS-BASED newspaper the *Free Speech* went to press, the paper's owner and editor, Ida B. Wells, had no reason to think that it would be the last. Wells, a black female schoolteacher turned journalist, had seen subscription rates rise as she devoted increasing attention to racial-justice issues and began printing the newspaper on pink paper to set it apart from other publications. For the May 21 edition, Wells penned an editorial that condemned the brutal lynchings of black men by white mobs and attacked the "old thread bare lie that Negro men assault white women."[1] The reason white men were torturing and executing black men was not, Wells wrote, because of the threat black men posed to white women; it was because of the threat they posed to white men's economic and sexual dominance. Wells intimated that black men were becoming successful rivals to white men in business as well as more intimate activities: "If Southern white men are not careful," she warned, "they will over-reach themselves and . . . a conclusion will then be reached which will be very damaging to the moral reputation of their women."[2]

Wells's words were reprinted a few days later in the *Memphis Scimitar*, a white-owned newspaper. The paper, which assumed that the editorial's author was a man, exhorted its readers to "tie the wretch who utters such calumnies to a stake at the intersection of

Main and Madison Streets and brand him in the forehead with a
hot iron and perform upon him a surgical operation with a pair of
tailor's shears."[3] On May 27, a mob of leading white businessmen
responded to this call by seizing Reverend Taylor Nightingale, a
former owner of the *Free Speech* they mistook to be the author of
Wells's piece, pistol-whipping him into denouncing the editorial as
a "slander against white women."[4] After Nightingale disclosed that
Wells was the actual author, the mob threatened to lynch her in
front of the courthouse[5] and burned the offices of the *Free Speech* to
the ground.[6] Wells, who happened to be away from Memphis at
the time, learned that the mob had "destroyed the type and fur-
nishings, and left a note behind saying that anyone attempting to
publish the paper again would be punished by death."[7]

The burning of the *Free Speech* was not an isolated occurrence;
instead, it was emblematic of the fate of fearless speech in America.
Throughout history, speakers who have given voice to racial and
sexual injustice have been mobbed, assaulted, and arrested. From
abolitionists before the Civil War to suffragists at the turn of the
twentieth century to contemporary protesters against racial injustice, the bravest advocates for true democracy have been persecuted
and prosecuted for their speech.

This is the story of not only our past, but our present. Today, in
America, college students protesting against genocide and racism
are being violently arrested, expelled, and evicted from their campuses. Demonstrators against police brutality are tear-gassed,
beaten, struck by vehicles, and thrown in jail. Women who expose
the abuses of powerful men are doxed, threatened, sued, and subjected to vicious harassment campaigns. Journalists reporting on
political misdeeds are vilified, assaulted, and surveilled. History
textbooks are being rewritten to erase the horrors of slavery, while
books that depict gay and lesbian relationships are being purged
from schools and libraries. Words, concepts, and entire disciplinary
fields relating to gender and race are being banished from classrooms. Federal and state officials are attempting to transform universities into factories of government-approved propaganda.
Teachers, school board members, and librarians are being defamed

as predators and threatened with arrest, ruinous litigation, and bodily harm.

How can this be true in America, the land of the First Amendment—that supposedly unassailable guarantor of our country's steadfast and singular dedication to freedom of expression? Are we not the nation whose law of free speech is "the most elaborate, the most doctrinally detailed, and the most speech protective of any nation on Earth, now or throughout history?"[8] Is it not true that "ours is the most outspoken society on Earth" and that "Americans are freer to think what we will and say what we think than any other people?"[9]

Unfettered free speech does indeed exist, but only for some Americans. Today, in America, delusional stalkers have a First Amendment right to terrorize their victims. Pornographers have a First Amendment right to glorify sexual violence for profit. Businesses have a First Amendment right to deny service to gay people and to advertise this fact. Antiabortion zealots have a First Amendment right to mislead pregnant women with fake pregnancy clinics and a First Amendment right to harass women attempting to access actual care. Corporations have a First Amendment right to spend unlimited funds to influence elections. Neo-Nazis have a First Amendment right to march through towns with majority Jewish populations wearing military-style uniforms and swastika armbands. The Ku Klux Klan (KKK) has a First Amendment right to burn crosses and call for violence against black people.

The principle often used to justify these kinds of speech is "freedom for the thought we hate." The implication is that "we" are an enlightened, democratic, liberal society and that misogyny, racism, religious zealotry, and plutocracy are despised minority viewpoints. But this is an inversion of our reality. When the drafters of the Constitution set out the rights of "*we the people*," they meant people like themselves: white, male, Christian, and wealthy.[10] And while great strides have been made over the centuries to transform America's false claim of democracy into a true one, the original ruling class has done everything it can to resist this. The values of white male supremacy and the speech that reinforces them have always received heightened protection in our society. It is speech that *challenges* hierarchies of gender, race, religion, and class—the radically democratic speech of equality and inclusion—that has been despised and violently suppressed throughout American history, up to and including in our present moment.

In the 1830s, abolitionism emerged as one of the first radical speech movements in America. On July 29, 1835, a vigilante group known as the Lynch Men broke into the Charleston, South Carolina, post office to seize abolitionist pamphlets that had been sent out by the Anti-Slavery Society of New York. Thousands of white supremacists gathered in the town square to burn the materials along with the effigies of three abolitionists. Soon after, South Carolina and other Southern states passed laws outlawing abolitionist literature. In 1836, Congress enacted a "gag rule" that immediately tabled petitions relating to slavery without consideration. The postmaster general censored antislavery materials with the approval of President Andrew Jackson, who also called on Congress to pass a law to shut down the "attempts to circulate through the mails inflammatory appeals addressed to the passions of the slaves, in prints and in various sorts of publications, calculated to stimulate them to insurrection and to produce all the horrors of a servile war."[11]

The fate of abolitionist Reverend Elijah Lovejoy in 1837 was a grim example of the drastic measures antiabolitionists were willing to take to suppress prodemocratic speech. Lovejoy had courageously persisted in publishing antislavery sentiments in his newspapers, first in St. Louis and then in Alton, Illinois, despite the destruction of several of his printing presses and repeated threats of violence. On November 2, 1837, responding to demands that he stop publishing his newspaper, Lovejoy eloquently defended his constitutional right to free expression: "I shall hold myself at liberty to speak, to write, and to publish whatever I please on any subject."[12] Five days later, he was shot to death by a proslavery mob.

The outraged response to speakers who endorsed racial equality was particularly intense when they also endorsed gender equality. Prominent leaders in these movements, such as William Lloyd

Garrison and Angelina Grimké Weld, were frequent targets of violent threats. Garrison and Grimké Weld were among the group of abolitionists and suffragists who joined the project to build a forum in Philadelphia "wherein the principles of Liberty, and Equality of Civil Rights, could be freely discussed, and the evils of slavery fearlessly portrayed."[13] The endeavor was praised by luminaries such as former president John Quincy Adams, who expressed his "fervent wishes that the Pennsylvania Hall may fulfil its destination, by demonstrative proof, that freedom of speech in the city of Penn shall no longer be AN ABSTRACTION."[14]

Pennsylvania Hall, heralded as the nation's first "Temple of Free Discussion,"[15] opened to the public on Monday, May 14, 1838. It was a grand edifice featuring a large lecture salon, several meeting rooms, galleries, and a bookstore. The Hall's inaugural events were to include several days of meetings and speeches on topics such as abolition and women's rights. On the same day as the opening of the Hall, Angelina Grimké, one of the featured speakers, married abolitionist Theodore Weld in an unconventional ceremony attended by guests of both races at a house a few blocks away. Two ministers, one black and one white, offered prayers in lieu of an officiant; the couple's spontaneous marriage vows emphasized equality between husband and wife; and the wedding cake was made with "free" (nonslave labor) sugar. Grimké Weld was a famous figure of the time, known for lecturing and writing with her sister, Sarah Grimké, about the evils of slavery and the importance of women's rights. The sisters were members of a Southern slave-owning family and had directly witnessed the brutal treatment of enslaved individuals. Earlier in 1838, Angelina had advocated before a committee of the Massachusetts legislature for the abolition of slavery and for women's right to petition, becoming the first woman in the United States to address a legislative body.

On Tuesday, May 15, rumors spread throughout Philadelphia about the nature of the antislavery speeches being made at the Hall, the mixed-race and mixed-gender audiences, and Grimké's "abolition wedding."[16] Placards appeared around the city urging citizens who "entertain a proper respect for the right of property, and the preservation of the Constitution of the United States," to gather the next day and "interfere, *forcibly* if they *must*, and prevent the violation of these pledges, heretofore held sacred."[17]

The Anti-Slavery Convention of American Women convened at the Hall on Wednesday morning. They discussed, among other issues, whether their meeting that night should take place before an audience of both men and women, which was controversial at the time. In light of objections, it was decided that the event, which would feature speeches by Grimké Weld and other prominent women on the topics of gender and racial equality, would proceed before a mixed-gender crowd, but not as an official meeting of the convention. By the time the session began, an angry mob, incensed by the sight of men and women, black and white, mixing together, had gathered outside the Hall. They were spurred also by erroneous reports that Grimké Weld had married a black man in an "amalgamation wedding."

Despite the mob howling and tossing rocks and bricks at the windows, Grimké Weld spoke calmly and defiantly, spontaneously incorporating the disruption into her remarks by observing that any violence she could suffer at the hands of the mob would pale in comparison to the suffering imposed upon the victims of slavery: "What is a mob? What would the breaking of every window be? What would the levelling of this Hall be? Any evidence that we are wrong, or that slavery is a good and wholesome institution? What if the mob should now burst in upon us, break up our meeting and commit violence upon our persons—would this be any thing compared with what the slaves endure? No, no: and we do not remember them 'as bound with them,' if we shrink in the time of peril, or feel unwilling to sacrifice ourselves, if need be, for their sake."[18]

As the mob continued to strike at the windows and doors, Grimké Weld went on, "There is nothing to be feared from those who would stop our mouths, but they themselves should fear and tremble."[19] Later in her speech, she urged the women of Philadelphia to exercise one of the only political means of communication then allowed to women—sending petitions to Congress—to call for the abolition of slavery. When Quaker abolitionist and women's rights advocate Lucretia Mott adjourned the session, she noted that due to "false notions of delicacy and propriety"[20] regarding the suitability of women speaking before male audiences, the event could not be considered an official meeting of the Anti-Slavery Convention of American Women. Mott expressed her hope that such objections "would not long obtain in this enlightened country" before adjourning the meeting.[21] Exiting the Hall, white women linked arms with black women who had attended the session, and they fought their way together through the jeering crowd.

The next morning, alarmed managers of the Hall sought assistance from the mayor of Philadelphia to provide security for the remaining scheduled events. The mayor demurred, suggesting that he could address the crowd in the evening but offering no further assistance. Angry crowds again assembled during the day, harassing women as they entered and exited the Hall. By Thursday evening, when the mayor arrived, the mob had swelled to the thousands. The mayor urged the Hall managers to cancel the events scheduled for the evening and close the building. The managers agreed, after which the mayor instructed the crowd to disperse. Within a half hour of his departure, the mob broke into the building, smashing windows, looting supplies, destroying books, and finally opening the gas jets of the building. The Hall soon roared into flame, the ignited zinc in its roof creating an unearthly blue haze over the city.[22] The light illuminated the crowds surging through the streets of Franklin Square carrying crowbars, torches, and bricks. The Liberty Bell, inscribed with the words that abolitionists had adopted as their call, "Proclaim Liberty Throughout All the Land Unto All the Inhabitants thereof," could be heard tolling in the dark, unanswered.[23]

Newspaper accounts of the incident, especially in the South, blamed the destruction on the "abominations" of black men mingling with white women: "Such practices, outraging the moral sense of the community, and if continued, tending inevitably to throw society into confusion, and to engender immorality and vice, it could not be expected, that any people, having respect for themselves or affection for their children, would permit to endure."[24]

After the Civil War and the formal abolition of slavery, anxieties and outrage regarding the association of black men and white
women took an even deadlier turn. As Wells detailed in the *Free
Speech*, vigilantes used fabricated accusations of rape of white
women by black men as pretexts to torture and lynch black men. In
Wilmington, North Carolina, a few years after the destruction of
the *Free Speech*, a white mob burned down the building that housed
another black-owned newspaper, the *Daily Record*. The violence
followed the publication of an editorial written by Alexander Manly,
the *Daily Record*'s owner and editor, that, like Wells's, referred to
consensual sexual relations between black men and white women.
Manly's piece was written as a response to a speech by socialite
Rebecca Felton that called for lynching "a thousand times a week if
necessary" to protect white women from supposed black rapists.[25]
Manly barely managed to escape Wilmington alive; other black
residents were not so fortunate. In what would later become known
as the 1898 Wilmington Massacre, white supremacists used Manly's editorial as a pretext to overthrow the city's democratically
elected biracial government, forcibly expel local black leaders, and
murder at least sixty black men, women, and children.

Jackson's appeal for a federal law to purge the mail of antislavery
content had gone unfulfilled in 1835, but in 1873, congressional
concern about sexual content led to the successful enactment of a
law prohibiting the distribution of "obscene, lewd [or] lascivious"
material through the mail, as well as the sale, transmission, and
possession of "obscene" material.[26] The Comstock Act was named
for Anthony Comstock, whose New York Society for the Suppression of Vice was represented by a split image on its seal depicting a
policeman shoving a reprobate into a cell on the left and a man in a
top hat throwing books into a fire on the right. The law did not
provide a definition of *obscenity*, but the majority of the books,
newspapers, magazines, advertisements, and photographs that
were burned or otherwise destroyed pursuant to the statute dealt
with women's rights, sexuality, and reproduction, including many
materials relating to birth control, sex education, and abortion.
More than three thousand individuals were arrested under the

Comstock Act between 1873 and 1915, including birth control advocate Margaret Sanger and suffragist Victoria Woodhull. Comstock boasted that his personal prosecution efforts had driven dozens of individuals to suicide.[27]

After Comstock's death in 1915, the influence of his namesake act began to wane, but another broad governmental restriction of speech soon came into force. The Espionage Act of 1917, expanded by the Sedition Act of 1918, imposed broad prohibitions against interference with military recruitment, operations, and order and forbade "disloyal" or "abusive" speech about the government.[28] Those jailed under the law included activists Charles T. Schenck and Dr. Elizabeth Baer for circulating flyers opposing the draft; socialist Kate Richards O'Hare for giving an antiwar speech; and labor leader Eugene V. Debs for telling his audience that they were "fit for something better than slavery and cannon fodder."[29]

Advocates for women's suffrage faced similar fates. In 1917, suffragist Alice Paul began leading silent protests of white-clad women at the White House six days a week. The women held signs that called for the right of women to vote and included statements such as "We Shall Fight for the Things Which We Have Always Held Nearest Our Hearts—for Democracy, for the Right of Those Who Submit to Authority to Have a Voice in Their Own Governments."[30] The peaceful protesters were frequently and violently attacked by angry men in full view of the police, who not only refused to intervene but arrested men attempting to aid the women. A number of the female picketers were arrested for the crime of "obstructing traffic" and imprisoned for several months at the Occoquan Workhouse in Virginia and the District of Columbia Jail. On November 14, 1917, during what was later referred to as the Night of Terror, those who protested the unsanitary conditions through hunger strikes were force-fed, and several of the women were physically assaulted by Occoquan prison guards.

In the post–World War I period, many states enacted "criminal syndicalism" laws that made it illegal to engage in the advocacy of political or economic changes by "criminal or violent means."[31] These laws were used predominantly against Communists, labor activists, and feminists. In 1919, Charlotte Anita Whitney, a white pacifist, suffragist, and advocate of racial and gender equality, gave a speech to the Women's Civic Center of Oakland. Like Wells before her, Whitney condemned "the economic and political disenfranchisement of African-Americans" and provided horrifying details about "the nation's abhorrent practices of lynching."[32] Whitney concluded her speech with an appeal to patriotism: "Let us then both work and fight to make and keep her right so that the flag that we love may truly wave 'O'er the land of the free / And the home of the brave.'"[33]

Whitney was arrested immediately following her speech and charged with violating California's Criminal Syndicalism Act for allegedly helping to establish the Communist Labor Party of America. Whitney's case generated considerable public sympathy and appeals for her to be pardoned. Whitney herself insisted that she had "done nothing to be pardoned for" and maintained that "if the Governor is disposed to pardon anyone, let him liberate the poor men who are now imprisoned for violation of this same law and whose guilt may be less than mine."[34] Whitney's case, like that of Schenck, Debs, and many other socialists and dissenters, made its way to the Supreme Court. In *Whitney v. California* (1927), her conviction, like theirs, was upheld. The Supreme Court reasoned that Whitney's speech had a "tendency" to cause harm, including by inciting crime, disturbing the peace, and endangering the government.

Throughout the civil rights movement of the 1950s and 1960s, advocates for racial justice were beaten, tortured, and killed, often at the hands of law enforcement. On March 7, 1965, in an attack now known as Bloody Sunday, peaceful protesters in Selma, Alabama, were brutally beaten by white state troopers and sheriff's deputies armed with tear gas, bullwhips, and billy clubs. During the "Freedom Summer" of 1964, a white Mississippi sheriff who belonged to the KKK arrested three civil rights activists—James Chaney, Andrew Goodman, and Michael Schwerner—and handed them over to his fellow Klan members to be executed. In 1968, South Carolina state troopers opened fire on a student protest against racial segregation at South Carolina State University, a historically black college in Orangeburg, killing three and injuring twenty-eight.[35] Two years later, four students were shot and killed at Kent State by the Ohio National Guard during a protest against the Vietnam War; eleven days after that, two more students were killed by police at Jackson State College, a historically black college in Mississippi, during a civil rights protest.[36]

This long legacy of suppression of prodemocratic speech demonstrates that the First Amendment's mythical status as the uncompromising guardian of free expression for all is the product of historical revisionism, selective attention, and limited imagination. What has been protected in the United States above all is not fearless speech in the service of equality but rather reckless speech in the service of racial and gender hierarchy.

Perhaps the most explicit illustration of the Supreme Court's endorsement of reckless speech over fearless speech is the 1969 case *Brandenburg v. Ohio*. In *Brandenburg*, the court drastically narrowed the scope of punishable speech by replacing the "bad tendency" test used to uphold Anita Whitney's conviction in 1927 with a much stricter "imminent lawless action test." The Brandenburg test permits punishment for advocating violence only when speakers *intend* to cause *imminent* violence and only in situations in which such violence is likely to occur.

The Brandenburg test is typically hailed as a great leap forward in progressive free speech doctrine, and because it overturned the court's decision in *Whitney*, it is also often treated as a vindication of Whitney. This impression is bolstered by the fact that the *Brandenburg* court seemed to embrace the logic of Justice Louis Brandeis's famous concurring opinion in *Whitney*: "Fear of serious injury cannot alone justify suppression of free speech and assembly."[37] But Clarence Brandenburg was no Anita Whitney, and the fact that the court chose to vindicate his free speech rights and not hers is neither a coincidence nor the outcome of a progressive evolution in the court's thinking.

Brandenburg was, if anything, the inverse of Whitney. He was a KKK leader who, in June 1964, invited a local reporter to come with a cameraman to a KKK rally he was going to hold on his farm.

The camera was rolling as Brandenburg addressed a crowd of hooded figures wearing full Klan regalia: "This is an organizers' meeting. . . . We're not a revengent [*sic*] organization, but if our President, our Congress, our Supreme Court, continues to suppress the white, Caucasian race, it's possible that there might have to be some revengeance [*sic*] taken."[38] The local news channel that broadcast Brandenburg's speech also included footage of the Klansmen, some of them visibly armed, marching around a burning cross and chanting racial slurs and phrases such as "Freedom for the Whites" and "Bury the n———rs."[39] In footage from another of Brandenburg's speeches, he states, "Personally, I believe the n———r should be returned to Africa, the Jew returned to Israel."[40] Portions of the footage were also broadcast on a national network.

Brandenburg was convicted under a law very similar to the California law used against Whitney. The Ohio Criminal Syndicalism statute made it illegal to advocate "crime, sabotage, violence, or unlawful methods of terrorism as a means of accomplishing industrial or political reform."[41] The Supreme Court, which had forty years earlier upheld the conviction of a female pacifist who condemned the lynching of black men, overturned the conviction of a KKK leader who encouraged white people to take "revengeance" against black people. This result did not vindicate Whitney, and this is not simply because Whitney's speech was antiracist and Brandenburg's was racist. It is because Whitney's speech did not call for violence against anyone, imminently or otherwise, in stark contrast to Brandenburg's. It is also because Whitney spoke on behalf of a cause and as a member of a group that had historically been violently silenced and suppressed, whereas Brandenburg endorsed and encouraged the powerful group that has historically perpetrated that suppression.

The difference between Whitney and Brandenburg illustrates the difference between fearless speech (parrhesia) and reckless speech. Fearless speakers like Whitney criticize the abuses of the powerful, risking harm to themselves in doing so; reckless speakers like Brandenburg attack vulnerable groups, creating a risk of harm to others.

For decades now, free speech in the American imagination has been defined by reckless speakers like Brandenburg. While the First Amendment in theory is neutral with regard to the subject matter of the speech it protects, in practice, it has been deployed most visibly and effectively in the service of powerful antidemocratic interests: misogyny, racism, religious fundamentalism, and corporate self-interest. Thanks in large part to the internet, this simplistic and reductionist promotion of reckless speech has also taken hold around the world. The convergence of civil and economic libertarianism has been a boon to the American-dominated tech industry, which sells the promise of free speech to billions of people around the world in order to surveil, exploit, and manipulate them for profit.

But it does not have to be this way. The First Amendment, like any law, is subject to interpretation, and as such, it can always be interpreted differently. Indeed, it has been interpreted so inconsistently over time that the doctrine has become almost unintelligible. This incoherence is both an indictment of the law and an invitation to improve upon it. It reveals that the doctrine is malleable enough to be molded in ways that advance the interests of democracy and limit the features that have undermined it.

One of the most valuable concepts in First Amendment doctrine is the right against compelled speech. In *West Virginia State Board of Education v. Barnette* (1943), the Supreme Court held that a public school could not punish students who refused to recite the Pledge of Allegiance. Justice Robert Jackson, writing for the majority, acknowledged that the government may have a legitimate desire to instill patriotism and national pride in its youth. But the attempt to compel such feelings is both futile and a violation of individual liberty. "If there is any fixed star in our constitutional constellation," he wrote, "it is that no official, high or petty, can prescribe what shall be orthodox in politics, nationalism, religion, or other matters of opinion or force citizens to confess by word or act their faith therein."[42] Compelled speech undermines all three of the primary values that freedom of speech is intended to vindicate: autonomy, truth, and democracy. Forcing private individuals to support

views or to associate themselves with ideas they find objectionable
infringes upon personal autonomy, distorts the truth and thus the
marketplace of ideas, and inhibits individuals' ability to participate
in democratic deliberation.

Another durable insight of First Amendment doctrine is that
offensiveness alone is not a sufficient justification for prohibiting
speech. In the 1971 case *Cohen v. California*, the court reversed the
conviction of a man who had been charged with disturbing the
peace for wearing a jacket displaying the words "Fuck the Draft"
inside a courthouse. The court rejected the argument that speech
could permissibly be restricted on the basis of its "offensiveness."
Among the court's reasons was the inherent indeterminacy of the
concept of offensiveness; as the court put it, "one man's vulgarity is
another's lyric."[43]

A third democracy-enhancing principle of First Amendment
doctrine is one that the court unfortunately tends to apply inconsistently and to disavow altogether when convenient: that speech can
and should be regulated when its harms outweigh its benefits. In
New York v. Ferber (1982), the court determined that child pornography is not entitled to First Amendment protection, finding that
whatever value such material provides is outweighed by the harms
it produces: the injury to the children depicted and the creation of
further demand for such material. But in striking down a law that
banned depictions of cruelty to animals in *US v. Stevens* (2010), the
court inexplicably denied that it ever engages in harm-benefit balancing in free speech analysis. The court claimed it relied instead
on history and tradition to determine which categories of speech
fall outside of full First Amendment protection. But the very existence of those unprotected or less protected categories, including
obscenity, defamation, fighting words, fraud, and true threats, cannot be explained without reference to harm-benefit analysis. While
defining and calculating the harms of speech in relation to its benefits is a complex and contested endeavor, the court's own rulings
demonstrate that it is neither impossible nor avoidable.

But while it is possible and important to make democracy-
enhancing improvements to First Amendment doctrine, this is only

part of the solution to our free speech dysfunction. Widespread misconceptions about what the First Amendment actually requires, combined with the widespread belief that the First Amendment should be the model for all free speech interactions, have constrained our ability to think broadly, creatively, and courageously about speech. It is imperative that we free ourselves from the stranglehold that the law has on our culture and our imagination.

The first step is being clear about what the First Amendment's free speech clause actually does. Like the rest of the Bill of Rights, the First Amendment protects individual rights from government infringement. Broadly speaking, it restrains the power of the government—and only of the government, a limitation known as the state action doctrine—to punish, prohibit, or regulate speech. Stated simply, the First Amendment means that the government cannot prohibit speech simply because it doesn't like it. This constraint is essential to the operation of democracy, because the government has tremendous power over private individuals, including the power to imprison or execute them. Allowing government officials to wield this asymmetrical power to silence or chill speakers they do not like would make democratic accountability impossible.

The next step is being clear about what the First Amendment does *not* do. First, it does not prevent all government restrictions of speech. The government is allowed to impose neutral regulations on speech, often referred to as "time, place, and manner" restrictions, as long as these regulations do not discriminate on the basis of viewpoint. An example would be requiring permits to hold parades and limiting when and where they can take place. The government is also sometimes allowed to prohibit or punish speech on the basis of content or viewpoint if there are compelling reasons for it to do so. An example would be criminal prohibitions against true threats. And finally, speech that is protected in some contexts may be prohibited in others. For example, the expression of racist views may be protected free speech in a public park but impermissible discrimination in the workplace.

Equally important, the First Amendment does not give private individuals free speech rights over other private individuals. When the government refuses to let private citizens speak simply because it doesn't like what they might say, this is censorship that violates their First Amendment rights. But when private citizens decline to listen to other private citizens, that is a personal choice that constitutes an exercise of their First Amendment rights. Talking to strangers can be pleasant, but it is not a duty. No one is obligated to respond to an unsolicited phone call or engage with a catcaller. Newspapers are not obligated to print every letter to the editor they receive. Book publishers aren't obligated to publish every manuscript sent to their offices. Universities don't have to hire everyone who applies for a job. Social media companies don't have to let spammers use their platforms. And none of these private entities are obligated to explain, to anyone, why they have chosen to engage with some speech and not others. We all have the right to develop our own standards and preferences about what speech we find valuable and to decide for ourselves what we want to hear, promote, ignore, or encourage.

But instead of emphasizing and celebrating the distinction between the speech *obligations* of the government on the one hand and the speech *freedoms* of private citizens on the other, contemporary civil libertarian discourse attempts to collapse it. According to the prevailing free speech orthodoxy, it is not only the government that should refrain from restricting harmful speech but private entities as well. Individuals, universities, and social media platforms are encouraged to emulate the First Amendment to the greatest extent possible, in particular by imposing government-like constraints on themselves regarding what speech they are allowed to reject or ignore. The designation of "speech protected by the First Amendment" is treated as though it were inherently valuable rather than a mere confirmation of lawfulness. And so free speech discourse in America is dominated by a legalistic, reactionary, and consumerist "more speech is better speech" model that promotes reckless speech above all.

Much of what is written about the American tradition of free speech tends to validate the widespread American belief that the United States is the best of all possible worlds when it comes to free expression. The harmful consequences of speech, when acknowledged at all, are often characterized as regrettable but necessary for the greater good—indeed, as proof of the doctrine's virtue and, by extension, that of its defenders.

This book offers a different and bolder perspective on free speech that takes power, harm, and history seriously. In place of abstract platitudes about the virtue or necessity of defending "controversial" or "unpopular" speech above all, the view of free speech presented in this book calls for rigorous investigation into the material facts and circumstances surrounding the speaker, the speech, and the impact on other people. This book emphasizes the distinction between what speech a democratic society should *protect* (a primarily legal question about the proper application of the First Amendment) and what speech a democratic society should *promote* (a broader question of what speech deserves attention and respect). It begins with an exploration of how existing First Amendment norms have consistently exalted and elevated reckless speech that benefits the powerful at the expense of the vulnerable. This exploration peels back the rhetoric of free speech to expose how it has perpetuated and maintained a neo-Confederate ideology of white male supremacy. Aided by a broken view of the First Amendment, this ideology has justified the subjugation of racial and religious minorities through intimidation and violence. It has provided refuge for all manner of misogynist abuse and exploitation. It has given cover to the censorship and the suppression of ideas. And it has ushered in an online dystopia where feckless tech platforms act with legal impunity.

This book then moves beyond the tired canon of Nazis and misogynists that typify reckless speech to develop a full-fledged notion of fearless speech that society should promote. In doing so, I offer a counternarrative that focuses on subversive, inspiring, and courageous speakers who have rarely been acknowledged as the exemplars of free speech that they are. They include an enslaved black woman who secured her own freedom, a journalist who challenged a rising American Nazi movement, a newspaper publisher who aided the cause of desegregation, a ferocious advocate for women's reproductive freedom, a groundbreaking feminist leader of state, a television journalist who broadcast unspeakable truths to an authoritarian government, and a young victim of gun violence who led a nationwide crusade for reform.

Their stories show us that there is no reason to allow reckless speech to define the boundaries of our law or our imagination when it comes to free speech. Throughout history and to the present day, extraordinary and inspiring speakers have risked their safety, their reputations, and in some cases their lives to call out injustice and hold the powerful accountable. Most of them were never plaintiffs in famous First Amendment cases, championed by the American Civil Liberties Union (ACLU), or lionized in Hollywood films. But their stories—and their speech—can enlarge our understanding and appreciation of the gift of speech and its role in the unfinished project of equality.

1

Burning Crosses

THE FOLLOWING PASSAGE IS AN EXCERPT FROM A 1916 PAMPHLET titled *The Rise and Fall of Free Speech in America*: "The right of free speech has cost centuries upon centuries of untold sufferings and agonies; it has cost rivers of blood; it has taken as its toll uncounted fields littered with the carcasses of human beings—all this that there might come to live and survive that wonderful thing, the power of free speech. In our country it has taken some of the best blood of our forefathers. The Revolution itself was a fight in this direction—for the God-given, beautiful idea of free speech."[1]

According to the pamphlet's author, the bloody and beautiful idea of free speech flourished almost without restriction throughout most of America's history. All this changed, however, with the invention of the motion picture, when moralistic panic about the impact of the new medium was "seized by the powers of intolerance as an excuse for an assault on our liberties."[2] Now, the author warns, the "pigmy child" of censorship has become "a giant whose forces of evil are so strong that he threatens that priceless heritage of our nation—freedom of expression."[3]

The pamphlet was written by D. W. Griffith, the son of a Confederate colonel and the director of the 1915 film *Birth of a Nation*. The film is notorious for its depiction of black men (played by white actors in blackface) as buffoonish thugs and sexually violent predators, Confederate soldiers and slave owners as noble victims, and the KKK as heroic defenders of social order and white womanhood. *Birth of a Nation* was a huge commercial success, playing to sold-out audiences in multiple cities and selected by President Woodrow Wilson as the first movie to be screened at the White House.

The film was also the subject of tremendous controversy and criticism. The play upon which it was based, Thomas Dixon Jr.'s *The Clansman*, had premiered in 1905, and performances were frequently followed by episodes of intense racial violence. One such uprising, the 1906 Atlanta Race Massacre, left dozens of black men dead and gutted black-owned businesses in the city. The newly formed National Association for the Advancement of Colored People (NAACP) feared that the film would similarly inflame racial prejudice and trigger violence. They pleaded with local censorship boards to prohibit *Birth of a Nation* from being shown in public. Perhaps unsurprisingly, these appeals to the white-dominated film review boards were largely unsuccessful. The NAACP also organized protests, boycotts, and public criticism of the film and sought to have it banned on public safety grounds.

Griffith wrote *The Rise and Fall of Free Speech in America* in direct response to the efforts of civil rights activists to censor his film. His impassioned defense of free speech and condemnation of censorship were thus colored by, and perhaps even entirely motivated by, self-interest: Griffith had both financial and ideological reasons for wanting *Birth of a Nation* and its glorification of white supremacy to reach as wide an audience as possible. The pamphlet characterizes his film as a work of courageous truth-telling attacked by ignorant groups merely because they "feel offended" by it and seek to "to foist their individual whims, hobbies, or prejudices on the suffering public."[4] Griffith's description of censorship as a "malignant pygmy" that has grown into a giant "caliban" (the brutish character in Shakespeare's *The Tempest* who is enslaved by Prospero after he attempts to rape Prospero's daughter) menacing the pure and beautiful heritage of American free speech is reminiscent of the center-piece scene of *Birth of a Nation*, when the formerly enslaved Gus pursues a young white woman until she leaps to her death to escape him.[5] Griffith declares that "so long as censorship holds the motion picture under its thumb, it is in every way enslaved,"[6] a grotesque choice of words in light of the film's presentation of actual slavery as a genteel and mutually beneficial institution.

But there were others who criticized the attempts to censor *Birth of a Nation* even though they found the film repugnant and dangerous. Some of these critics focused on the unintended consequences of censorship: in the short term, as a practical matter, censorship may backfire by inadvertently increasing the visibility and influence of the expression being censored as well as by making martyrs of hateful speakers.

An even more serious concern, in the civil libertarian view, was the danger that government censorship on behalf of one group today would be used against that group and others in the future. In a letter to the NAACP, ACLU cofounder Roger Baldwin warned that "if an anti-Negro film could be so suppressed a pro-Negro one . . . can also be so suppressed."[7] In Baldwin's opinion, laws designed to protect a minority group "always stir up more prejudice than they prevent."[8] "We earnestly urge our Negro friends," Baldwin wrote, "to confine themselves" to measures such as "boycott, picketing, demonstration, [and] letters of protest to motion picture proprietors" rather than seeking government intervention that "creates bad legal precedents that can be turned as easily against Negroes as for them."[9]

It was on these grounds that the ACLU opposed a 1939 ordinance that allowed films to be censored for encouraging "race prejudice," arguing that such a law "will work against films favourable to Negroes, opposed by the other side."[10] Some commentators maintain that this was precisely the fate of *Within Our Gates*, a 1920 film by black director Oscar Micheaux that exposed the brutality of the KKK and lynch mobs. The film "was banned in several places for the same reasons as *Birth*: It could incite racial tension. Thus the weapons taken up against a racist film were turned on an anti-racist one."[11]

While the "bad precedent" theory is superficially compelling, it falls apart on scrutiny. One of its fundamental flaws is that it reduces complex speech conflicts to simplistic matters of taste or morality. If *Birth of a Nation* is just "speech that black people don't like," then it is easy to claim that restricting it will lead to restricting "speech black people do like," such as *Within Our Gates*. But the NAACP's campaign against *Birth of a Nation* did not stem from mere aesthetic or moralistic objections; it was based on well-grounded fears of racialized violence and discrimination. The NAACP's national secretary, May Childs Nerney, warned that if the film "goes unchallenged it will take years to overcome the harm it is doing. . . . The entire country will acquiesce in the Southern program of segregation, disenfranchisement and lynching."[12]

History has proved Nerney correct. As the NAACP had feared, violence erupted around screenings of *Birth of a Nation*. Lynchings and riots increased in cities where the movie was shown, including in Lafayette, Indiana, where a white man shot and killed a fifteen-year-old black boy upon leaving the movie theater. The film also contributed to the resurgence of the KKK. *Birth of a Nation* portrayed the Klan as a heroic organization and supplied them with dramatic new iconography, including white hooded robes and burning crosses, neither of which was associated with the original Klan.[13] Counties that screened the film were 60 percent more likely to be home to a branch of the KKK by 1930, and the film's romanticization of the group boosted recruitment for decades.[14] The film's violent, paranoid fantasies of a world under the heel of predatory black men and craven intellectuals have been replicated in books like the *Turner Diaries* and on white supremacist websites, inspiring mass murderers from Timothy McVeigh to Dylann Roof. Roof's explanation of why he shot nine African American parishioners to death after they welcomed him into their church is an eerie echo of *Birth of a Nation*'s storyline: "Well I had to do it because somebody had to do something because, you know, black people are killing white people every day on the streets, and they rape white women, 100 white women a day. . . . The fact of the matter is what I did is so minuscule to what they're doing to white people every day, all the time."[15]

In addition to conflating harmfulness with offensiveness, the "bad precedent" theory is also often a form of historical gaslighting.

To speak of *creating* a bad precedent implies that precedent, up until this point, has not been bad. The warning that censoring anti-black speech today will lead to censorship of pro-black speech in the future tacitly asserts that this repression has not happened yet.

But the censorship of black people's speech was already firmly in place by 1915. The ACLU's patronizing warning to the NAACP about the harms of censorship would have been better directed at the white people who had created censorship review boards and enacted censorship ordinances years before the NAACP began its protest of *Birth of a Nation*. These forces had already made clear that they would not hesitate to ban "films favourable to Negroes."

On July 4, 1910, in one of the most anticipated events in sports history, Jack Johnson, the first black world heavyweight champion of boxing, faced off against James J. Jeffries, the white, previously undefeated world heavyweight champion. The fight was years in the making. Johnson had begun demanding that Jeffries face him in the ring in 1904, but Jeffries had persistently refused on racial grounds: "I don't think the public wants me to defend my title against any one but a white man. Don't think I am afraid of a negro. I'm not. They can be licked just as easily as anybody else. I simply have promised myself that I would fight only white men, and I won't break my word."[16] Sticking to that vow, Jeffries retired when there were no more white men left for him to fight. But after Johnson knocked out the white fighter who had succeeded Jeffries as champion—becoming the first black world heavyweight champion in a match that prompted writer Jack London to declare that "Jack Johnson proved that in the ring he was the master of the white man"—Jeffries came out of retirement to try to reclaim the title.[17]

The match was dubbed the Fight of the Century. More than eighteen thousand people crowded into the Reno stadium that had been built specifically for the fight. Cameras had been set up to film the match so that copies could be distributed and viewed around the country. Press attention leading up to the event was intense and racially charged. A *New York Times* editorial expressed a common sentiment: "If the black man wins, thousands and thousands of his ignorant brothers will misinterpret his victory as justifying claims to much more than physical equality with their white neighbors."[18] Or, as Jeffries put it: "I am going into this fight for the sole purpose of proving that a white man is better than a Negro."[19]

But Jeffries wasn't able to deliver. Johnson brought Jeffries down in the fifteenth round, defeating the "Great White Hope." Immediately, numerous city officials around the country announced plans to prohibit the film of the fight from being shown. Within a few days, "at least nine states and forty-one towns banned prizefight films or were about to adopt such censorship laws to prevent the exhibition of the Johnson-Jeffries Fight Film."[20] The outcry was still going strong in 1912, when Congress passed the Sims Act, banning the distribution of prizefighting films across state lines.[21] The law was not repealed until 1940.[22]

When black civil rights leaders protested against *Birth of a Nation* in 1915, they sometimes directly referenced the censorship of the Johnson-Jeffries fight film. For example, in an open letter to the Denver community requesting that the film not be shown there, the activists appealed to the sensibilities of white citizens by reminding them of their objection to "the Jack Johnson prize fight pictures," which "will interpret our feelings on this occasion to you."[23] Of course, the two situations were not actually symmetrical. The fight film was a recording of an actual historical event, one that white audiences had been eager to see as long as they believed that it would demonstrate white athletic superiority. The sole basis for repressing it was wounded racial pride. By contrast, *Birth of a Nation* was a work of fiction that deliberately distorted historical events to justify and glorify white supremacy and violence against black people. As one commentator astutely noted, the activists' appeal "strategically suppressed the significant differences between the censorship of fight films featuring the boxer Jack Johnson and *The Birth of a Nation* in order to position African Americans' protest as an appeal for equal treatment, not special treatment."[24]

This history highlights the absurdity of the claim that the civil rights campaign against *Birth of a Nation* paved the way for the censorship of pro-black films. The white ruling elite were not holding back from censorship prior to the rise of civil rights advocacy in 1915: white government officials had already created film censorship boards; an all-white, all-male Supreme Court had already ruled that motion pictures were not protected by the First Amendment;[25] and white authorities had already literally censored a factual documentary record of black athletic excellence. It is delusional to think that antiracist movies like *Within Our Gates* would have been safe from suppression if not for the NAACP's largely unsuccessful attempt to ban *Birth of a Nation*.

Griffith's fiery 1916 pamphlet denouncing film censorship makes no mention of the banning of the Johnson-Jeffries fight film, despite it being perhaps the most notorious, high-profile case of film censorship of the time. Griffith was surely aware of Johnson, a flamboyant character who boldly flouted racial norms and social conventions. Johnson's multiple marriages, most of them to white women, caused significant scandal, especially after his first white wife committed suicide. He was charged for violating the Mann Act in 1912 after traveling with a white woman across state lines; his later marriage to that woman prompted a Georgia congressman—one of the sponsors of the Sims Act—to draft federal legislation banning interracial marriage.[26] Some film scholars have suggested that Griffith was so outraged by Johnson's famous exploits that he modified the portrayal of Gus, the large, imposing black man who pursues the pure, innocent, white woman through the woods, to evoke the famous boxer.

The repression of the Johnson-Jeffries fight film is only one of the many acts of censorship pointedly overlooked in Griffith's celebration of free speech in America. Griffith also fails to mention the Comstock Act of 1873, that sweeping and notorious censorship law prohibiting the distribution of "obscene," "immoral," and "indecent" material through the mail and the possession, sale, or circulation of "obscene" materials. Nor does he acknowledge the banning of abolitionist literature by Southern states prior to the Civil War, or Congress's "gag rule" on antislavery petitions in 1836, or the destruction of printing presses, threats to newspaper editors, and lynching of advocates of racial equality by white mobs. Also

absent from Griffith's rosy picture of free speech in pre-motion picture America is the long-standing denial of the most basic expressive
rights, including the right to vote, to women and nonwhite men.

Accordingly, when Griffith claims that there were virtually no
restrictions on free speech between the founding of America and
the motion picture era, he can only be talking about free speech for
white men. As detailed in the Introduction, women and nonwhite
men who attempted to lay claim to the right of free speech were
met with mob violence, legal suppression, or both. It is only by
erasing the long history of censorship of women and nonwhite men
that Griffith can paint a picture of a free speech paradise suddenly
in danger of being despoiled by censors. That Griffith should pro-
pound such a selective, self-serving, victim-claiming[27] reading of
history is hardly surprising: it is the same tactic he used to popular-
ize neo-Confederate Lost Cause mythology in *Birth of a Nation*.

The civil libertarian "bad precedent" theory of censorship similarly relies on a depoliticized, ahistorical account of reality that erases
acts of oppression by powerful groups in the past and assigns a false
power to vulnerable groups in the present. Whether expressed to
discourage subordinated groups from attempting to limit the power
of oppressive groups or to reassure the same groups that such restraint
will keep them safe, this theory at best creates a false equivalence
between asymmetrical parties and at worst inverts the relationship
of perpetrators and victims entirely. As such, it perfectly converges
with the neo-Confederate agenda to co-opt free speech for violent,
antidemocratic purposes.

For almost as long as white supremacists have promoted themselves as the brave defenders of the First Amendment and free
speech, groups like the ACLU, which calls itself the "largest and
oldest civil liberties organization" in the United States, have aided
them. After successfully arguing on behalf of Brandenburg that
marching around a burning cross in KKK regalia while calling for
"revengeance" against black and Jewish people was protected by the
First Amendment in 1969, the ACLU helped establish that neo-
Nazis have a First Amendment right to terrorize a town full of
Holocaust survivors in 1976. That year, the National Socialist Party

of America (NSPA) announced its intention to march through the town of Skokie, Illinois, wearing Nazi-style uniforms, displaying banners featuring swastikas, and carrying placards reading "Free Speech for the White Man."[28] Members distributed pamphlets and harassed Skokie residents with Jewish-sounding names with telephone calls about the march. At the time, more than half of Skokie's population was Jewish, thousands of whom were Holocaust survivors. The town of Skokie passed a series of ordinances to prevent the march from taking place. But in what is widely considered to be a high watermark of First Amendment free speech case law, the ACLU successfully argued on behalf of NSPA that the march was an exercise of free speech and thus protected by the First Amendment.

In striking down Skokie's efforts to prevent the neo-Nazis from wearing swastika armbands during the march, the Illinois Supreme Court analogized the issue presented to that of the famous 1971 Supreme Court case *Cohen v. California*, discussed briefly in the Introduction. In reversing the conviction of a man who had been charged with disturbing the peace for wearing a jacket displaying the words "Fuck the Draft" inside a courthouse, the court rejected the argument that speech could be restricted on the basis of its "offensiveness."[29] It was just as impermissible, according to the Illinois Supreme Court, to prohibit the display of swastikas in public demonstrations as it was to punish Cohen for the "four-letter word" on his jacket. To make its point, the Illinois court rewrote a key passage of the *Cohen* decision focused on the profane word, supplementing it with the word *emblem*: "How is one to distinguish this [the swastika] from any other offensive word (emblem)? . . . While the particular four-letter word (emblem) being litigated here is perhaps more distasteful than most others of its genre, it is nevertheless often true that one man's vulgarity is another's lyric. Indeed, we think it is largely because governmental officials cannot make principled distinctions in this area that the Constitution leaves matters of taste and style so largely to the individual."[30] Though the court claimed it was simply following the holding of *Cohen*, the two cases differed in significant ways. The "offensive word" in *Cohen* was a single profanity on one man's jacket. The "emblem" that Frank Collin, NSPA's leader, and his neo-Nazi confederates wanted to wear on their military-style uniforms was the swastika, the most immediately recognizable symbol of the Holocaust. And while Cohen's speech was not addressed to any particular individual or group, Collin specifically targeted the town of Skokie because of its Jewish population. As one expert testified in the Skokie case, "The words of any Nazi to any Jew have, by definition, lost the usual intent and limitation of words: they are symbolic continuations of the Holocaust, literal perpetuations of the climate of the Holocaust, and preparations for a new Holocaust. No matter what words their placards bear, when Nazis march in Skokie, their presence and their regalia say to Jews: 'You thought you escaped. You did not. We know where you are. When our strength is sufficient and when the time is ripe, we will come and get you.'"[31]

In the Illinois Supreme Court's view, a profane political statement on a jacket and an organized attempt to terrorize the targets of a genocide were both simply "matters of taste and style." In essence, the court found that "offense" and "injury" were the same for the purposes of the First Amendment. But this conflation of offense and injury is profoundly depoliticizing and ahistorical. A lone citizen criticizing an official governmental policy is a classic example of speaking truth to power. The greatest harm the act could inflict is to offend bystanders particularly sensitive to profanity or to criticism of the government. An organization dedicated to white supremacy engaging in a show of force against a vulnerable minority—invoking a genocide that many of them had barely escaped—is the very antithesis of speaking truth to power.

But civil libertarianism tends to flatten these distinctions; profanity, swastikas, sit-ins, burning crosses, pacifism, and Confederate flags are all swept up together. Indeed, in the civil libertarian view, the more repulsive the expression, the *more* protection it deserves. This claim relies not just on "bad precedent" theory ("censoring Nazis today means censoring Jews tomorrow") but also on the specious "speech we hate" defense.

In explaining why it often defends "controversial and unpopular entities" such as neo-Nazis and the KKK, the ACLU emphasizes that it is not "because we agree with them; rather, we defend their right to free expression and free assembly. Historically, the people whose opinions are the most controversial or extreme are the people whose rights are most often threatened. Once the government has the power to violate one person's rights, it can use that power against everyone. . . . We subscribe to the principle that if the rights of society's most vulnerable members are denied, everybody's rights are imperiled."[32] The rhetorical slippage of what and who is being defended—from "unpopular entities" to "controversial or extreme" opinions to "threatened rights" to "society's most vulnerable members"—in this passage is noteworthy. It is a skillful sleight of hand: *unpopular entities* with *controversial and extreme opinions* are *vulnerable people* whose *rights are threatened.* But "popularity" and "controversy" are highly subjective concepts, and being unpopular is not the same as being vulnerable, and being disliked is not the same as being threatened. Given that racial and sexual bigotry is foundational to American identity, it is simply not the case that neo-Nazis, KKK members, and pornographers are universally "unpopular" or "disliked." Racism and misogyny have never been anything less than firmly mainstream in America. While individual purveyors of white male supremacy may not always be openly embraced by society, the ideology emphatically is.

Reflecting in April 2017 on the significance of the ACLU's defense of the Skokie neo-Nazis, Aryeh Neier, the ACLU executive director at the time of the litigation, stated that "in a country where free speech generally prevails, it is best to take hate speech in stride. Ignoring it sometimes works, as does overwhelming it with the peaceful expression of contrary views."[33] The Skokie march never took place; it was called off for unexplained reasons by Collin. But only a few months after Neier's 2017 remarks, the ACLU again fought successfully for the right of white supremacists to hold a demonstration, this time in Charlottesville, Virginia. Unlike the Skokie march, the Unite the Right rally did take place, and it was neither ignored nor overwhelmed by the peaceful expression of opposing views.

The protest began as an objection to Charlottesville's removal of a statue of Robert E. Lee and the renaming of Lee Park as Emancipation Park. A push to remove Confederate statues from public spaces had begun in the wake of Roof's 2015 racist massacre in South Carolina, although only eight statues out of approximately seven hundred had been removed by 2017. Critics of the removals claimed that they constituted a form of censorship and an erasure of history. Those advocating for removals pointed out that these monuments were never intended to be neutral commemorations of Civil War history but were erected as acts of racial intimidation. "The political will that enabled these monuments to be placed in front of courthouses, state capitals, schools, town squares, and other public civic places shows that communities in the Jim Crow era wanted clear visual images in important public spheres emphasizing white supremacy and the subjugation of Black communities as part of the post–Civil War order."[34] Confederate monuments are physical manifestations of "white backlash to Black demands for rights," and the contemporary defense of them is an expression of "white identity politics" that transcends geographical borders: "The South is everywhere now, and so are its worst political pathologies."[35]

The organizers of the Unite the Right rally wanted to hold the event in Emancipation Park itself. The city of Charlottesville, citing concerns for public safety, refused to grant the permit unless the rally was moved to a different, larger park away from the city's Downtown Mall, a busy pedestrian-only shopping area. The ACLU intervened on behalf of the organizers to ensure that the rally took place in Emancipation Park, arguing that the far-right organizers' "choice of location is critical to the message of the rally" and that holding the rally in another location "would dilute and alter" their message.[36]

During the rally, armed demonstrators waved Confederate flags and swastikas, chanted Nazi slogans, and attacked counterprotesters. A white supremacist deliberately drove his car into the crowd, killing a woman named Heather Heyer. Three people died in total, nearly fifty people were injured, and the city suffered millions of dollars of damage. Then-President Donald Trump evoked Lost

Cause ideology when he notoriously declared that there were "very fine people on both sides" of the protest and praised the "people in that group that were there to protest the taking down, of to them, a very, very important statue and the renaming of a park from Robert E. Lee to another name."[37] This was one of many instances in which Trump endorsed neo-Confederate ideology—characterized by investment in racial hierarchy, strong attachment to traditional gender roles and gender conformity, idealization of the pre–Civil War South, Christian nationalism, and hostility to democracy[38]—and connected it to the exercise of free speech.

The 2017 rally emboldened white supremacists in Virginia and beyond, prompting more armed demonstrations in the years that followed. More than twenty-two thousand gun rights activists flooded Richmond, Virginia, in January 2020 to protest the state's democratically enacted gun control laws. Governor Ralph Northam, concerned about a repeat of the violence and unrest that erupted in Charlottesville in 2017, declared a state of emergency and announced that no firearms could be brought to capitol grounds. While the several thousand protesters on the grounds were unarmed, many more thousands of protesters outside of the capitol grounds brought sniper rifles and AR15s. They also brought Confederate flags, a battle tank, and a homemade guillotine inscribed with "The penalty for treason is death."[39] Attendees included the Proud Boys and other white supremacist groups as well as right-wing conspiracy theorist Alex Jones. While conservative commentators and media outlets described the event as "peaceful,"[40] several journalists noted that counterprotests, Martin Luther King Jr. Day celebrations, and normal activities were canceled out of fear of violence.

In hindsight, the Richmond rally appears to have been a kind of dress rehearsal for the 2021 US Capitol insurrection. As in Richmond, a white supremacist mob attempted to subvert the democratic process through violence. On January 6, thousands of Trump supporters swarmed the US Capitol in an effort to stop the certification of the 2020 presidential election. The rioters, waving Confederate, American, and Trump flags, attacked police officers with a fire extinguisher, dragged one officer down several steps and beat him with a flagpole, attempted to locate and assassinate Speaker of the House Nancy Pelosi, constructed a gallows on Capitol grounds and called for the hanging of Vice President Mike Pence, ransacked congressional offices, looted federal property, and forced terrified elected officials and their staff into hiding for several hours.[41] Four people died during the riot, and five law enforcement officers who responded to the event died in the days and weeks that followed.[42]

One of the most searing images for many Americans was "the sight of a man casually carrying the Confederate battle flag outside the Senate floor. . . . It was a piercing reminder of the persistence of white supremacism more than 150 years after the end of the Civil War."[43] Commentators warn that the insurrection has become the "New Lost Cause," which, "like the old one, seeks to convert a shameful catastrophe into a celebration of the valor and honor of the culprits and portray those who attacked the country as the true patriots. . . . Just as neo-Confederate revisionism shaped racial violence and oppression after the war, Trump's New Lost Cause poses a continuing peril to the hope of 'one Nation under God, indivisible, with liberty and justice for all.'"[44]

As is often the case with acts of coordinated brutality, the January 6 insurrection had many fathers. These include, of course, the extremists who physically carried out the attack but also the political figures who encouraged or excused it, the intelligence community that failed to warn or protect against it, and the online platforms that allowed the organizers to plan and promote it. The through line of these actions and omissions is a reckless, antidemocratic conception of free speech. "Under the guise of the First Amendment, domestic violent extremists recruit supporters, and incite and engage in violence,"[45] testified a Department of Homeland Security official during a congressional investigation into the attack, and federal authorities treated online threats of violence toward government personnel and property as "First Amendment protected speech."[46] On the grounds of free expression, social media platforms allowed these extremists to broadcast their propaganda and coordinate plans for violence. Federal agencies failed to produce a threat assessment of this activity because they regarded it as

"First Amendment protected speech."[47] Even after the extent of the carnage became clear, Republican National Committee members defended the insurrection as "legitimate political discourse."[48] The paltry attempts of a handful of tech companies to address the damage after the fact, including by banning then-President Trump from their services, were condemned by high-profile individuals across the political spectrum as "censorship."

The First Amendment has been hijacked by the white male supremacist agenda that seeks to return exclusive political, legal, economic, and social power to those who were considered "the people" at the time of the country's founding and to keep it out of the hands of those they feel are seeking to "replace" them. The number of people who fully and explicitly embrace this agenda may be small compared to the number who reject it, but it is essential to recognize that this vocal minority of white supremacists are in fact advancing an agenda that is consistent with American history, is overwhelmingly embraced by today's GOP, receives wide-ranging and generous support from wealthy individuals, and is embedded in American society's dominant institutions. The civil libertarian fetishization of "the speech we hate" has granted it further outsized influence and power. Interpreting the First Amendment as a right of reckless speech has paved the way for the violent reaffirmation of racial patriarchy.

2

Burning Women

"FEAR OF SERIOUS INJURY CANNOT ALONE JUSTIFY SUPPRESSION OF free speech and assembly. Men feared witches and burnt women. It is the function of speech to free men from the bondage of irrational fears."[1] These lines from Brandeis's concurring opinion in *Whitney v. California* (1927) are among the most famous and eloquent in First Amendment history. They are also notable as a rare acknowledgment by the Supreme Court of the long and violent suppression of women's speech by men.

According to historian Amanda Foreman, "the silencing of women is as old as civilization itself. . . . The first laws to have come down to us included a speech code for women."[2] The Sumerian law codes, which date back four thousand years, command that "a woman who speaks out of turn to a man will have her teeth smashed by a burnt brick."[3] Historian Mary Beard highlights a scene in Homer's *Odyssey*, written almost three thousand years ago, in which a young Telemachus commands his mother Penelope to stop talking and go to her room to weave: "Speech will be the business of men, all men, and of me most of all; for mine is the power in this household."[4] Ancient Greek and Roman societies, Beard notes, endeavored "not only to exclude women from public speech but also to parade that exclusion."[5] While permitted to speak in limited circumstances, such as in defense of family or prior to being martyred, a woman was generally expected to "as modestly guard against exposing her voice to outsiders as she would guard against stripping off her clothes."[6]

As Beard writes in *Women & Power: A Manifesto*, "When it comes to silencing women, Western culture has had thousands of years of practice."[7] Greek mythology is rife with examples of male suppression of female speech, from Tereus cutting out Philomela's tongue after he rapes her to Apollo's curse on Cassandra after she rejects his sexual advances that her truthful prophecies will never be believed. The Christian tradition is replete with stories of the grisly fates of virgin martyrs who resisted sexual assault: St. Agnes, who was stabbed in the throat and then thrown into a fire for rejecting the sexual advances of a Roman official's son; St. Petronilla, tortured on the rack for refusing to marry the pagan king Flaccus; and St. Agatha, whose breasts were cut off after she resisted a Roman prefect's sexual overtures. Medieval literature scholar and gender theorist Roberta Magnani concludes that "this brutality was done to silence them. Much like they are now, women's voices were seen as troubling,"[8] a sentiment reinforced by St. Paul's declaration that "I suffer not a woman to teach, nor to use authority over the man: but to be in silence. For Adam was first formed; then Eve."[9]

William Blackstone's *Commentaries on the Laws of England* note the offense of being a "common scold" (*communis rixatrix*), punishable by being "placed in a certain engine of correction called the trebucket, castigatory, or cucking stool, which in the Saxon language signifies the scolding stool; though now it is frequently corrupted into ducking stool, because the residue of the judgment is, that, when she is so placed therein, she shall be plunged in the water for her punishment." The offense, which involves arguing noisily with one's neighbors, was understood to be almost exclusively committed by women.[10]

And then, of course, there were the witch hunts. Author Stacy Schiff explains that while "witches and wizards extend as far back as recorded history," the figure conjured up by the Salem trials married general superstition with specific fear of women: "As is often the case with questions of women and power, elucidations here verged on the paranormal. Though weak willed, women could emerge as dangerously, insatiably commanding."[11] Women were considered so dangerous, in fact, that they could be hanged for offenses such as "having more wit than their neighbors."[12] The events that led to the Salem witch trials in 1692 began with an investigation of schoolgirls who had interrupted a sermon with screams and contortions. Though women had few rights compared to men and lived highly constrained lives, their words were believed to be so powerful that they made milk spoil, crops fail, children corrupt, and men impotent. By the time the trials concluded, twenty people had been executed, several people had died in jail, and nearly two hundred people had been accused of practicing "the Devil's magic." In Salem and elsewhere in New England, more than two-thirds of the individuals who were accused and found guilty of witchcraft were women.

But the witch hunts never really ended.[13] In December 2018, actress and activist Amber Heard published an op-ed in the *Washington Post* titled "I Spoke Up Against Sexual Violence—and Faced Our Culture's Wrath. That Has to Change."[14] The editorial detailed the harassment Heard had received in the wake of speaking up about domestic abuse. While the op-ed did not name any perpetrators or specific events, it was widely assumed that Heard was referring to the verbal and physical abuse allegations she made about her then-husband, actor Johnny Depp, during their highly publicized divorce in 2016. Depp denied the allegations and sued a UK tabloid, the *Sun*, in June 2018, for referring to him as a "wife-beater."[15] After hearing testimony from both Heard and Depp, the UK court ruled in favor of the *Sun*, finding that its characterization of Depp was "substantially true."

Heard's op-ed, published two years after her divorce from Depp, mostly focused on the progress of the #MeToo movement and the need for stronger legal protections for women and girls who have experienced abuse. It also included Heard's claim that "two years ago, I became a public figure representing domestic abuse, and I felt the full force of our culture's wrath for women who speak out." The op-ed recounts the negative career consequences and threats to her safety she endured as a result: "I had the rare vantage point of seeing, in real time, how institutions protect men accused of abuse."[16]

In February 2019, Depp sued Heard over this op-ed for $50 million, claiming that Heard's allegations of abuse were a defamatory "hoax" and that Heard was actually the abusive party in their relationship.[17] The trial garnered intense, around-the-clock public scrutiny, greatly facilitated by the presiding judge's decision to allow the proceedings to be televised live over Heard's objection. Among the evidence brought to light by the trial were text messages from 2013 that Depp sent to actor Paul Bettany stating "Lets burn Amber!!!," "Let's drown her before we burn her!!!," and "I will fuck her . . . burnt corpse afterwards to make sure she is dead."[18]

And burn her they did. Depp had vowed to a different friend in 2016 that Heard was "begging for global humiliation. . . . She is going to get it,"[19] and the two-month trial delivered on this promise. Heard was forced to describe, on the witness stand and in front of the world, graphic details of sexual assault and physical abuse— details that were then widely mocked by social media influencers, celebrities, and even corporate brands. Heard was called a liar, a drug addict, a whore, and a monster. She was professionally blacklisted, constantly surveilled by the press and the public, and subjected to death threats and harassment.

All of this happened because Heard wrote something that people did not like—the kind of speech that, according to American free speech orthodoxy, should be most robustly protected by the First Amendment. But in a decision that chilled the speech of sexual abuse and domestic violence victims everywhere, Heard was found liable for defamation and ordered to pay Depp $15 million.

One might have thought that Heard's case would have been an ideal one for a prominent free speech organization like the ACLU to take up: Heard was punished legally, financially, reputationally, and psychologically for making factually true statements in an op-ed. A multimillion-dollar defamation award was granted to a powerful man who was never named in the piece. Heard had been globally vilified and harassed with unprecedented savagery. In addition to all this, it was the ACLU that had asked her to write the op-ed in the first place.

The ACLU had asked Heard in 2018 to become an artist ambassador and to sign an op-ed to raise awareness of domestic violence. It was revealed at trial that the organization had been substantively involved with the drafting of the op-ed. And yet, when Depp sued Heard over the op-ed, the ACLU offered no public support, not even to highlight the obvious and important free speech stakes of the suit. Indeed, in response to one liberal commentator's head-spinning claim that involvement with Heard's op-ed stood in shameful *contrast* to the organization's "apolitical willingness to stand up for all speech, regardless of the speaker's identity, and to stand up for those accused, no matter what the accusation,"[20] ACLU national legal director David Cole defended the organization by highlighting its free speech work for white supremacists and homophobes—and said nothing about the importance of defending the free speech rights of domestic violence victims.[21]

The Heard op-ed was a unique and high-profile opportunity for the ACLU to defend fearless speech and to demonstrate that its theory of free speech does not consistently privilege men's speech over women's. While Heard has the advantages of being famous, wealthy, and white, her experience of domestic abuse and harassment by a man with considerably more power and status rendered her vulnerable. But apart from a single sentence buried at the bottom of an unsigned ACLU statement—"As the nation's oldest free speech organization, we fight for the freedom to speak out about barriers to gender justice"[22]—the organization barely acknowledged the free speech stakes of Depp's lawsuit and its chilling effect on all victims of domestic abuse. Worse still, when other self-styled civil libertarians said the quiet part loud and characterized support for domestic violence victims as *standing in opposition* to the civil libertarian commitment to free speech,[23] the ACLU's response was to offer reassurances that the organization was just as devoted to Nazis as it always had been.[24]

Given the ACLU's abandonment, it was hardly surprising when, soon after beginning the process to appeal the decision, Heard announced that she had made the "very difficult decision to settle" the case. In a statement posted to social media, she explained,

> I never chose this. I defended my truth and in doing so my life as I knew it was destroyed. The vilification I have faced on social media is an amplified version of the ways in which women are re-victimized when they come forward. Now I finally have an opportunity to emancipate myself from something I attempted to leave over six years ago and on terms I can agree to. . . . I make this decision having lost faith in the American legal system, where my unprotected testimony served as entertainment and social media fodder.
>
> For too many years I have been caged in an arduous and expensive legal process, which has shown itself unable to protect me and my right to free speech. I cannot afford to risk an impossible bill—one that is not just financial but also psychological, physical and emotional. Women shouldn't have to face abuse or bankruptcy for speaking her truth, but unfortunately it is not uncommon.
>
> I will not be threatened, disheartened, or dissuaded by what happened from speaking the truth. No one can and no one will take that from me. My voice forever remains the most valuable asset I have.[25]

Though the ACLU and other civil libertarians had little to say about the trial's devastating free speech consequences, not just for Heard but for all women considering speaking out about men's abuse, many women did. As journalist Moira Donegan wrote in the *Guardian*,

> Lost in the scandal and spectacle of the lawsuit has been this reality: it is Heard, not Depp, who has been put on trial, and she is on trial for saying things whose truth is evidenced by the very fact of the lawsuit itself. Depp's frivolous and

punitive suit, and the frenzy of misogynist contempt for Heard that has accompanied it, have done a great deal to vindicate Heard's original point: that women are punished for coming forward. What happens to women who allege abuse? They get publicly pilloried, professionally blacklisted, socially ostracized, mocked endlessly on social media and sued. Wrath, indeed.[26]

Donegan knows of what she speaks. She, too, was sued for defamation by a man over #MeToo allegations. In October 2017, as the #MeToo movement was gaining force, Donegan created an anonymous Google spreadsheet for women to share allegations about abusive men in the media industry. Donegan included a disclaimer that the document was "only a collection of misconduct allegations and rumors" that should be taken "with a grain of salt."[27] She intended the document to only be shared within her social circles; she took the document offline twelve hours after creating it, once she realized it was going viral.[28] After she learned that writer Katie Roiphe planned to out her as the creator of the list in *Harper's Magazine*, Donegan preempted her by identifying herself as creator of the spreadsheet in a January 2018 essay. One of the men named on the list, Stephen Elliot, sued Donegan for $1.5 million in damages in October 2018. The litigation dragged on for more than four years before the parties finally settled.

"Men feared witches and burnt women," *and they are still doing it.* Brandeis himself was doing it even as he wrote those words; despite championing the right to engage in injurious speech, Brandeis concurred in the decision to "burn" Anita Whitney for hers. As the Heard case revealed in excruciating detail, when it comes to women's speech, the protection of the First Amendment is little more than hollow rhetoric.

By contrast, the First Amendment is always available to defend men's misogynist expression and sexual exploitation. In 2012, in an early precursor to "deepfake porn,"[29] the hardcore pornographic magazine *Hustler* published a doctored photo of female conservative commentator S. E. Cupp performing oral sex on a man. The caption described Cupp as a "lovely young lady" whose "hotness is diminished when she espouses dumb ideas like defunding Planned Parenthood. Perhaps the method pictured here is Ms. Cupp's suggestion for avoiding an unwanted pregnancy." The photo was accompanied by a disclaimer that stated that "no such picture . . . actually exists."[30] The photo drew criticism from many quarters, including from feminists across the political spectrum. *Hustler*'s owner, Larry Flynt, defended the photo as "protected free speech,"[31] citing the 1988 Supreme Court case that found that his magazine's satirical ad describing how minister Jerry Falwell had lost his virginity to his mother in an outhouse was protected by the First Amendment.[32]

Hustler has been a frequent target of both criticism and litigation since its launch in 1974. The magazine has featured nude photos of women without their consent (including of Jacqueline Kennedy Onassis[33]), graphic depictions of women being raped, beaten, and tortured, racist caricatures, Holocaust jokes, and a long-running cartoon titled *Chester the Molester*, which detailed the exploits of a middle-aged pedophile as he hunts and assaults young girls. The cartoonist who created *Chester* was convicted of molesting his teenage daughter in 1990. One of Flynt's daughters accused Flynt of molesting her as a child, and two of his other daughters also indicated that he had engaged in inappropriate behavior with them.[34]

But Flynt, who died in 2021, invariably and largely successfully invoked the First Amendment in the defense of his magazine's content. For this, he enjoyed widespread acclaim as a champion of free speech rights, especially following his portrayal by Woody Harrelson in the highly successful and award-winning 1996 Hollywood film *The People versus Larry Flynt*. In the words of cultural critic Laura Kipnis, "it wasn't the Left or the avant-garde that played a decisive role in expanding free speech. . . . It was the pornographer, Larry Flynt."[35]

In a 2011 interview, journalist Johann Hari asked Flynt if he could explain the motivation for two of *Hustler*'s most controversial publishing decisions. One was the depiction of a gang rape of a woman on a pool table that some claimed inspired the real-life rape of a woman on a pool table a few months later in New Bedford (the case that served as the basis for the movie *The Accused*). Flynt responded to the criticism by publishing fake postcards of a woman nude on a pool table with the caption "Greetings from New Bedford, Massachusetts, The Portuguese Gang-Rape Capital of America" in the next issue of *Hustler*.[36] The other was a photo spread that depicts a woman being "forcibly shaved, raped, and apparently killed in a concentration camp."[37] Flynt answered that the shoots were "satire" but struggled to explain who or what was being satirized, eventually invoking the First Amendment and the *Hustler v. Falwell* (1988)[38] case (which had not involved any sexual images):

> That is satire. That's what I went to the United States supreme court for. It was a landmark judgment. It was a unanimous decision. Supreme Court Justice William Rehnquist, one of the most conservative justices, said sometimes things are done under the name of the First Amendment that are less than admirable but that doesn't give the government the right to suppress it. . . . I don't know how many different ways I can say this—the First Amendment gives me the right to be offensive. If you're not going to offend somebody you don't need the First Amendment.[39]

Ever the self-promoter, Flynt was happy to play up the suggestion that he played a singularly important role in vindicating First Amendment rights: "If the 1st Amendment will protect a scumbag like me . . . then it will protect all of you, because I'm the worst."[40] This is a succinct expression of one of the fundamental tenets of American free speech orthodoxy—that protecting the rights of the "worst" speakers is the only way to assure the rights of everyone else. "Ensuring the free speech rights of anyone, including a racist or misogynist, secures the same rights for everyone else, including an intended victim," wrote ACLU leaders Mary Ellen Gale and Nadine Strossen in 1989.[41] Neier, a former ACLU executive director, similarly claimed, "The people who most need the ACLU to defend the rights of the Klan are the blacks. The people who most need the ACLU to defend the rights of Nazis are the Jews."[42]

Like many sacred tenets, the claim that protecting harmful speakers is necessary to protect those they harm, a version of the "bad precedent" theory discussed in chapter 1, tends to be treated as self-evident. But the evidence that safeguarding the rights of one group necessarily safeguards the rights of other groups is unpersuasive. It is particularly hard to discern when the group whose speech is supposedly in need of protection has far more power than the group it targets—for example, the famous male owner of a multi-million-dollar pornography business versus a relatively obscure female political commentator. The claim also presumes that legal protections are self-executing, stable, and consistently applied to people regardless of wealth, status, gender, or race. But this is not now nor has it ever been true in the United States, a reality that progressive organizations such as the ACLU generally tend to recognize outside of the First Amendment context.

How exactly does the right to publish fake pornography of a woman without her consent advance the free speech rights of the woman depicted? Perhaps the answer is that the First Amendment would protect Cupp if she responded to her depiction by publishing a fake pornographic depiction of Flynt. But such a "I know you are but what am I?" approach to the First Amendment is an absurdly impoverished and adolescent conception of free speech.

The more sophisticated argument is that protecting misogynist speech guarantees the protection of speech criticizing misogyny. The claim was explicitly made by a federal court in dismissing a lawsuit against *Hustler* involving a crude sexual portrayal of another woman with views that Flynt didn't like, feminist advocate Andrea Dworkin: "The First Amendment works both ways. While feminists cannot sue pornographers because they find the materials offensive and harmful to women, neither can other members of society who find feminist literature offensive and potentially harmful to their way of life sue feminists for publishing their views. In a society with such diverse opinions and life-styles as flourish in these United States, the protection of free speech guaranteed by the

First Amendment is perhaps the most important component of the free society envisioned by our founders as set forth in the United States Constitution."[43]

But as the Heard, Donegan, and countless other #MeToo cases prove, the First Amendment does not, in fact, "work both ways." First, misogynists have asymmetrical tools at their disposal; they can publish humiliating and degrading images of women for profit with no consequences—a license to inflict extrajudicial punishments under the protection of the First Amendment. This in itself is a profound, structural asymmetry. Second, as evidenced by the Depp-Heard case and many others, men can and do sue women for speech they find "offensive and potentially harmful to their way of life." The "bad precedent" theory is as specious with regard to sexist speech as it is with racist speech.

Instead of robustly protecting women's speech criticizing men's abuse, civil libertarians affirmatively seek to protect violent or exploitative expression targeting women and other vulnerable groups and block attempts to mitigate the harms of myriad forms of abuse, including harassment, stalking, and nonconsensual pornography.

These efforts underscore the long and complex relationship between feminism, free speech, and the mainstream porn industry. During the so-called sex wars of the 1970s and 1980s, feminists battled over whether pornography was a liberating and progressive form of expression or a cynical and dangerous form of misogynist exploitation. Those in the pro-pornography camp lauded men like Hugh Hefner, the founder of the pornographic magazine *Playboy*, who many viewed as a feminist and a free speech champion. His daughter, Christie Hefner, established the Hugh M. Hefner First Amendment Award in 1979 "to honor individuals who have made significant contributions in the vital effort to protect and enhance First Amendment rights for all Americans."[44] Among the first recipients of the award in 1980 was David Goldberger, the ACLU attorney who represented the neo-Nazis in Skokie; several other ACLU attorneys have been recipients or judges of the award over the years, including former ACLU director Neier and former ACLU president Strossen.

Hefner, who died in 2017, apparently admired *The Feminine Mystique*, Betty Friedan's 1963 feminist manifesto, and was sympathetic to the frustrations imposed by domestic femininity, especially the restrictions on their sexual freedom. Eight years before *Roe v. Wade* (1973) was decided, Hefner published a feature story that supported the right to abortion and often featured abortion experts in the magazine. The Playboy Foundation provided $40,000 to start the ACLU's Women's Rights Project and provided printing services for the organization's pamphlets and abortion rights materials.[45]

At the same time, Hefner commissioned several articles to attack what he labeled "militant" feminists. In a 1970 memo, he denounced "the highly irrational, emotional, kookie trend that feminism has taken in the last couple of years. These chicks are our natural enemy and there is . . . nothing we can say in the pages of *Playboy* that will convince them that we are not. It is time to do battle with them and I think we can do it."[46] One of these battles was *Playboy*'s publication of an editorial by a male writer ridiculing the women's liberation movement as "so frivolous and yet so earnest, so absurd and yet so justified, so obsessed on the one hand with trivia and, on the other, with the radical restructuring of male-female relationships, of family life and of society itself. . . . Don't deceive yourself that it's nothing but the exhibitionism of a handful of neurotics, uglies and dykes."[47]

Hefner's reputation as a "feminist" is also undermined by the fact that *Playboy*'s success began with the publication of nonconsensual pornography. Hefner purchased nude photos of Marilyn Monroe that she had hoped would never see the light of day; they had been taken when she was a struggling actress still known as Norma Jean Baker. The publication of these photos in *Playboy*'s first issue did much to ensure the magazine's success. Hefner's penchant for revenge porn also extended to women he knew personally, as detailed by Holly Madison and confirmed by Hefner's widow, Crystal Hefner. Hefner would routinely use disposable cameras to take photos of women at the Playboy Mansion while they were intoxicated and distribute them to guests. According to Crystal

Hefner, there were "thousands" of such photos.[48] The existence of these compromising photos had a coercive effect: "When I lived at the mansion, I was afraid to leave," said Madison. "If I left, there was just this mountain of revenge porn just waiting to come out."[49] Even more seriously, the 2022 A&E docuseries *Secrets of Playboy* included detailed allegations from multiple sources that Hefner routinely drugged and raped women at his mansion. According to Miki Garcia, Playboy's head of promotions from 1973 to 1982, Hefner "never wanted a woman to become so powerful that he couldn't control her. And it was so wrong and so against what he espoused to everyone—I mean, all about protecting women and non-exploitation. All that, that was nothing but garbage. . . . I think he hated women underneath it all."[50]

Whatever kind of "feminism" that could be attributed to Hefner, then, would be highly selective. Selective feminism can be understood as a form of *interest convergence*, a term used by critical race scholar Derrick Bell Jr. to describe white people's willingness to support some racial equality goals and not others. According to Bell, white people will support measures to address racism so long as those measures also benefit white interests but will not support measures that undermine those interests. So, for example, white business owners might embrace the desegregation of businesses, because there is an economic benefit in increasing customer size. But the same white people might cling to racially discriminatory practices in bank loans and zoning restrictions out of fear of having to compete with black businesses. "The interest of blacks in achieving racial equality will be accommodated only when it converges with the interests of whites,"[51] revealing, Bell suggests, white people's fundamentally instrumentalist and opportunistic approach to racial equality goals. White people will endorse remedies for racial injustice only to the extent that they "will secure, advance, or at least not harm societal interests deemed important by middle and upper class whites."[52]

Bell's interest convergence theory demonstrates that white supremacy does not exclusively take the form of radical and overt hostility to racial minorities; it can also take a "liberal" form that superficially and selectively embraces some racial equality goals while ensuring that white interests remain the ultimate priority. Male supremacy can be understood the same way. The selective feminism of liberals like Hefner embraces the advancement of women's interests so long as they converge, or at least do not conflict, with men's interests. Liberal male supremacy, like liberal racial supremacy, is about *primacy*: men's interests should *take precedence* over women's. Advancement in women's rights, elevation of women's status, dedication of resources to women's welfare—all of these may be acceptable in the male supremacist framework, so long as they match men's interests or do not deplete resources dedicated to men's interests. What is not acceptable in a male supremacist framework is any improvement in women's rights, status, or welfare that would conflict with men's interests or result in men getting less than they believe they deserve.

In seeking funding from Playboy, then-ACLU president Aryeh Neier made sure to highlight the ACLU cases he thought would most appeal to Hefner—"sexual civil liberties cases involving abortion, voluntary sterilization, birth control, and 'bralessness.'"[53] As Neier so cannily understood, such interests converge with—or at least do not diverge from—certain male interests. For men who are invested in increased sexual access to women, expanding women's reproductive rights or loosening sexual norms has considerable appeal. The same men might well object, as Hefner did, to exercises of women's rights that are less useful to men's interests, especially those that might challenge rather than enhance men's sexual objectification of women.

One of the most famous of these challenges resulted in a First Amendment case that illustrated just how fully the male subject preoccupies free speech doctrine. In the 1980s, advocacy efforts led by Catharine MacKinnon and Andrea Dworkin resulted in the passage of the Minneapolis Antipornography Civil Rights Ordinance, which provided a right of action to individuals who had been injured by trafficking, coercion, or assault in pornography. The ordinance defined pornography as "the graphic sexually explicit subordination of women" that included one or more of six defined factors, many of which involved presenting women as "sexual objects" that enjoyed pain, humiliation, mutilation, or degradation.[54] The Seventh Circuit struck down the ordinance on First Amendment grounds in *American Booksellers Association v. Hudnut* (1985),[55] a ruling that was summarily affirmed by the Supreme Court.[56]

Judge Frank Easterbrook, writing for the majority in *Hudnut*, accepted the claim that pornography caused harm to women. "Depictions of subordination tend to perpetuate subordination. The subordinate status of women in turn leads to affront and lower pay at work, insult and injury at home, battery and rape on the streets."[57] Quoting the statute, Easterbrook agreed that "pornography is central in creating and maintaining sex as a basis of discrimination. Pornography is a systematic practice of exploitation and subordination based on sex which differentially harms women. The bigotry and contempt it produces, with the acts of aggression it fosters, harm women's opportunities for equality and rights."[58]

But the fact that pornography causes such serious harm, wrote Easterbrook, "simply demonstrates the power of pornography as speech."[59] Along with other forms of harmful speech, including "racial bigotry, anti-semitism, violence on television, and reporters' biases,"[60] pornography must be protected by the First Amendment because the alternative "leaves the government in control of all of the institutions of culture, the great censor and director of which thoughts are good for us."[61]

The Minneapolis ordinance and the *Hudnut* decision was a flash point in the porn wars: in popular perception, the case was a clash between free speech and moralism, and free speech won. The law was derided as an attempt to legislate morality or to censor "offensive" speech, and Easterbrook's decision has been praised as an example of unyielding commitment to the principle of free speech.

But among the great ironies of the case is that the statute was struck down precisely because it did *not* legislate morality or focus on offensiveness. The ordinance was invalidated because it did not fit into a preexisting category of exception to the First Amendment's protection. In finding the ordinance unconstitutional, Easterbrook compared the definition of pornography in the ordinance to the definition of obscenity provided in *Miller v. California* (1973). Obscenity is one of the oldest categorical exceptions to First Amendment protections, and *Miller* held that speech is obscene if "the average person, applying contemporary community standards" would find that the work, taken as a whole, "appeals to the prurient interest," depicts sexual conduct "in a patently offensive way," and "lacks serious literary, artistic, political, or scientific value."[62] Easterbrook noted, disapprovingly, that the Minneapolis ordinance "does not refer to the prurient interest, to offensiveness, or to the standards of the community,"[63] and it "is irrelevant under the ordinance whether the work has literary, artistic, political, or scientific value."[64] These differences, he said, doomed the statute.

But as MacKinnon herself explained clearly, she made a deliberate choice to reject the obscenity framework because of its male-dominated morality. "Obscenity law is concerned with morality, specifically morals from the male point of view, meaning the standpoint of male dominance."[65] The statute, and MacKinnon's objection to pornography generally, was not based on morality but on *harm*—specifically, the harm that pornography inflicted on particular women in particular circumstances. As such, the ordinance represented a divergence between men's interests (concerned with the offensiveness of obscenity) and women's (concerned with the harm of pornography).

The court did not hold that the statute violated the First Amendment because it attempted to regulate speech; it found that the statute violated the First Amendment because it attempted to regulate speech based on demonstrated harm to actual women rather than on a demonstration of its offensiveness to the "community." That is, narrowly defined harm to women is not an adequate basis to regulate speech, but harm to the moral sensibilities of an imagined community is. The government cannot be trusted to determine "what is good for us" but can be trusted to make determinations about "offensiveness" or what constitutes literary, artistic, political, or scientific value.

As MacKinnon wrote of the decision, "Feminism doubts whether the average person, gender neutral, exists; has more questions about the content and process of definition of community standards than about deviations from them; wonders why prurience counts but powerlessness doesn't; why sensibilities are better protected from offense than women are from exploitation; defines sexuality, hence its violation and expropriation, more broadly than does any state law and wonders why a body of law that can't in practice tell rape from intercourse should be entrusted with telling pornography from anything else."[66]

The *Hudnut* case vividly illustrates how, despite pretensions to absolutism, the courts have always limited First Amendment protection according to assessments of harm. The only questions are which harm and to whom. Free speech protections can always be "outweighed by other interests," particularly "harm to someone who matters."[67] The someone who matters, it is no doubt clear at this point, is the male subject. Very often, it is not men's supposed power but their claimed *vulnerability* that occupies the field. The hidden man in law is not some superhero fantasy; he is often, in fact, remarkably fragile. And what the hidden man considers to be harmful is treated as the objective standard for harm.

Hudnut illustrates this with regard to obscenity, but it is true of other categorical exceptions to First Amendment protection, such as defamation. As feminist scholar Ann Scales writes, "The defamation exception is like an affirmative action program for wealthy or important people. Defamation law officially recognizes *their* subjective experience of the worthlessness of . . . the use of 'more speech' to prevent injuries to their reputations."[68] This is a conclusion reinforced by the Depp-Heard trial and the wave of defamation lawsuits against other women who have spoken out about men's abuse.

The "fighting words" exception is yet another category clearly defined by masculine perceptions of offensiveness.[69] As the court stated in *Chaplinsky v. New Hampshire* (1942), "The word 'offensive' is not to be defined in terms of what a particular addressee thinks. . . . The test is what men of common intelligence would understand would be words likely to cause an average addressee to fight. . . . The English language has a number of words and expressions which, by general consent, are 'fighting words' when said without a disarming smile. . . . Such words, as ordinary men know, are likely to cause a fight. So are threatening, profane or obscene revilings."[70] Cynthia Grant Bowman observes that the fighting words doctrine is "male-biased in its central concept—the assumption that the harm of personally abusive language either consists in, or can be gauged by, its tendency to provoke a violent response."[71]

It is no accident that the "categorical exceptions" approach to the First Amendment, according to which all speech is by default protected unless it falls into one of a few narrow and "historically recognized" exceptions, primarily reflects and serves the interests of white men. It is the approach most often invoked to invalidate attempts to address harm to women and minorities, as the Supreme Court did most recently by striking down stalking prohibitions in *Counterman v. Colorado* (2023).[72]

Stalking is a crime disproportionately committed by men against women, one so often correlated with murder that experts call it "slow motion homicide."[73] Victims rarely seek assistance from law enforcement out of the well-grounded fear of not being taken seriously, and those who do are often ignored. In the tiny fraction of reported cases in which law enforcement does choose to intervene, restraining orders, arrests, and convictions can mean the difference not only between speech and silence but between life and death. But in June 2023, the Supreme Court declared that this speech-affirming, lifesaving intervention violated the First Amendment rights of delusional stalkers.[74]

Counterman v. Colorado effectively not only legalized stalking but valorized it as a form of free speech. The case involved a woman named Coles Whalen, who had been a thriving Colorado musician until a stranger named Billy Counterman became obsessed with her. For years Counterman bombarded Whalen with thousands of unwanted messages, interrogating her about her personal life, implying that he was physically surveilling her, and telling her he wanted her to die. As Whalen had no idea who Counterman was or what he looked like, she became increasingly anxious about performing live and connecting with her fans out of fear that he might be in the audience. She tried to ignore the messages, but after learning that Counterman had twice been arrested for threatening other women with bodily harm (including threats that he would "put your head on a fuckin sidewalk and bash it in" and "rip your throat out on sight"), she contacted law enforcement.[75] Counterman was eventually arrested and convicted of stalking, but not before Whalen had stopped performing, begun varying her daily routes, and reluctantly started carrying a gun for protection.

Counterman was convicted under a Colorado law that prohibits repeatedly communicating with another person in "a manner that would cause a reasonable person to suffer serious emotional distress and does cause that person . . . to suffer serious emotional distress."[76] Counterman argued that even though his communications were objectively distressing, they should be protected by the First Amendment because he did not actually intend for them to be perceived that way. The state of Colorado maintained that proving that the communications were objectively terrifying was sufficient for conviction. Supported by amicus briefs from stalking experts, First Amendment scholars, and other states that also used an objective standard, Colorado emphasized that stalkers often sincerely believe that their behavior is welcome or benevolent. These delusional beliefs make them more, not less, dangerous to their victims.

But the Supreme Court ruled against Colorado, holding that the First Amendment did require proof that a stalker consciously disregarded a substantial and unjustified risk that his communications would be perceived as terrifying. Stated more plainly, the court declared that stalking is protected free speech if the stalker truly believes that his repeated, objectively terrifying conduct is welcome. The more deluded the stalker, the more constitutionally protected the stalking.

Rather than taking into account any of the actual harms to actual victims of stalking, the majority opinion focused on the hypothetical fear of hypothetical speakers whose speech could hypothetically be mistaken for threats: "The speaker's fear of mistaking whether a statement is a threat; his fear of the legal system getting that judgment wrong; his fear, in any event, of incurring legal costs—all those may lead him to swallow words that are in fact not true threats."[77] Tellingly, the majority offered no empirical evidence of this supposed "chilling effect" that must be prioritized above all else, most likely because, as numerous scholars have pointed out, very little evidence of this exists.[78] The average individual does not consult legal statutes and their enforcement before deciding how or if to speak. What is more, an exploration of stalking prosecutions would lead to the opposite conclusion: stalking, like other abuses disproportionately committed by men against women, is among the most underreported and underprosecuted crimes.[79] Long before the court's decision in *Counterman*, abusers could already feel confident that they could act with near impunity in the vast majority of cases. This certainly seems to have been true of Counterman himself, whose previous convictions for making violent threats against female family members clearly did not deter him from stalking Whalen.

The court also notably failed to consider the chilling effects on the speech of stalking *victims*. The targets of stalking are forced to weigh every interaction, every public appearance, every word against the possibility that their stalker is listening, watching, waiting. Can they continue to do the work they love if it keeps them on their stalker's radar? Can they advertise a speaking engagement that reveals their physical location? Can they share a joyous family event that might trigger a delusional escalation?

It was not particularly surprising that the conservative Supreme Court under Chief Justice John Roberts—which had made its hostility to women clear when it ruled that the Constitution provides no right against forced birth in *Dobbs v. Jackson Women's Health* (2022)—delivered another decision so callously indifferent to women's lives. The outcome was presaged by the oral arguments, during which Roberts read some of Counterman's threatening messages out loud as punch lines. Justices Neil Gorsuch and Clarence Thomas chuckled frequently through the arguments, affecting a serious tone only when opining that hypersensitivity was surely a far graver threat to society than stalking.[80]

But the decision in *Counterman* was not, as with *Dobbs*, the product of the conservative supermajority. Justice Elena Kagan authored the opinion, joined by the two other liberal justices on the court along with four of their conservative colleagues. It was a stark contrast to *Dobbs*, in which Kagan had joined the liberal justices in a dissent that decried the conservative supermajority's specious use of history and tradition to deny constitutional protections to women. The *Dobbs* dissenters pointedly observed that "'people' did not ratify the Fourteenth Amendment. Men did," and "when the majority says that we must read our foundational charter as viewed at the time of ratification . . . it consigns women to second-class citizenship."[81] But the *Counterman* majority failed to acknowledge that this is no less true for the First Amendment. The dissenters' conclusion in *Dobbs* applies equally to *Counterman*: "One result of today's decision is certain: the curtailment of women's rights, and of their status as free and equal citizens."[82] Tragically, it seems that one of the only things that can unite conservatives, liberals, and libertarians today is that the First Amendment protects men's speech at the expense of women's speech and men's delusions at the expense of women's lives.

Even as stalking experts and victim advocates emphasized that the decision against Colorado meant that more women would die at the hands of their stalkers, civil libertarians across the political spectrum celebrated the outcome as a victory for the First Amendment. An ACLU attorney praised the court for guaranteeing that "inadvertently threatening speech cannot be criminalized" and for "provid[ing] essential breathing room for public debate."[83] A Foundation for Individual Rights and Expression (FIRE) attorney rejoiced that "fewer prosecutors will be able to criminalize speech tomorrow than was possible yesterday" and praised the majority for "ensur[ing] that Americans would not face prosecution for parody or political commentary."[84]

The *Counterman* decision is another example of the First Amendment victim-claiming tactic that allows the ACLU to portray pornographers and white supremacists as persecuted minorities. As MacKinnon has archly noted, it is quite remarkable to take

"the position that the pornographers are the rebels, the disenfran-
chised, and the hated, rather than the bearers and defenders of a
ruling ideology of misogyny and racism and sexualized bigotry,"
when they are "hated to the tune of eight billion dollars a year."[85] It
is equally remarkable to take the position that a stalker, not his victim, is the truly vulnerable party when it comes to free speech. The
Counterman court's solicitude for the free speech of stalkers over
the safety and speech of their victims makes overt what the trickle-
down free speech theory attempts to obscure—namely, that civil
libertarianism chooses certain speakers *over* others. The assertion
that protecting the pornographer protects the feminist has always
been a hollow pretense, but in cases like *Counterman*, even that thin
disguise is discarded: the court explicitly sides with the harmful
speaker over the one he harms.

In the 2010 case *US v. Stevens*, Roberts referenced the "historic
and traditional categories long familiar to the bar," including
obscenity, defamation, fraud, incitement, and speech integral to
criminal conduct, which the court considers to be "well-defined and
narrowly limited classes of speech, the prevention and punishment
of which have never been thought to raise any Constitutional problem."[86] While Roberts admitted that this list of classes was not
entirely exhaustive, noting in particular the court's ruling in *New
York v. Ferber* regarding child pornography, he disparaged the idea
that the court has "a freewheeling authority to declare new categories of speech outside the scope of the First Amendment."[87] But the
list in *Stevens* does not come close to capturing all the categories of
exceptions that the court has recognized in the context of First Amendment protections—forty-eight, by the count of one First Amendment expert.[88] Even that longer list of exceptions does not capture
the vast amount of expression that the court has simply never subjected to First Amendment scrutiny, including securities regulation,
criminal conspiracy, and products liability, just to name a few.

The "historic and traditional categories" approach artificially
freezes First Amendment doctrine in place and attempts to preempt any "new" claims of harm from the calculus of free speech.[89]
Indeed, in *Stevens*, the court made the surprising claim that it never

engages in harm balancing when deciding First Amendment cases. Roberts characterized the government's suggestion that the case turned on "a categorical balancing of the value of the speech against its societal costs" as "startling and dangerous": "The First Amendment's guarantee of free speech does not extend only to categories of speech that survive an ad hoc balancing of relative social costs and benefits. The First Amendment itself reflects a judgment by the American people that the benefits of its restrictions on the Government outweigh the costs. Our Constitution forecloses any attempt to revise that judgment simply on the basis that some speech is not worth it."[90]

Despite Roberts's protestations to the contrary, balancing has played a central role in First Amendment cases. In *Chaplinsky*, the court explained that fighting words do not receive the full protection of the First Amendment because "such utterances are no essential part of any exposition of ideas, and are of such slight social value as a step to truth that any benefit that may be derived from them *is clearly outweighed* by the social interest in order and morality."[91] And it is hard to see how the other categories of speech considered to be exceptions to First Amendment coverage can be justified if not by some balancing of potential harms versus potential benefits.

Accepting poorly defined and dubiously justified categories such as obscenity but rejecting a narrow definition of harm to women as a sufficient ground for the regulation of speech is yet another illustration of how, as law professor Lucinda Finley writes, "male-based perspectives, images, and experiences are often taken to be the norms in law. Privileged white men are the norm for equality law; they are the norm for assessing the reasonable person in tort law; the way men would react is the norm for self-defense law; and the male worker is the prototype for labor law."[92]

We can add to this that the white male speaker is the norm for First Amendment law and that his perception defines the boundaries of its protection. "The more a non-white person can be talked about as the same as a white male, the more deserving she or he is to be treated equally to, or the same as, white males. This language not only uses white males as the reference point, but it also exalts them. To be the same as white males is the desired end. To be different from them is undesirable and justifies disadvantage."[93]

As we have seen, when assessments of the value and harm of speech are made with a white male subject in mind, the result is that speech valued by white men but harmful to women and minorities is likely to be characterized as protected speech, whereas speech that diverges from the interests of white men tends to be classified as an exception to First Amendment protection.

It was predictable, then, that the ACLU would resist efforts to prohibit what is colloquially referred to as "revenge porn," the unauthorized distribution of sexually explicit, private images. After all, two of the pornography moguls lauded by the ACLU as free speech heroes, Flynt and Hefner, used this form of exploitation to sell their magazines. Since 2013, when the movement to criminalize nonconsensual pornography began in earnest, the ACLU has argued that this abuse is free speech protected by the First Amendment. When it was unsuccessful in convincing legislatures that no restriction of nonconsensual pornography was constitutionally permissible, the ACLU used its considerable influence to push a narrow definition of the crime that limited punishment to distributors who expressly intended to harm their victims.

On the other side were advocates and First Amendment scholars (including myself) who argued that motive was irrelevant to the crime. Whether a perpetrator intended to harm the victim, make money, or obtain sexual gratification or some other form of validation was beside the point; as with other sexual acts, the key element was the victim's lack of consent.

The ACLU's lobbying efforts against nonconsensual pornography bills did not stop nearly every state from passing a law between 2014 and 2024. Unfortunately, their pressure tactics regarding motive requirements did succeed in ensuring that most of those laws are too narrow to be genuinely effective. They also helped ensure that the state laws that were not limited in this way were challenged on constitutional grounds. To date, however, every constitutional challenge to a nonconsensual pornography law has

failed. Courts have so far refused to endorse the view that this hor-
rific form of sexual exploitation is free speech protected by the First
Amendment, despite the ACLU's best efforts.[94]

Occasionally, civil libertarians themselves seem to question
whether their robust defense of pornographers and white supremacists is truly justifiable. Gale and Strossen, for example, briefly consider whether

> the Klan, the Nazis, and the pornographers, at some deeper
> level of our national psyche, are not really despised fringe
> groups at all, but centrists in extremists' clothing, purveyors
> of the denied truth that we as a nation are still hostages to
> our history of racial and sexual xenophobia and oppression.
> By allowing them to speak freely, while overtly and sancti-
> moniously denouncing their message, we covertly accept it.
> Because the political and social context in which they speak
> is not and never has been neutral, we cannot comfortably
> contend that they alone are the enemy of equal rights and
> freedoms. The enemy is still us.[95]

But almost as soon as they raise this compelling possibility, Gale
and Strossen dismiss it and revert back to civil libertarian orthodoxy. Echoing Neier's assertion that black people and Jews "need"
the ACLU to protect the KKK and Nazis, they conclude their essay
by suggesting that feminists like Dworkin should be grateful "that
for almost seventy years the real ACLU has been working to make
the world safe for her to write."[96]

Self-congratulatory narcissism aside, civil libertarians also fail
to recognize the world is not in fact safe for feminists—or for any
woman who steps into the minefield of men's anger—when men's
reckless speech can be weaponized against women with impunity.
This is particularly true for men of great wealth, power, and public
popularity. Stalking, sexual harassment, rape threats, nonconsensual pornography, "doxing" (the publication of private or personally
identifying information, often with malicious intent), and "deepfake porn" (visual imagery that is digitally manipulated to falsely

depict a person as nude or engaged in sexual conduct) do not only inflict severe psychological, economic, and reputational harm on individual victims; they also silence women as a group, deterring them from pursuing educational and professional opportunities, reporting abuse, engaging in intimate expression, and participating in civic life. How much of women's art, literature, teaching, and leadership have we lost because of misogynist abuse? And why should we settle for any free speech theory that doesn't even ask that question?

3

Burning Books

In May 2023, in keeping with the long tradition of white male supremacists who have burned books, printing presses, and people in their furious determination to preserve the racial, sexual, and economic inequality on which the United States was founded, Florida lawmakers enacted a law making it illegal for public colleges and universities in the state to teach that "systemic racism, sexism, oppression, and privilege are inherent in the institutions of the United States and were created to maintain social, political, and economic inequities."[1] The law is only one of hundreds of measures passed in recent years by conservative lawmakers attempting to censor what can be taught, thought, or spoken in the United States. Many of these efforts have focused on schools and universities, but they have also targeted private businesses, social media platforms, and public spaces. They have sought not only to purge these places of ideas that challenge or offend conservative sensibilities but also to dictate the values and perspectives that Americans must adopt instead.

"The role of the university is not to shield students from speech that makes them uncomfortable. . . . The cure for speech that one disagrees with lies not in prescription but in open debate and free inquiry."[2] The prominent politician and Harvard Law School graduate who made this statement in 2019 urged all the public colleges and universities in his state to adopt a version of the Chicago Statement, a widely praised free speech resolution issued in 2015 by the University of Chicago Committee on Freedom of Expression that pledged the institution's "commitment to a completely free and open discussion of ideas."[3] The speech and the call drew praise from civil liberties organizations, including the influential organization known at the time as the Foundation for Individual Rights in Education (FIRE),[4] who "applaud[ed]" the public official's efforts to "lead the way in promoting open discussion and civil discourse."[5]

The year was 2019, and the speaker was Florida governor Ron DeSantis, the man who would soon begin an all-out censorship campaign against the educational institutions in his state. The man who stood by DeSantis's side as he vowed to "protect student speech and the open exchange of ideas on our campuses,"[6] Florida commissioner of education Richard Corcoran, stated in a May 2021 speech that it was necessary to "police" teachers to ensure they were not indoctrinating students with a liberal agenda.[7] Referring to a teacher who had put up "Black Lives Matter" signs in her classroom, Corcoran bragged that he "made sure she was terminated."[8] In June 2021, the Florida Board of Education banned public schools from teaching about "critical race theory" (CRT).[9]

In 2021, Florida enacted a "free speech" law that forbids educators from *limiting* discussion "of ideas and opinions that they may find uncomfortable, unwelcome, disagreeable, or offensive," including those propounded by the KKK and Nazis,[10] but in 2022, DeSantis signed the Individual Freedom Act—more popularly known as the "Stop WOKE (Wrongs to Our Kids and Employees) Act"—*forbidding* instruction that might cause individuals to feel "discomfort, guilt, anguish, or any other form of psychological distress on account of his or her race, color, sex, or national origin" and classifying such instruction as discrimination.[11] DeSantis also signed a bill that would impose stiff criminal penalties on nonviolent protesters and those who damage Confederate monuments while providing criminal and civil immunity to people who kill or injure protesters with their vehicles.[12]

Also in 2022, DeSantis signed the euphemistically titled "Parental Rights in Education" law (dubbed the "Don't Say Gay" bill by its detractors), which prohibits school districts from encouraging classroom discussion about "sexual orientation or gender identity . . . in a manner that is not age appropriate or developmentally appropriate for students."[13] DeSantis's press secretary, Christina Pushaw, referred to critics of the bill as "groomers," sparking a nationwide trend of right-wingers accusing Democrats and liberals of being pedophiles and groomers.[14]

DeSantis also signed a law that seeks to punish the Walt Disney Company for criticizing his "Don't Say Gay" bill and a law that attempts to force private social media companies to carry speech against their will.[15] In addition, DeSantis fired an elected state prosecutor in 2022 on the basis of his political views, a move that a federal judge determined to be a violation of the prosecutor's First Amendment rights.[16] DeSantis has also openly declared his desire to change defamation law in direct opposition to the Supreme Court's ruling in the landmark case *New York Times Co. v. Sullivan* (1964),[17] leading one of his allies to propose a bill, H.B. 951,[18] that would allow the state to ignore Supreme Court precedent on defamation.[19]

DeSantis's efforts to censor schools and universities in particular are part of a larger trend of what PEN America terms "a legislative war on education in America."[20] Bills restricting what subjects teachers can teach and students can learn, both in kindergarten through twelfth grade and higher education, began proliferating in 2021 and intensified in 2022. Between January and August 2022, "lawmakers in 36 different states . . . introduced a total of 137 educational gag order bills, an increase of 250 [percent] over 2021."[21] To date, nearly all of the bills introduced that attempt to censor topics such as the role of racism and sexism in American institutions, discussions of sexual orientation or gender identity, and other "divisive concepts" have been sponsored by Republicans.[22] Many are so vaguely and broadly worded that it is impossible to know in advance what they prohibit and what they permit. Some of the bills create financial incentives for parents or other parties to sue for the removal of "offensive" educational material. Supporters of these educational gag orders routinely smear teachers, administrators, librarians, and school board members as indoctrinators, "groomers," and "pedophiles," which has led to harassment, firings, doxing, threats, and physical assaults.[23]

Since the Trump administration and continuing to the present day, Republicans have openly pursued an agenda of aggressive, state-sponsored suppression of speech and worked to curtail press freedoms, limit the rights of protesters, and punish dissenters. These efforts have many targets but have increasingly taken aim at educational institutions. The current anti-education movement began in earnest in September 2020, after an obscure journalist named Christopher Rufo appeared on Tucker Carlson's show to demand an executive order from Trump to abolish "critical race theory," which he characterized as an "existential threat to the United States."[24] Rufo chose the term not because it accurately described the curriculum of the corporate antibias trainings he had been examining but because he considered it to be, as Benjamin Wallace-Wells wrote in the *New Yorker*, "a promising political weapon." Wallace-Wells explained, "Its connotations are all negative to most middle-class Americans, including racial minorities, who see the world as 'creative' rather than 'critical,' 'individual' rather than 'racial,' 'practical' rather than 'theoretical.' Strung together, the phrase 'critical race theory' connotes hostile, academic, divisive, race-obsessed, poisonous, elitist, anti-American. . . . Critical race theory is the perfect villain."[25]

Three weeks after Rufo's appearance, Trump delivered exactly what Rufo demanded. His 2020 Executive Order on Combating Race and Sex Stereotyping was shamelessly Orwellian, denouncing those who acknowledge the centrality of slavery in America's founding and the lasting legacy of racism as slavery apologists whose views "were soundly defeated on the blood-stained battlefields of the Civil War." Tucked among the spluttering denunciation of various straw-man claims, including "that America is an irredeemably racist and sexist country; that some people, simply on account of their race or sex, are oppressors; and that racial and sexual identities are more important than our common status as human beings and Americans," and innocuous-sounding platitudes about racial and gender equality are the order's real targets: the discussion of "divisive concepts" or "scapegoating" relating to race or sex.[26]

According to the order, such divisive concepts include suggestions that "an individual, by virtue of his or her race or sex, bears responsibility for actions committed in the past by other members of the same race or sex" and that "any individual should feel discomfort, guilt, anguish, or any other form of psychological distress on account of his or her race or sex."[27] Race or sex scapegoating means "assigning fault, blame, or bias to a race or sex, or to members of a race or sex because of their race or sex," and includes claims that "consciously or unconsciously, and by virtue of his or her race or sex, members of any race are inherently racist or are inherently inclined to oppress others, or that members of a sex are inherently sexist or inclined to oppress others."[28]

Trump's executive order marked the beginning of a nationwide legislative assault against educational institutions. "Schools and universities are being threatened today to a degree that has no recent parallel," wrote Jeffrey Sachs and Jonathan Friedman of PEN America in February 2022. "There is a willingness, and even *eagerness*, to bring the weight and power of government to bear on controlling classroom speech."[29]

PEN America maintains a comprehensive database of what it has termed "educational gag orders," laws that restrict what can be taught, read, or discussed in the classroom.[30] According to PEN's database, nearly two hundred such laws were introduced in forty different states between 2021 and August 2022, nineteen of which became law in fifteen states, affecting 122 million Americans.[31] Additionally, governors, attorneys general, and administrative agencies in several states have issued numerous orders, statements, and guidelines seeking to censor school speech relating to social justice and diversity.[32] These laws and policies, often vaguely and broadly worded to ensure maximum chilling effect, are primarily aimed at repressing speech that acknowledges or condemns the influence of racism, sexism, homophobia, and transphobia in American society.[33]

Between the beginning of 2023 and the beginning of 2024, a wave of bills has been introduced aimed at reducing or eliminating diversity, equity, and inclusion efforts. As of January 2024, nearly sixty such measures have been introduced and eight have become law. Utah's law, as one example, makes race- or gender-specific student support services illegal and "prohibits any program, office or initiative that has 'diversity, equity and inclusion' in its name."[34] Several states have also limited tenure protections for faculty along with diversity initiatives.[35]

In two cases decided together in 2023, *Students for Fair Admissions v. Harvard* and *Students for Fair Admissions v. University of North Carolina*, the conservative supermajority of the Supreme Court held that Harvard and the University of North Carolina's race-conscious college admissions policies violated the Equal Protection Clause of the Fourteenth Amendment. The decision severely restricts the ability of American universities, most of which had historically excluded nonwhite students, to diversify their student bodies and address long-standing racial inequalities in higher education. In her dissent, Justice Sonia Sotomayor wrote, "Ignoring race will not equalize a society that is racially unequal. What was true in the 1860s, and again in 1954, is true today: Equality requires acknowledgment of inequality."[36]

A neo-Confederate mentality—ahistorical, revisionist, censorious, and intent on reinstating a rigid racial and gender hierarchy—has spread across the conservative establishment. The attacks on education have had a predictably chilling effect on teachers and students alike, who cannot be sure what topics they are allowed to discuss or what questions they are allowed to answer in the classroom. Many of the censorship bills give parents and other parties the right to sue over alleged violations,[37] and tip lines[38] and watch lists[39] have been established to encourage reporting and facilitate the tracking of incidents. The politicized hysteria over critical race theory has converged with hysteria over transgender bathroom access and COVID-19 measures, creating a climate of animosity against teachers, administrators, and school board members.

Teachers have been defamed, threatened, and physically attacked; many educators have left the profession in the wake of the anti-CRT movement.[40] Librarians have been harassed for the inclusion of books with LGBTQ+ themes in their collections and confronted by armed extremist groups for hosting Pride-themed events.[41] Republican state lawmakers have instigated harassment campaigns against school board members they consider to be insufficiently deferential to the governor's edicts. In one example, Florida state representative Randy Fine posted the cell phone number of a young Brevard County School Board member on his Facebook page after the district instituted COVID-19 mask mandates in defiance of DeSantis's ban, urging residents to contact her.[42] Angry protesters called and confronted the board member at board meetings and at her home, calling her a pedophile and threatening to "make you beg for mercy. If you thought January 6 was bad, wait until you see what we have for you!"[43] One protester outside the board member's home coughed in her face, while another shouted "Give her covid!" and a third swung a "Don't Tread on Me" flag toward her face. At one point, someone made a false report that the board member had abused her five-year-old child, leading to a visit from the Florida Department of Children and Families.[44]

———

In the manner of all authoritarians, neo-Confederates seek to use the power of the state to censor speech that threatens their values and to compel speech that serves them. But they also do not want to be clearly perceived as doing this. Being (accurately) identified as authoritarian censors depriving the American people of their constitutional rights threatens the political domination and cultural legitimacy that neo-Confederates crave. By casting themselves in the role of heroic defenders of freedom and the Constitution, they reduce the risk of unifying opposition across the political spectrum of nonextremist Republicans, centrists, and liberals.

Beginning around 2020, the convenient spectacle of "cancel culture" emerged to justify and distract from the Republican-led, highly coordinated, well-funded governmental assault on freedom of expression generally and on education in particular. A seemingly endless stream of op-eds, think pieces, media coverage, social media commentary, speeches, academic conferences, academic articles, and expert panels helped establish cancel culture as the *real* threat to free speech.

Like "safe spaces," "trigger warnings," and "political correctness," cancel culture is an amorphous concept, often used loosely and interchangeably with censorship and silencing to describe a wide range of negative reactions, from mild criticism to job loss. As was the case with those previous targets of cultural hand-wringing, the evidence of the existence and impact of cancel culture derives primarily from self-reported anecdotes about individuals being silenced, criticized, or punished by some private, nongovernmental force, usually traceable to a form of "liberal intolerance."[45]

Focusing on nongovernmental "censorship" turns the spotlight away from Republicans' blatant use of state power to control speech, and the reliance on subjective reports gives pride of place to those with the thinnest skin and greatest sense of grievance—a group that happens to include a large number of conservatives who feel persecuted by nonconservative individuals and ideas.[46] That feeling of persecution drives the hyperbolic rhetoric of the cancel-culture narrative, reinforcing the message that the shadowy left is an enemy that must be fought with force. This is in some ways the most pernicious aspect of the "thought-terminating cliché,"[47] to use Robert Jay Lifton's term, of cancel culture—the vilification that helps justify not only censorship of but violence against the alleged perpetrators of evil. It explains why cancel culture is a favorite topic among conservatives, from Fox News talking heads[48] to *Wall Street Journal* op-ed writers[49] to Trump.[50]

While president, Trump referred to cancel culture as a "political weapon" of the left. In 2020, Trump claimed that cancel culture was "driving people from their jobs, shaming dissenters, and demanding total submission from anyone who disagrees" and declared that this was "the very definition of totalitarianism, and it is completely alien to our culture and our values, and it has absolutely no place in the United States of America."[51] Trump invoked cancel culture again in his speech accepting the 2020 Republican presidential nomination, asserting that because "the goal of cancel culture is to make decent Americans live in fear of being fired, expelled, shamed, humiliated and driven from society as we know it," it must be countered with "patriotic education."[52]

The effect of a disproportionate focus on private "censorship" and the continued insistence that it poses an equal or greater threat to free speech than government censorship is to minimize and ultimately rationalize government censorship as the answer to private censorship. And as long as the focus is on the sins of the intolerant student, the biased teacher, or the coddling administrator, it stays off the powerful government official and the vast and powerful machinery of the state. Cancel culture is a shell game designed to distract from the Republicans' neo-Confederate agenda.

The shell game is one of the oldest confidence tricks in history.[53] There are many variations, but in general, spectators are instructed to keep their eye on a ball as it is covered by a shell or other container and then shuffled around with other identical containers. The seductive premise of the game is that you only have to pay attention to win; the con, of course, is that paying attention to the game is exactly how you lose. The con artist is in control of the ball at all times and is skilled at distracting players' attention so that they do not notice when the ball is slipped beneath another identical shell or off the table altogether. The con artist will sometimes occasionally let a player win (or allow a shill posing as a player to win) to convince the crowd that the game isn't rigged. Inevitably, though, those sucked into the game will find themselves on the losing end, because a shell game by definition cannot be won.

Those who have studied shell games and other cons note that two types of people are particularly susceptible to becoming dupes: the naïve and the arrogant. The naïve are easily swayed by the appearance of legitimacy (professional attire, official-sounding vocabulary) or sympathetic stories (tales of woe),[54] while the arrogant are done in by their conviction that they possess unique powers of perception or skills that allow them to see what others cannot.[55] But the players are not the only marks; so too are the spectators so absorbed by the con artist's game that they fail to notice his confederates in the crowd robbing them blind.

Some people fall for the cancel-culture con because they are entranced by sensationalist stories about liberal censorship; some because they believe that their instincts about the threat to free speech are unerring. Still others may see through the sham but decide to participate in it for personal, financial, or reputational gain. But whatever the motivation for playing the cancel-culture game, the spoils will always go to the neo-Confederate ideologues eager to deprive Americans of their rights.

One of the most useful features of cancel-culture discourse as a propaganda tool is its fundamental ambiguity. The term is used to describe everything from students "feeling uneasy"[56] in class to professors being fired for innocuous remarks.[57] As Osita Nwanevu writes, "cancel culture . . . seems to describe the phenomenon of being criticized by multiple people. . . . Neither the number of critics, the severity of the criticism, nor the extent of the actual fallout from it seem particularly important."[58] That kind of imprecision makes substantive analysis impossible, which is exactly the point of the con. Those sucked into cancel-culture discourse are certain that they are following a real object—*Cancel culture is here, in this tense classroom! No wait, it's over there, in those vicious social media posts!*—oblivious to the reality that the only real object all along is what the con(servative) artist wants them to see, or rather, *not* to see: the Republican theft of democracy.

"To say 'cancel culture,'" writes Ligaya Mishan, "is already to express a point of view, implicitly negative. Although cancel culture is not a movement—it has neither leaders nor membership, and those who take part in it do so erratically, maybe only once, and share no coherent ideology—it's persistently attributed to the extremes of a political left and a fear-mongering specter of wokeness, itself a freighted term, originally derived and then distorted from the Black vernacular 'woke,' which invokes a spirit of vigilance to see the world as it really is."[59] Using "wokeness" as a pejorative, along with "critical race theory," "cultural Marxism," and "socialism," reinforces the message that the *real* censors and traitors are not the Republican leaders repressing dissent and compelling conformity but shadowy leftists laying siege to our schools.

Cancellation is such a slippery concept that conservatives can invoke it as a justification for conduct that, if undertaken by anyone other than a conservative, would itself be labeled cancellation. For example, after reading about a student protest of an event involving the anti-LGBTQ organization Alliance Defending Freedom at Yale Law School in March 2022, DC Circuit Judge Laurence Silberman emailed a list of nearly all US federal judges encouraging them to blacklist the student protesters: "The latest events at Yale Law School in which students attempted to shout down speakers participating in a panel discussion should be noted. . . . All federal judges—and all federal judges are presumably committed to free speech—should carefully consider whether any student so identified should be disqualified for potential clerkships."[60]

Some months later, Fifth Circuit Judge James Ho proclaimed that he would no longer hire clerks from Yale Law School to protest "rampant 'cancel culture' on its campus and incidents in which students had disrupted conservative speakers."[61] Ho later doubled down on this position, writing in a *National Review* piece coauthored with Eleventh Circuit Judge Elizabeth Branch that "students who practice intolerance don't belong in the legal profession."[62] One occasion for the judges' screed was a March 2023 event at Stanford Law School in which conservative Fifth Circuit Judge Kyle Duncan, a Trump appointee, was met with angry student protesters.[63] Notably, these judges did not express similar sentiments when, in 2021, members of the Stanford Federalist Society—the same organization that had invited Duncan to speak—successfully pressured the law school to withhold a student's diploma because he had mocked the organization with a satirical flyer.[64]

As Trump declared in March 2022, "If we allow the Marxists and Communists and Socialists to teach our children to hate America, there will be no one left to defend our flag or to protect

our great country or its freedom." Accordingly, Trump issued a call
to arms: "Getting critical race theory out of our schools is not just a
matter of values, it's also a matter of national survival. We have no
choice, the fate of any nation ultimately depends upon the willingness of its citizens to lay down and they must do this, lay down
their very lives to defend their country."[65]

Distraction, justification, vilification: cancel culture is, for good
reason, one of the most powerful tools in the conservative propaganda playbook. But its effectiveness would be limited if it were
only promoted or internalized by the conservative faithful. To
achieve true cultural and political domination, partisan propaganda requires legitimation by external sources. Accordingly, the
cancel-culture con game requires confederates, shills, and dupes,
and there is a seemingly endless supply of liberals and civil libertarians who have lined up to volunteer.

It is laudable that organizations like the ACLU and FIRE have
intervened in meaningful ways against the most recent wave of
conservative attacks on schools, challenging the constitutionality
of educational gag orders[66] and representing faculty who have been
fired for First Amendment–protected speech.[67] But these same
organizations, by internalizing and amplifying conservative propaganda about campus intolerance and cancel culture, helped bring
the current state of crisis into being.[68] These organizations have disproportionately highlighted isolated anecdotes of liberal intolerance over widespread, systematic evidence of harassment and
censorship by conservatives. Even worse, they have at times directly
supported the imposition of laws and policies that purport to counter the supposed excesses of liberal intolerance by restricting students' right to protest.[69] While never failing to admonish women
and minority students that "the best answer to bad speech is more
speech," liberals and libertarians have helped delegitimize counterspeech and vilify student protesters.[70]

Particularly in the context of education and social media, liberals and libertarians have increasingly joined conservatives in vilifying counterspeech and conflating (private) reactions to speech with
(governmental) restrictions of speech. The ACLU and FIRE have

played a significant role in deflecting attention from conservative attacks on democracy and free expression by focusing their opprobrium on the supposed liberal excesses of political correctness, campus "safe spaces," and now cancel culture. Whether these groups have been genuinely taken in by neo-Confederate propaganda or are motivated by cynical self-interest is unclear. The anti-cancel-culture movement has become a veritable cottage industry, inspiring books, op-eds, feature articles, podcasts, policy papers, seminars, legislative proposals, and academic conferences. Taking up the mantle of a free speech defender against the ominous and amorphous threat of cancellation can be tremendously lucrative not only financially but also in terms of social, intellectual, or moral capital. Far from being ostracized or silenced, the provocateur, the "heterodox" thinker, and the "balanced" journalist are often rewarded with cultural accolades and impassioned fan bases: "Being outrageous has never cost so little or earned professional contrarians and provocateurs so much."[71] Indeed, sometimes speakers deliberately invoke the imaginary threat of cancellation as a means of preemptively legitimating their views and the retaliatory steps they will take to defend them.

Denouncing the most extreme and obvious excesses of the right's coordinated attack on schools and educators while reprimanding the left for isolated incidents of private recrimination is a version of the "both sides-ism" also exhibited by media outlets like the *New York Times*. In a March 2022 op-ed titled "America Has a Free Speech Problem," the *Times* editorial board acknowledged the right's coordinated censorship campaign against schools and educators while suggesting that isolated incidents of private recrimination were equally condemnable. "Many on the right," the board wrote, "for all their braying about cancel culture, have embraced . . . laws that would ban books, stifle teachers and discourage open discussion in classrooms," while "many on the left refuse to acknowledge that cancel culture exists at all." The board concludes based on this evidence that "the political left and the right are caught in a destructive loop of condemnation and recrimination around cancel culture."[72] This kind of false equivalence is what historian Thomas Zimmer refers to as journalism's "neutrality dogma"—"the privileging of 'nonpartisanship' over accuracy, the tendency to present both sides as essentially the same when they are evidently not, the distortion-by-'balance.'"[73] That distortion, Zimmer argues, consistently both favors and obscures "the radicalizing rightwing forces in American life."[74]

The op-ed veered beyond distortion into outright error by claiming that "Americans are losing hold of a fundamental right as citizens of a free country: the right to speak their minds and voice their opinions in public without fear of being shamed or shunned."[75] No such right has ever existed, in America or anywhere else. The First Amendment protects the right of private citizens against governmental restrictions of speech; it does not bestow a right to an audience, and certainly not to an adoring, uncritical one. In fact, the First Amendment protects the right of private citizens to criticize, ridicule, or ignore other people's speech, including by shaming and shunning. This is a point that liberals and civil libertarians have traditionally understood and defended: when private actors object to or avoid speech they do not like, including through protests and boycotts, they are engaging in quintessential exercises of free speech and individual liberty.

That the editorial board of the most prominent liberal-leaning newspaper in the United States believes the First Amendment confers a wide-ranging constitutional entitlement to express oneself without criticism helps explain why it regularly runs pieces like "I Came to College Eager to Debate. I Found Self-Censorship Instead," in which a University of Virginia student described losing her former confidence to speak her mind because of the "steep consequences" for doing so. According to the student's self-reported account, those consequences were observing her fellow students "shift in their seats" and seeming "to get angry" after she expressed an opinion in a class discussion.[76] At a time when students at campuses across the nation are grappling with the chilling effects of sexual harassment and abuse,[77] white supremacist recruitment efforts,[78] gun violence,[79] professor "watchlists,"[80] and unauthorized surveillance,[81] it is telling that the national paper of record chose to amplify an allegation of censorship based on little more than the subjective feelings and anecdotal observations of one undergraduate student.

In a February 2023 op-ed, the CEO of PEN America, Suzanne Nossel, praised Florida governor DeSantis for his 2019 endorsement of the Chicago Statement before criticizing him for now "embrac[ing] the very tactics he once decried, putting the weight of government power behind efforts to repress viewpoints that offend him and his supporters."[82] Nossel's observation that promoting the tolerance of uncomfortable ideas on campus on the one hand while ruthlessly purging entire concepts from schools on the other are inherently contradictory positions is of course correct. But to the authoritarian, they are in a meaningful sense the *same position*: the classic authoritarian position is "free speech for me but not for thee," with the added twist that the *me* here are government officials who can bring the power of the state to bear against ideas that do not serve their interests. DeSantis himself made his authoritarian commitments clear in 2018 when he pledged to defend "First Amendment speech rights against those in academia, media and politics who seek to *silence conservatives*."[83]

Like many civil libertarians who are deeply concerned about the impact of private intolerance on free expression, Nossel criticizes government censorship. But hyperfocusing on the supposedly intolerant acts of private individuals, especially students, helps drive the demand for and justification of government censorship as a response. Nossel writes that "the cure that DeSantis and his backers favor—intrusive legislation to muzzle the opposite set of views—is worse than the disease,"[84] but characterizing private intolerance as a "disease" in the first place is the kind of rhetoric that encourages, however inadvertently, this very cure. And even as she criticizes the cure, Nossel devotes much of the piece to agreeing with DeSantis and his supporters about the disease: "They are not wrong to call out the quest for a more inclusive and equitable society when it veers into the outright suppression of speech and ideas. Progressives too often forget that the movements they wage—whether for racial justice, gender justice, climate or anything else—depend upon free speech protections to guarantee the space for dissent; and that such protections must apply equally to speech with which they disagree. Some fail to acknowledge, too, that worthwhile perspectives and solutions can emerge from outside their own ideological spheres."[85]

Even when acknowledging Republicans' aggressive, multi-pronged, state-sponsored attacks on educational institutions, many liberals and civil libertarians continue to emphasize anecdotes of private intolerance as if they were equal or even greater threats to freedom of expression. As free speech in schools and universities is literally under attack by partisan government forces in direct viola-tion of the First Amendment—Republicans throughout the coun-try are using the force of law to remove books, ban words, strip curriculums, silence faculty, and compel speech in educational institutions—influential figures across the political spectrum con-tinue to fulminate about the dangers of intolerant students, liberal bias among professors, and cancel culture.

The reality that "for all the fear that cancel culture elicits, it hasn't succeeded in toppling any major figures—high-level politicians, corporate titans—let alone institutions"[86] points toward yet another motivation for ostensibly nonconservative entities to participate in the cancel-culture shell game: ideological alignment with at least some neo-Confederate goals. The attachment to white male supremacy often transcends political affiliation,[87] and much of what passes for liberalism in the United States is simply a less extreme, and less crudely expressed, version of conservatism. Power in America, whether political, cultural, or economic, has always pri-marily been the province of white men, and plenty of people across the political spectrum think that it should stay that way. Some-times the only meaningful difference between conservatives and liberals on this point is whether they are willing to admit this.

There are plenty of liberals as well as conservatives who are, to use philosopher Regina Rini's evocative term, *status quo warriors*. What unites status quo warriors is sometimes their objection not to *what* is being canceled but to *who* is doing the canceling.[88] Part of the power, or threat, of the #MeToo and #BlackLivesMatter movements is the centering of women and minorities' voices and experiences. As Nwanevu writes, "The critics of cancel culture are plainly threatened not by a new and uniquely powerful kind of public criticism but by a new set of critics: young progressives, including many minorities and women who, largely through social media, have obtained a seat at the table where matters of justice and etiquette are debated and are banging it loudly to make up for lost time. The fact that jabs against cancel culture are typically jabs leftward, even as conservatives work diligently to cancel academics, activists, and companies they disfavor in both tweets and legislation, underscores this."[89]

It can sometimes be difficult to determine whether participation in the cancel-culture con is driven by naïveté, opportunism, ideological alignment, or some combination of these factors. What is clear, however, is the cumulative impact of this collaboration: the hijacking of free speech for neo-Confederate ends. As the Lost Cause myth reframes the Civil War as the War of Northern Aggression, the cancel-culture myth reframes the conservative assault on education as an attack by liberal censors. Over and over again, racist, sexist, homophobic, transphobic expression is characterized as "free speech" that must be defended, while challenges to white male supremacy are characterized as indoctrination that must be rooted out.[90] "The power to cancel is nothing compared to the power to establish what is and is not a cultural crisis," writes Nwanevu. "And that power remains with opinion leaders who are, at this point, skilled hands at distending their own cultural anxieties into panics that—time and time and time again—smother history, fact, and common sense into irrelevance."[91] Stripped of its rhetorical flourishes, the upshot of cancel-culture discourse is that power—and speech—belongs where it always has been: in the hands of white men.

The loudest proponents of the need to "protect the speech we hate" are those with no intention of honoring that commitment themselves. Every successive phase of moral panic over insufficiently tolerant students and left-leaning faculty, however sincere, ultimately serves the interests of the most regressive and antidemocratic groups in society. Good faith concerns about ideological diversity and intellectual fortitude are all too easily instrumentalized in reactionary propaganda aimed at vilifying institutions of higher education, their faculty, and their students as simultaneously perverted and puritanical, crude and censorious, hopelessly fragile, and dangerously aggressive.[92]

The hijacking of the free speech conversation is crucial to the right's war on schools, drawing attention away from Republicans' coordinated campaign of state-sponsored censorship and painting "leftist indoctrination" as the real enemy. The persistent invocation of liberal intolerance, whether in the form of "political correctness," "snowflake students," or "cancel culture," not only distracts from but is used to justify repressive measures against students and teachers. The right's de-education campaign depends on the support and amplification of liberal collaborators. Unintentionally or not, every participant in the cancel-culture shell game contributes to the delegitimization of protest, the rewriting of history, the vilification of educators, and the deepening of a reactionary political agenda.

4

Burning Down the Public Square

In April 2022, while his offer to buy the social media platform Twitter (which he renamed X) was pending, billionaire and self-proclaimed "free speech absolutist" Elon Musk was asked how he would handle the question of free speech on the site.[1] Musk answered, "A good sign as to whether there is free speech is, is someone you don't like allowed to say something you don't like? If that is the case, we have free speech. . . . That is the sign of a healthy, functioning free speech situation."[2] When the deal went through, Musk stated, "Free speech is the bedrock of a functioning democracy, and Twitter is the digital town square where matters vital to the future of humanity are debated."[3]

The next day, Musk added, "By 'free speech,' I simply mean that which matches the law. I am against censorship that goes far beyond the law. If people want less free speech, they will ask government to pass laws to that effect. Therefore, going beyond the law is contrary to the will of the people."[4] Some commentators wondered if Musk mistakenly thought that the First Amendment restrained private business, while others assumed he was aware that the First Amendment only restrains government entities (the state action doctrine) but was voluntarily choosing to adopt the First Amendment as a guide for his private company.

It didn't take long, however, for Musk to start banning accounts of users who criticized him, journalists who reported on him, or people who used terminology he didn't like. At the same time, Musk reinstated the accounts of users who promoted conspiracy theories, posted sexually explicit images of people without consent, and espoused neo-Nazi ideology. While this led to criticism that Musk was betraying the First Amendment principles he claimed to champion, his handling of the platform tracks First Amendment doctrine—in its overpromotion of reckless, bigoted speech that conforms to the preferences of powerful, white, wealthy men and simultaneous repression of speech that does not—pretty well.

Given the radical potential of technology to create new ways of seeing, communicating, and interacting, why does the tech industry cling so desperately to the regressive, limiting, and unimaginative principle of free speech dictated by the First Amendment? Why do virtually all of the giant tech companies, with their nearly infinite resources, conform to all the same conventional ideas about free speech and censorship? Why, for that matter, does the public continue to congregate and communicate on these commercialized, predatory platforms mining our speech for profit?

In 2021, the five largest US companies by market capitalization were Apple, Microsoft, Alphabet, Amazon, and Facebook.[5] In that year, those five tech companies "constitute[d] 20 percent of the stock market's total worth, a level not seen from a single industry in at least 70 years."[6] Google, Apple, and Microsoft all enjoyed record-breaking profits that year, while Facebook "doubled its profits and reported its fastest growth in five years."[7]

The dominance of the tech industry extends far beyond economic markets, shaping how people work, vote, socialize, learn, shop, and communicate. In 2005, only 5 percent of Americans reported using social media; by 2021, that number was 72 percent.[8] The majority of individuals on social media use the platforms every day.[9] As the influence and power of Big Tech has continued to expand, calls to reform the industry have emerged with increasing frequency and urgency across the political spectrum. A 2021 Pew Research survey found that 68 percent of Americans think that "major tech companies have too much power and influence in today's economy" and that more than half of Americans think that major tech companies should be more highly regulated.[10] President Joe Biden signed an executive order in July 2021 urging the Federal Trade Commission (FTC) to examine anticompetitive restrictions, unfair data collection, and surveillance practices by dominant internet platforms,[11] and the FTC filed an antitrust suit against Facebook in August 2021.[12] Several bills have been introduced in Congress aimed at reducing the liability shield afforded to tech companies by Section 230 of the Communications Decency Act.[13] Executives from Facebook, Twitter, and Google have been summoned before Congress multiple times in recent years to address issues such as anticompetitive practices, misinformation, and algorithmic amplification.[14]

But despite the thirty-one congressional hearings on the tech industry held between 2017 and 2022 and increasingly impassioned calls for reform, "no major legislation has been passed to address privacy, antitrust issues, children's harms online, or to strengthen federal regulatory agencies that oversee social-media firms" in that time.[15] And the profit, power, and influence of major tech companies continue to grow.

The tech industry dominates the national and global economy in part because it has successfully framed free speech as a product and itself as its most important provider, convincing the American public and many legislators to view regulation of the industry as literal censorship. Social media and other communications platforms encourage and amplify reckless speech, including white male supremacist rhetoric, terrorist content, doxing and harassment campaigns, and coordinated attacks on journalists, politicians, and activists, because doing so is profitable for them. By conflating social media engagement with the exercise of constitutional rights, the tech industry has taken a lead role in the rise of reckless speech.

The tech industry's unprecedented economic, political, and cultural dominance relies in significant measure on its successful—and successfully disguised—commodification of free speech. From the earliest days of the commercial internet, techno-libertarians

asserted that cyberspace was the true home of free speech, an assertion wrapped in antiregulatory sentiment. Tech companies invoked
laissez-faire First Amendment principles to justify their long-
standing failure to address extremism and abuse, elevating passivity into a virtue.

From the early "hacker ethic" that "prized the free flow of information" to a Twitter executive's (in)famous 2012 characterization
of the site as the "free speech wing of the free speech party,"[16] free
speech values are frequently invoked by the tech industry to justify
the flourishing of harmful content.[17] John Perry Barlow, a cofounder
of the influential libertarian organization Electronic Frontier
Foundation, offered a poetic vision of free speech in his influential
1996 manifesto, Declaration of the Independence of Cyberspace: "All
the sentiments and expressions of humanity, from the debasing to
the angelic, are parts of a seamless whole, the global conversation
of bits. We cannot separate the air that chokes from the air upon
which wings beat."[18]

In 2012, then-CEO of Reddit Yishan Wong defended a sub-
reddit devoted to sexualized and surreptitious photographs of und-
eraged girls by stating, "We stand for free speech. This means we
are not going to ban distasteful subreddits. We will not ban legal
content even if we find it odious or if we personally condemn it."[19]
In 2014, Fredrick Brennan, creator of the site known at the time as
8chan, referred to pedophiliac content on his site as "simply the
cost of free speech."[20] Newer social media sites like Gab and Parler,
home to vast amounts of violent white male supremacist content,
are even more explicit about their professed First Amendment ideals; Gab's terms of service mentions the First Amendment no fewer
than eight times;[21] Parler's community guidelines state its "mission
is to create a social platform in the spirit of the First Amendment
to the United States Constitution."[22]

Tech companies offer the illusion of "free speech" in a dual
sense: free of cost and free of censorship. But as has been painstak-
ingly detailed by investigative journalists, whistleblowers, and
scholars, there is nothing free about tech industry practices. As
succinctly if not intentionally expressed in Mark Zuckerberg's

testimony before a 2018 joint hearing before the Senate Judiciary and Senate Commerce, Science, and Transportation committees, the business of social media platforms isn't free speech, but profit. When asked by Senator Orrin Hatch, "How do you sustain a business model in which users don't pay for your service?," Facebook's CEO answered, "Senator, we run ads."[23]

The tech industry masks its corporate manipulation, extraction, and exploitation of speech through an increasingly wide range of "free" services promising connection, entertainment, and convenience. "With all of these opportunities for speech, it is sometimes easy to forget that, whatever users wish to do and to be through the use of these platforms, their interests are always subject to the grace of the platform."[24] Tech companies are committed to free speech primarily as a source of free labor. When individuals post on social media sites, believing that they are engaging in freedom of expression, billion-dollar corporations mine that speech for data to be used for marketing, advertising, and surveillance purposes. Online speech is filtered, arranged, promoted, altered, and labeled in accordance with corporate interests.[25] The objective is not the promotion of free speech or the protection of the public interest but rather the harvesting of data for profit. Search engines and social media platforms create nothing; they amplify, sort, and sell the speech of "users" who increasingly cannot conceptualize a right of free speech that exists apart from the internet: "To exist is to be indexed by a search engine."[26]

These industry players operate "commercial enterprises designed to maximize revenue, not defend political expression, preserve our collective heritage, or facilitate creativity."[27] The commodification of free speech is an essential element of what Shoshana Zuboff calls "surveillance capitalism." It is "a boundary-less form that ignores older distinctions between market and society, market and world, or market and person. It is a profit-seeking form in which production is subordinated to extraction as surveillance capitalists unilaterally claim control over human, societal, and political territories extending far beyond the conventional institutional terrain of the private firm or the market."[28] What is more, the relentless pursuit of what is euphemistically referred to as *engagement, community,* or *user-generated content* places a premium on extremist content that disproportionately targets vulnerable populations for abuse and harassment, endangering public welfare and undermining democracy itself.

This extremism has a decidedly partisan slant. Contrary to oft-repeated claims that social media is biased against conservatives, the algorithms of major social media sites disproportionately amplify right-wing content, with catastrophic results.[29] Internal Twitter research demonstrates that its algorithms amplify right-wing content more than left-wing content.[30] Research by the Tech Transparency Project found that YouTube algorithms create a much more robust filter bubble for right-wing content than left-wing content and that Fox is by far the most recommended information channel on YouTube.[31] Researchers have suggested that the Fox News channel dominates YouTube because it traffics in conspiracy theories and employs more polarizing and inflammatory language than left-leaning channels like MSNBC.[32] The influence of Fox News illustrates that the ecosystem of extremism and disinformation is not limited to social media. Indeed, in many ways, Fox News pioneered the strategies of outrage, engagement, and virality that now characterize social media.[33]

Meta has deliberately promoted conservative sites on its platforms, even changing Facebook's algorithm to reduce the visibility of left-leaning news sites[34] and allowing right-wing sites to "skirt the company's fact-checking rules, publish untrustworthy and offensive content and harm the tech giant's relationship with advertisers," despite the efforts of its own employees to convince the company to consistently apply its own policies.[35] Internal Facebook research, titled "Carol's Journey to QAnon," demonstrated how quickly Facebook's algorithm recommended extremist conspiracy theories to an account set up for an imaginary woman with interests in Fox News and Sinclair Broadcasting.[36] The day after the 2020 election, 10 percent of all political content posts viewed on Facebook in the United States falsely claimed that the vote was fraudulent.[37] As one Facebook employee wrote in an internal document, if the company "takes a hands-off stance for these problems . . . then the net result is that Facebook, taken as a whole, will be actively (if not necessarily consciously) promoting these types of activities. The mechanics of our platform are not neutral."[38]

The mechanics of social media platforms are indeed not neutral, and neither are the offline consequences. The lopsided political amplification of right-wing content on social media is all the more troubling given the disproportionate incidence of right-wing violence: "Since 2015, right-wing extremists have been involved in 267 plots or attacks and 91 fatalities," more than four times the number of plots and attacks associated with left-wing viewpoints.[39] The list of deadly events announced, planned, or live streamed on social media is seemingly endless: the 2014 Isla Vista "incel"-inspired killings of six people, the 2017 Unite the Right rally in Charlottesville that left three dead, the 2018 Tree of Life synagogue mass shooting that killed eleven, the 2019 Christchurch massacre that killed fifty-one, the 2019 El Paso mass shooting that killed twenty-three, the January 6 insurrection that contributed to nine deaths, the 2022 mass murder of ten black shoppers at a grocery store in Buffalo, and the 2022 Uvalde elementary school massacre that killed nineteen children and two adults. But no amount of bloodshed seems to shake the resolve of Meta CEO Mark Zuckerberg, who told an audience at Georgetown University in 2019 that while others might "decide the cost is simply too great," Facebook would "continue to stand for free expression, understanding its messiness, but believing that the long journey towards greater progress requires confronting ideas that challenge us."[40]

It is notable that white supremacists were among the earliest internet adopters, having quickly recognized the potential of decentralized and anonymized communication for increasing their numbers, disseminating propaganda, and planning attacks. One of the first online bulletin board systems (BBS) to go live, the Aryan Liberty Net, was founded by a KKK leader named Louis Beam in 1984. Beam boasted that he was able to make racist material that had been banned in Canada and European countries available on the US-based computer network.[41] The *New York Times* reported in

1985 that the Aryan Liberty Net had "established a computer-based network to link rightist groups and to disseminate a list of those who it says 'have betrayed their race.'"[42] The lists included the names, telephone numbers, and addresses of individuals the organization considered to be "race traitors" and "informers." The group described itself as "a pro-American, pro-White, anti-Communist network of true believers who serve the one and only God—Jesus, the Christ"; membership was restricted to "Aryan patriots only."[43] An early message posted to the site proclaimed, "Finally, we are all going to be linked together at one point in time. Imagine, if you will, all the great minds of the patriotic Christian movement linked together and joined into one computer."[44]

The tactics used by far-right extremists today—doxing, trolling, coded memes, decentralized communication strategies to avoid detection and disruption (what Beam referred to as "leaderless resistance"[45])—were developed decades ago on online bulletin boards like this.[46] As Adam Clark Estes writes, "You can draw a line from the first neo-Nazi online bulletin boards to the online hate forum Stormfront in the '90s to the alt-right movement that helped Donald Trump rise to power in 2016."[47] Social media platforms have accelerated the distribution of extremist content through engagement tools such as "like" buttons, which teach algorithms to feed users more content similar to what they have viewed before.

The tech industry has accelerated and promoted violent white male supremacist rhetoric for its own ends. While the true religion of corporations is profit, not politics, indifference to the destruction wrought by the ruthless pursuit of self-interest is the very definition of recklessness. In its colonization and commodification of free speech, the tech industry unites corporate recklessness with individual recklessness.

———

On October 14, 2021, in the midst of widespread criticism and scrutiny over violent extremism, dangerous misinformation, and sexual exploitation on its platform, the company known at the time as Facebook announced the launch of a new artificial intelligence project called Ego4D.[48] The name derives from the project's focus on "egocentric," or first-person, perception, and Facebook planned to use the resulting dataset to, among other things, equip augmented reality glasses and virtual reality headsets with the capacity to transcribe and recall audio and visual recordings of individuals around the user. When asked whether Facebook had implemented measures to address privacy concerns regarding these capabilities, a spokesperson replied that the company "expected that privacy safeguards would be introduced further down the line."[49]

As underscored by multiple internal documents released by whistleblowers in the weeks preceding the project's announcement, this approach—to aggressively push new, untested, and potentially dangerous products into the public realm and worry about the consequences later, if at all—was typical of Facebook. Documents that former Facebook employee Frances Haugen shared with the Securities and Exchange Commission revealed what Adrienne LaFrance called in the *Atlantic* the "'asymmetrical' burden placed on employees to 'demonstrate legitimacy and user value' before launching any harm-mitigation tactics—a burden not shared by those developing new features or algorithm changes with growth and engagement in mind."[50] While the company may have abandoned Facebook's official motto, "move fast and break things," it still seems to accurately describe the company's philosophy.

Even so, it was particularly brazen of Facebook, which renamed itself Meta a few weeks later, to launch a project that makes it easier for individuals to record people around them without consent on the heels of multiple revelations about the company's troubling privacy, security, and moderation practices. One such revelation was that the company had allowed nude images of an alleged rape victim to be viewed fifty-six million times without her consent before taking them down because the man she accused of the crime was a famous soccer star.[51]

Such brazenness results not merely from callousness but also confidence—confidence that no matter what is revealed about Meta's role in irreparable harms to individuals or the breakdown of our democracy, it will face no real consequences. This has held true throughout revelations about the company's amplification of deadly disinformation about COVID-19, the endangerment of teens' mental health, the acceleration of dangerous conspiracy theories, the preferential treatment of powerful elites, and the promotion of violently racist and sexist propaganda.

The lesson that Meta and other ad-based social media companies such as Twitter and Google have learned every time they are implicated in scandal is that the media attention will be intense for a while, company representatives will be called before Congress to answer uncomfortable questions, the occasional fine will be levied and easily paid, there will be talk of reining in the tech industry—and business will proceed as usual. As a Facebook communications official allegedly stated while dismissing criticism of the company's facilitation of Russian interference in the 2016 US presidential election, "It will be a flash in the pan. Some legislators will get pissy. And then in a few weeks they will move onto something else. Meanwhile we are printing money in the basement, and we are fine."[52]

What accounts for the tech industry's continued insouciance even as the social and human costs of its central profit model, based on the euphemism of "engagement," have become undeniably clear? It is now public knowledge that social media and other telecommunications platforms contribute to genocides, suicides, mass shootings, international and domestic terrorism, public health crises, insurrections, election interference, sexual exploitation, reputational ruin, psychological trauma, and misinformation on an unprecedented scale—and yet, the tech industry not only survives but thrives. While legislative efforts to regulate the industry have increased in recent years, these have mostly originated outside the United States, where many dominant tech corporations are based. In the United States, even as criticism of Big Tech has reached a fever pitch across the political spectrum, very little has actually been done to date to impose real accountability on the tech industry.

Part of the explanation for this is simple: Big Tech is big business, and in the United States, the rule seems to be that the greater the profits, the more diminished the responsibility. But the tech industry's ability to inflict so much injury with so much impunity turns on more than just raw corporate power. In fact, its success is largely contingent on obscuring the commercial nature of its enterprises. As many scholars, journalists, and advocates have detailed, the supposedly free services offered by tech companies allow them to extract vast amounts of data from unsuspecting users for profit. But perhaps even more importantly, the tech industry (in particular the user-generated content tech industry) appeals to an additional and even more powerful sense of "free": free speech. Social media platforms have created the impression that they are indispensable for, if not indistinguishable from, free speech.

This consumerist constitutionalism—the conflation of a commercial product with a constitutional right—serves corporate interests in multiple ways. First, given the deep emotional attachment Americans have to their constitutional rights, convincing them that they need a particular product in order to exercise those rights is sure to be a lucrative enterprise. This is especially true if the public believes that they are always on the verge of losing those rights and that the only way to avert this crisis is to consume more of the product. Consumerist constitutionalism leads individuals to not only acquire but also to identify with certain products and services, creating an endowment effect that makes any interference with access feel like an existential threat. The halo of constitutional rights also helps disguise corporate interests as noble principles, sidestepping the wariness many Americans would typically exhibit toward overtly commercial enterprises. This disarming effect is promoted and reinforced by civil liberties advocates and organizations that lobby in favor of industry interests in the name of protecting constitutional rights.

Consider, for example, the firearms industry's successful conflation of Second Amendment rights with gun ownership. Working in tandem with organizations such as the National Rifle Association, gun manufacturers and distributors have been so successful in associating the purchase of weapons with the Second Amendment that every modern debate over firearms regulation inevitably becomes a debate over the Second Amendment. This is despite the fact that the Second Amendment's text and history make plain that it addresses the collective right of bearing arms as part of a militia, not an individual right to purchase or use weapons. Even after the Supreme Court's mystifying and activist reinterpretation of the right as one of individual self-defense in *District of Columbia v. Heller* (2008), the conflation of that complex and nuanced right with the right to purchase and use firearms remains insupportable.[53] But as debates over gun safety have demonstrated, the minority of individuals who own the majority of firearms in America view guns not as products, but as extensions of their identities.[54] In this fetishized view, even the most modest public safety reforms are perceived as unconstitutional intrusions on a fundamental right. The NRA's fact-free assertion that "the only thing that stops a bad guy with a gun is a good guy with a gun"[55] is designed to appeal to the fears and delusions of the average gun owner, which makes it very effective advertising for the billion-dollar firearms industry.

Consumerist constitutionalism that conflates social media activity and free speech follows much the same pattern. From the earliest days of the internet, tech developers invoked the First Amendment and free speech principles in their visions for cyberspace.[56] The Electronic Frontier Foundation and the ACLU touted the internet as the truest medium for free speech. Early legislative attempts to regulate the internet were quickly struck down on First Amendment grounds. Modest efforts to address egregious online abuses continue to be condemned as censorship, while billion-dollar tech companies fund research and scholarship to further boost the link between freedom of expression and the use of commercial social media services. The shopworn civil libertarian claim that "the best answer to bad speech is more speech," an echo of the NRA's more-guns myth, is a gift to the corporations whose business model is extracting valuable data from internet users by means of their free labor.

Consumerist constitutionalism helps explain the deferential and preferential treatment Congress has bestowed upon both the firearms industry and the tech industry. The findings section of the

Protection of Lawful Commerce in Arms Act (PLCAA), which broadly immunizes the firearms industry from liability, explicitly invokes both the Second and First Amendments.[57] Similarly, Section 230 of the Communications Decency Act, which broadly immunizes the tech industry from liability, emphasizes the internet as "a forum for a true diversity of political discourse."[58] Both of these laws have served not only to close the courtroom door on individuals who have suffered injuries due to the actions or inactions of industry actors but also to create perverse incentives for those industries to be as reckless as they wish in their pursuit of profit.

———

In *Packingham v. North Carolina* (2017), the Supreme Court declared the internet to be "the modern public square."[59] This claim has been repeated so often by politicians, tech industry leaders, civil libertarians, and scholars that it has achieved the status of conventional wisdom. Proponents of the claim point to the vast array of activities now conducted online and to the public's increasing reliance on social media platforms such as Facebook and Twitter for discussion and debate on matters of public importance. The public square, in this view, is presumed to be the quintessential site of democratic deliberation and civic participation—a physical "marketplace of ideas."

But as architecture historian Tom Wilkinson asks, "When we say 'public square,' . . . who or what is this public? Who owns this space, what makes it public? . . . This is the essence of democracy: the ability to question power, and the power to do so."[60] Because the concept of the digital public square is often presented as both a descriptive and a prescriptive assessment, the doctrinal and policy consequences that flow from the analogy are significant. The internet-as-digital-public-square view chiefly emphasizes the principle of openness to all people and all ideas. Accordingly, adherents of this perspective tend to view restrictions and regulations of online forums as antidemocratic and censorious. This is particularly true of governmental attempts to exclude certain speakers or listeners, such as the North Carolina law invalidated in *Packingham* that prohibited sex offenders from accessing commercial social networking sites. A more expansive version of the digital public square maintains that exclusion by private actors, such as major social media companies, is equally or even more detrimental to democratic deliberation than exclusion by government actors.[61]

But if the goal is to promote a space for democratic deliberation and to realize the values underlying the First Amendment, the public-square analogy is both misleading and misguided. First, the significant differences between social media forums—virtual spaces owned by for-profit corporations—and physical public squares have important consequences for free speech. Second, the extent to which social media forums do resemble physical public squares is not necessarily a virtue. After all, the public square has historically tended to reinforce legal and social hierarchies of race, gender, class, and ability rather than foster radically democratic and inclusive dialogue.[62] In the United States in particular, the public square has frequently served as a site for the assertion of violent white male supremacy.[63] Relatedly, focusing on the public square as a uniquely significant site for meaningful democratic discourse and debate obscures the importance of governmental forums and nonpublic spaces that generate democratic discourse, debate, and activism, including homes, schools, workplaces, bookstores, hair salons, and clubs.

These troubling realities of the public square are glossed over when the concept is invoked to criticize forums deemed insufficiently "open." This increasingly includes social media forums when they attempt to address online misinformation, abuse, and violations of their terms of service. These attempts are pejoratively framed as introducing regulation, interference, or censorship into the public square. But the public square, like all public spaces, has never been unregulated; it has always been *selectively* regulated, and in ways that tend to benefit more powerful members of society at the expense of less powerful members.

In its most literal sense, the public square is a physical space, open to the public and usually managed by the government, where people gather. Famous public squares include the ancient Agora in Athens, the Piazza San Marco in Venice, and Scollay Square in Boston.[64] The term *public square* can also refer to other publicly accessible and governmentally managed locations, such as parks and sidewalks.[65]

It is certainly true that people also gather on social media, but beyond that, the analogy to the physical public square is strained. The dominant social media platforms, including Facebook, Twitter, and YouTube, are virtual spaces owned by private enterprises that operate for profit.

Despite marketing rhetoric that emphasizes inclusion, community, and communication, these platforms are designed to serve corporate, not public, interests. With few exceptions, this means that they are designed to extract as much attention and information from people as possible for commercial purposes. The prioritization of "engagement" above all else creates perverse incentives for harassment, invasions of privacy, and false information that can destroy reputations, lives, and democracy itself.

A second obvious difference between the public square and the internet is that the former is a physical location where identifiable and observable individuals interact in person, whereas the latter is a virtual environment in which individuals rarely see each other face-to-face and are often completely anonymous and untraceable.[66] The disinhibition, amplification, permanence, and captivity of virtual interactions have a significant impact on the dynamics of communication in real-world spaces.[67] While online communication expands the boundaries of public discourse in many ways, it also allows for destructive forms of abuse that chill expression and inhibit participation in public debate.

The fact that social media forums do not provide face-to-face interactions in physical spaces can have salutary effects on free speech and debate. Large gatherings such as marches and protests present risks of physical harm, may require travel or long hours of standing, and can be challenging for older individuals and those with disabilities.[68] Organizing such events often requires time-consuming paperwork, intensive planning, and resources.[69] In person, individuals may feel intimidated by speakers who are phys-ically larger, aggressive, or armed.[70] Some people need time to reflect before expressing themselves, which is not always available in person.[71]

In contrast, online communication can happen anywhere, including from the comfort of one's own home. While virtual com-munication can pose risks to physical safety, it does not do so in the same immediate physical sense as in-person communication. Many social media platforms have few or no barriers to entry or participa-tion, flattening the hierarchy between elites and the general public and making it possible for people to contribute to or join discussions almost instantly. Online platforms also make it easier to conduct asynchronous conversations, allowing for increased possibilities to ponder, prepare, and revise one's thoughts. And because online communication is global, interactions on social media platforms often involve a much wider range of people and ideas than would be possible in physical gatherings.

At the same time, many characteristics of virtual interactions negatively impact communication and debate. Chief among these is the "online disinhibition effect," or "how people say and do things in cyberspace that they wouldn't ordinarily say and do in the face-to-face world."[72] Numerous studies have demonstrated that people are more likely to engage in abusive behavior when they feel insu-lated from the consequences, including when their identity is con-cealed.[73] This anonymity facilitates disinhibition, which can have positive effects on the free exchange of ideas but can also encourage reckless and destructive behavior that many individuals would eschew in person.[74] Anonymity also makes detection, intervention, and accountability with regard to such behavior much more difficult.

Abusive behavior often has a chilling effect on targeted indi-viduals' expression. This effect can be more severe online than in person due to the amplification afforded by the internet.[75] The internet provides abusers with loudspeakers and extensive opportu-nities to invite others to join in their abuse.[76] The internet and social media make it possible to "crowdsource" harassment, an aggregat-ing effect that greatly increases the negative impact of harassing behavior. Social media platforms in particular "give cyber harassment campaigns the ability to go viral, because they allow for 'near instantaneous, widespread dissemination.'"[77]

The nature of the internet also extends the shelf life of abusive content. It is extremely difficult, if not impossible, for abusive or privacy-violating content to be removed once it has been posted online.[78] Such permanence creates the possibility that targets of harassment may never regain peace of mind, thrusting them into a constant state of anxiety or fear about the exposure of their private information. Technology scholar David Douglas notes that "entering a doxing victim's name into a search engine may reveal her personal details and the abuse associated with the doxing attack for years."[79] As University of Virginia law professor and privacy expert Danielle Keats Citron writes, "Harassing letters are eventually thrown away, and memories fade in time. The web, however, can make it impossible to forget about malicious posts. Search engines index content on the web and produce it instantaneously. Indexed posts have no built-in expiration date; neither does the suffering they cause."[80]

Finally, the global reach of the internet can make abuse and harassment virtually impossible to escape. Unlike offline harassment, which may be restricted by geography or time, online harassment can manifest anywhere at any time. If, as is often the case, the online abuse is indexable by a major search engine, it is accessible to almost anyone (the target's coworkers, fellow students, clients, children), almost anywhere (at the target's place of work, her school, her home, her doctor's office).[81]

The significant differences between physical and virtual spaces provide compelling reasons to design and govern them in different ways. Features of online interaction such as disinhibition, amplification, permanence, and captivity create powerful incentives for harassment and abuse, especially of vulnerable individuals and groups.[82] Given the relatively unbounded nature of online forums as opposed to physical forums and the increased potential for lasting and irreparable harm, social media forums are justified in taking a more assertive role in moderating or curating content so as to avoid chilling expression and inhibiting participation in public debate.

The significant differences between social media platforms and the physical public square illuminate not only the limitations of the public-square analogy but also the potential for innovation and experimentation that moves beyond it. As nongovernment entities, private enterprises have tremendous freedom to design their platforms to encourage free speech and democratic deliberation in far more radical ways than actual public squares.

From the Greek agora to the city sidewalk, the physical public square has been a site of exclusion, hostility, surveillance, and silencing of vulnerable and minority populations, including women, nonwhite men, the poor, and the disabled.[83] In the United States, slavery and segregation excluded black people outright from public spaces;[84] later, selectively enforced surveillance and stop-and-frisk practices deterred black people from entering them.[85] Women in early America were relegated to the "private sphere" of the home[86] and deprived of significant opportunities to earn money,[87] receive an education,[88] or move freely in public without a male companion. Women in public spaces were targeted by antiprostitution and other public-decency laws,[89] and today they continue to contend with pervasive street harassment and sexual assault.[90] Vagrancy laws targeted the poor and unemployed for harassment and arrest,[91] and hostile architecture has rendered many public spaces inaccessible to those without homes and those with disabilities.[92] Public spaces are also heavily marked with symbols of whiteness, masculinity, and dominance, from the names of streets and parks to the subjects of statues and monuments.[93] Indeed, as discussed in chapter 1, white male supremacy is so fundamentally intertwined with the public square that attempts to challenge or remove symbols of racial and gendered hierarchy have been met with violence.

With regard to unchecked racism, sexism, and extremism, the digital public square does often indeed resemble the physical public square. Those same forces are potent online, causing similar intimidation and silencing. White male supremacism dominates the online landscape, from Facebook groups planning insurrections to

Nazi propaganda on Twitter to QAnon videos on YouTube.[94] Rampant sexist and racist harassment—including rape threats, nonconsensually distributed intimate imagery, doxing, and organized campaigns of racial hatred—on these forums silences women and minorities and pushes them out of public discourse.[95] When social media platforms fail to address these abuses in the name of "free speech,"[96] the result is not open debate and democratic deliberation but rather an exclusionary and elitist echo chamber.

On January 8, 2021, two days after the US Capitol attack, Twitter permanently banned Trump's personal account.[97] Twitter had first temporarily locked the @realDonaldTrump account on January 6, after Trump posted a video and a statement repeating false claims about the election and expressing his "love" for the rioters,[98] requiring Trump to delete the tweets before he could post again. At the time of the lockout, the Twitter safety team noted that if Trump violated Twitter's policies again, his account would be banned.[99] In a January 8 blog post, Twitter explained that it had determined that two of Trump's tweets following the riots, one referencing "American Patriots" and another stating that Trump would not be attending President-elect Biden's inauguration, were "likely to inspire others to replicate the violent acts that took place on January 6, 2021, and that there are multiple indicators that they are being received and understood as encouragement to do so."[100]

Twitter's decision to ban Trump came after Facebook's announcement that it would be suspending Trump's account indefinitely.[101] More social media bans—not just of Trump, but of other individuals who promoted lies about the election, endorsed white supremacist rhetoric and violence, or encouraged further insurrection efforts—quickly followed.[102] On January 9, Google and Apple removed the right-wing-dominated social media site Parler from their app stores after the site refused to moderate violent content, and Amazon removed the site from its web-hosting services later that same day, citing the platform's multiple violations of Amazon's terms of service.[103]

In the view of those who had been sounding the alarm about online extremism and abuse for decades, these efforts were too little, too late, but they did signal a sense of responsibility that could potentially mitigate future damage to public safety and democracy. But any muted praise for the tech industry's overdue attempt at course correction was drowned out by a crescendo of accusations that tech companies were engaged in a partisan attack on free speech and the First Amendment.[104]

Many of these critics expressed themselves on Twitter, including then–Secretary of State Mike Pompeo, who posted that "silencing speech is dangerous. It's un-American. Sadly, this isn't a new tactic of the Left. They've worked to silence opposing voices for years."[105] Trump's son, Donald Trump Jr., tweeted, "Free Speech Is Under Attack! Censorship is happening like NEVER before! Don't let them silence us."[106] Congressman Matt Gaetz proclaimed, on Twitter, "We cannot live in a world where Twitter's terms of service are more important than the terms in our Constitution and Bill of Rights."[107] Many conservatives were particularly aggrieved by the drop in their follower counts, likening the enforcement of Twitter's terms of service to the actions of totalitarian regimes.[108] For example, former White House press secretary Sarah Huckabee Sanders tweeted on January 9, "I've lost 50k+ followers this week. The radical left and their Big Tech allies cannot marginalize, censor, or silence the American people. This is not China, this is United States of America, and we are a free country."[109]

But the criticism did not only come from conservatives. Following Facebook's indefinite suspension of Trump's account, whistleblower Edward Snowden tweeted, "Facebook officially silences the President of the United States. For better or worse, this will be remembered as a turning point in the battle for control over digital speech."[110] The Electronic Frontier Foundation somberly observed that "we are always concerned when platforms take on the role of censors."[111] A senior legislative counsel for the ACLU opined that "it should concern everyone when companies like Facebook and Twitter wield the unchecked power to remove people from platforms that have become indispensable for the speech of billions."[112] Prominent ACLU attorney Ben Wizner criticized Amazon's decision to cut off Parler, telling the *New York Times* that "we should recognize the importance of neutrality when we're talking about the infrastructure of the internet."[113]

It is quite a testament to the power of consumerist constitutionalism that when the backlash against the tech industry finally came, it was not over tech companies' decades of decisions to leave up massive amounts of extremist speech but over a handful of decisions taking a tiny portion of it down. The highly personal sense of grievance that permeates outrage over social media "censorship" makes clear the degree to which Americans have come to view posting on social media as an activity to which they have a proprietary and constitutional entitlement.

As discussed in the introduction, while the protection of speech provided by the First Amendment was once understood as a right against government prohibition, it has been increasingly reinterpreted in the digital age as the right to private promotion. A 2019 Freedom Forum Institute survey found that 65 percent of respondents erroneously believe that "social media companies violate users' First Amendment rights when they ban users based on the content of their posts."[114] While much First Amendment doctrine is unstable and ambiguous, the state action doctrine is not. But the "private censorship is as bad or worse than government censorship" narrative serves antidemocratic interests in three ways: it minimizes, distracts from, and justifies actual government censorship; it discounts the First Amendment rights of private actors, including tech companies, against compelled speech and forced association; and it ultimately reinforces, rather than challenges, the reduction of free speech to social media activity.

The backlash against social media platforms for removing or restricting speech is in some sense an instance of the tech industry being hoisted with its own petard. It is the outsized influence of the internet over daily life that leads individuals to think of online platforms and tech companies not as the premises and products of private businesses but as public forums controlled by quasigovernmental actors. Modern society is so thoroughly dependent on social media for communication, news, commerce, education, and entertainment that any restriction of access *feels* like a matter of constitutional significance.[115] And, of course, the tech industry has carefully cultivated the illusion that social media activity is synonymous with free speech and has actively encouraged the public to think of online platforms as natural, essential, and unmediated outlets for free speech. Even as representatives of major tech companies are repeatedly summoned before Congress and asked how they can justify their "censorship" of various speech and speakers, they hedge, apologize, and avoid providing the obvious answer: that their decisions to ignore, remove, or restrict speech are exercises of their own First Amendment right to free speech.

What accounts for their reluctance to provide this answer, when it has the virtue of being both the truth and a valuable opportunity to educate the deeply misinformed American public about what the First Amendment actually protects? The answer lies in the fact that it is still ultimately in the tech industry's best interests to maintain the illusion that they are in the business of protecting users' free speech rights rather than their own. That, after all, is the myth that allows tech companies to pretend that their hands are tied when it comes to violent and abusive content except in the most extreme circumstances. That is the myth that ensures that the public opinion will be on their side when they return to their usual practices of amplifying and monetizing harmful content in the guise of respecting free speech.

The tech industry tolerates and at times openly embraces the narrative that private censorship is as bad as or worse than government censorship because it reinforces the perception that social media engagement is the truest and most important form of free speech. Criticism of Big Tech "censorship," whether from the right or the left, takes dependence on social media as a given and seeks only to make it "fairer." More transparency, enhanced due process protections, detailed explanations of content moderation policies, and proof that these policies are being enforced consistently would all require sinking more time, more labor, and more attention to technology and submitting to even greater technological domination over every aspect of our lives.

In addition to reducing free speech to social media consumption, the backlash against "Big Tech censorship" is harmful for two other, intertwined reasons. As previously discussed, the First Amendment protects the right of private actors to speak and not to speak, to associate with speech and to not associate with speech, and to include speech and to exclude speech. Though they are very powerful, tech companies are still private actors, not government actors. They should be criticized for doing too little, not too much, to keep reckless speech off their platforms. They should be encouraged wherever possible to take *more* responsibility for the speech they promote, not less, not only to reduce harm to the public but also to vindicate their own First Amendment rights to decide for themselves what kind of speech they want to amplify. The concept of private censorship is inherently contradictory; it is a claim that the First Amendment right not to listen violates the First Amendment right to speak.

As Orwellian claims lead to Orwellian solutions, if allowing private actors to make decisions about speech is censorship, then forbidding them from making those decisions must be free speech. This is the logic of multiple high-profile lawsuits against Facebook, Twitter, Google, and others for alleged free speech violations;[116] Trump-era executive orders aimed at curtailing "social media censorship";[117] and, most chillingly, legislation in states such as Florida and Texas authorizing the government to force social media platforms to carry speech against their will.[118] Indeed, in upholding Texas's law, the Fifth Circuit explicitly derided the right of private companies to make decisions about what content to allow on their platforms as censorship and characterized the Texas law as a vindication of free speech.[119]

The January 6 insurrection demonstrated in brutal detail how a consumerist conception of free speech serves the interests of white male supremacy. The tech industry helped to promote a reckless and radically individualistic conception of free speech that fueled the organization, execution, and legitimation of a violent assault on democracy. The tech industry certainly should have been criticized in the wake of the Capitol attack, but for its decades-long, reckless promotion of extremist and abusive content for profit, not its belated attempts to rein it in. The Big Tech censorship narrative denigrates the First Amendment rights of all private actors against compelled speech and forced association, paving the way for actual censorship by the government and further reducing free speech to reckless consumerism.

The story of Big Tech is a story about recklessness. In law, recklessness is defined as acting with a conscious disregard for a substantial and unjustified risk of harm to others.[120] It is a mental state considered less culpable than an actual intent to cause harm but more culpable than a negligent failure to be aware of the risk of harm. Recklessness can be described as a product of selfishness more than malice; it is a risk calculation that values the potential of self-benefit more highly than the potential of harm to others. The possibility of being held accountable for the negative consequences of risky activities tends to serve as an important restraint on the reckless pursuit of self-interest. Accordingly, the more remote the possibility of accountability, the greater the risks one will take. Economists refer to the perverse incentives created by the ability to off-load the costs of risky conduct onto others as a "moral hazard," and it explains why the tech industry moves so fast and breaks so many things: it is never responsible for picking up the pieces.[121]

This moral hazard is largely a creation of federal law. In 1996, Congress attempted to regulate pornographic content on the internet by passing the Communications Decency Act. While the Supreme Court soon invalidated nearly all of the act on First Amendment grounds, a bipartisan provision, now popularly known as Section 230, remained. Section 230 limits how and when online intermediaries ("interactive computer services"[122]) can be held legally accountable for the actions of those who use their platforms and services. The majority of courts over the last three decades have interpreted Section 230's provisions to grant sweeping legal immunity to what the statute refers to as "providers or users of an interactive computer service" for content created by other users.

But this interpretation directly contradicts the statute's purported goal, which is to serve as a "Good Samaritan" law for the internet.[123] Good Samaritan laws in the American legal system provide individuals with immunity from civil liability for reasonable attempts made in good faith and without legal obligation to aid others in distress. Without such protection, Good Samaritans might be discouraged from offering assistance out of fear of being held liable for unintentional consequences. For example, a bystander who knows CPR may hesitate to perform it on a gunshot victim for fear of being sued for any inadvertent injury caused by the technique. The aim of Good Samaritan laws is to provide an incentive, or at least remove a disincentive, for people to render assistance when they have no legal obligation to do so.

Section 230's operative provision is titled "Protection for 'Good Samaritan' blocking and screening of offensive material." The law was originally conceived as a reward for online intermediaries who take affirmative steps to restrict harmful content on their platforms with immunity from liability for those actions. For nearly thirty years, however, courts have instead interpreted the law to preemptively absolve online intermediaries of liability for harms facilitated by their sites and services, even when they could easily have chosen to prevent them and even when they solicit, amplify, or profit from them. Such unqualified immunity not only erases the incentive to help that Section 230 was intended to provide but also creates an incentive to harm. Doing nothing is always cheaper than helping, and harmful content can be very profitable. As long as tech platforms are allowed to enjoy the benefits of doing business without any of the burdens, they will have little incentive to take care and every incentive to be reckless in their pursuit of profit.

This immunity is a dramatic exception to the general rules of liability and gives the tech industry a competitive advantage over virtually every other industry and over most private individuals. Most people, most of the time, can be held liable for causing harm. This is true even if they cause it indirectly and unintentionally, and especially if they benefit in some way from the harm. As Justice Elena Kagan asked during the oral argument in *Gonzalez v. Google* (2023), "Every other industry has to internalize the costs of its conduct. Why is it that the tech industry gets a pass?"[124] Car manufacturers can face liability for making engines that catch fire. Hospitals can be sued for botched surgeries. Grocery stores can be held accountable for failing to maintain safe premises. Employers can be held liable for failing to respond to reports of discrimination. While there is no general duty to aid in US law, third parties can be held both criminally and civilly liable for their role in harmful acts they did not cause but did not do enough to prevent. This potential for liability encourages us to take care, to internalize risk, and to prevent foreseeable harm.

Interpreting Section 230 as a preemptive immunity shield constitutes an astonishingly effective kind of tort reform, though it is not typically characterized as such. Tort reform efforts generally seek to alter civil law to make it more difficult for injured parties to bring claims, receive compensation, or obtain jury trials. Tort reform has historically been championed by conservatives in the name of protecting the free market. A common tactic of tort reform is to portray the civil system as being overrun by greedy, unscrupulous plaintiffs and to cast corporations in the role of the victim. "Corporate victimhood deflects attention away from the true victims: those who suffered from defective products, negligent medicine, investor fraud or unreasonably risky financial activities."[125] By contrast, progressives have historically decried tort reform as privileging corporate interests over individual welfare. As a general matter, progressives recognize that "tort liability encourages industries to develop new safer technologies"[126] and emphasize the constitutional significance of access to the courts, especially for marginalized groups.

And yet when it comes to the tech industry, progressives have largely turned a blind eye to how Section 230 has been interpreted to close the courtroom door on some of the most vulnerable members of society. This includes women, racial minorities, and minors, many of whom have been irreparably harmed by the action or inaction of powerful corporations. As politicians on both sides of the aisle have begun to criticize Big Tech's power and influence—though often for very different reasons—they have rarely acknowledged how both parties' decades-long, enthusiastic embrace of Section 230 has helped create it.

The sweeping interpretation of Section 230 immunity ensures that the drive to create safer or healthier online products and services will never be able to compete with the drive for profit; as long as tech platforms are allowed to enjoy the benefits of doing business without any of the burdens, they will have little incentive to take care. The devastating fallout of this moral hazard is an online ecosystem flooded with lies, extremism, racism, and misogyny fueling offline harassment and violence. The tech industry's continued immunity from liability in the face of this reality is a testament to the extraordinary degree to which lawmakers and the public continue to believe that when it comes to free speech, corporate interests align with constitutional ones.

The champions of Section 230 insist that protecting the tech industry from liability is even more necessary today than it was in 1996 to ensure that the internet remains the most powerful medium of free expression. Section 230 enthusiasts refer to the law as the "Magna Carta of the Internet,"[127] the "foundation of the Internet,"[128] the "cornerstone of Internet freedom,"[129] and "the First Amendment of the Internet."[130] Unpacking these claims about the importance of Section 230 for free speech requires a clear understanding of the statute's operative provisions and the very different protections they provide.

Section 230 has been interpreted to broadly shield online intermediaries from criminal and civil liability in two situations:

- When they allow certain content on their platforms—230(c)(1) states that "no provider or user of an interactive computer service shall be treated as the publisher or speaker of any information provided by another information content provider."

- When they do not allow certain content on their platforms—230(c)(2) shields providers and users of an interactive computer service from civil liability with regard to
any action that is "voluntarily taken in good faith to
restrict access to or availability of material that the provider or user considers to be obscene, lewd, lascivious,
filthy, excessively violent, harassing, or otherwise objectionable" or "taken to enable or make available to information content providers or others the technical means
to restrict access" to such material.[131]

While (c)(2) should be considered the heart of Section 230, as it
most clearly expresses the law's Good Samaritan goals, it is (c)(1)
that dominates the popular understanding of the law. This provision has been used to protect online classifieds sites from facing
liability for sex trafficking,[132] online firearms sellers from facing
liability for facilitating unlawful gun sales,[133] online message
boards like 8chan (now renamed 8kun) from facing liability for live
streaming massacres and spreading terrorist propaganda,[134] and
online marketplaces from facing liability for putting defective
products into the stream of commerce.[135] Section 230(c)(1) has been
invoked to protect online firearms marketplaces such as Armslist,
which facilitates the illegal sale of weapons used to murder domestic violence victims,[136] and to classifieds sites like Backpage (now
defunct), which was routinely used by sex traffickers to advertise
underage girls for sex.[137]

The closest analog to what Section 230(c)(1) does for the tech
industry is what the PLCAA does for the firearms industry: it provides a super immunity for powerful corporations, encouraging
them to pursue profit without internalizing the costs of that pursuit. Just as the PLCAA eliminates incentives for manufacturers to
develop safer guns or secure storage, Section 230(c)(1) eliminates
incentives for tech corporations to design safer platforms or develop
more secure products. Private individuals are left to deal with the
fallout—including life-destroying harassment, publicized sexual
exploitation, and ubiquitous surveillance—of a reckless tech

industry moving fast and breaking things, just as they are forced to absorb the costs of deaths and injuries associated with a reckless firearms industry.

Rather than encouraging the innovation and development of measures to fight online extremism and abuse, Section 230(c)(1) removes incentives for online intermediaries to deter or address harmful practices no matter how easily they could do so. The moral hazard created by the law stifles the development of a duty of care for the tech industry and eliminates the incentives for the best-positioned party to develop responses to avoid foreseeable risks of harm.[138]

Section 230 also denies those injured by reckless tech practices access to the courts. In *Chambers v. Baltimore & O. R. Co.* (1907), the Supreme Court stated that "the right to sue and defend in the courts is the alternative of force. In an organized society it is the right conservative of all other rights, and lies at the foundation of orderly government. It is one of the highest and most essential privileges of citizenship."[139] Tort law, John Goldberg and Benjamin Zipursky write in *Recognizing Wrongs*, "is a mechanism of account-ability" that provides victims of wrongdoing a direct path to redress, not contingent on "the solicitude of those who injure them or on the beneficence of charitable organizations or government benefits programs."[140] But Section 230(c)(1) preempts plaintiffs from ever bringing suit in many cases and ensures that those suits that are brought will rarely survive a motion to dismiss on Section 230 grounds.

Section 230 defenders counter that these procedural obstacles are justified because plaintiffs should be suing the direct source of the content that caused their injuries, not the intermediaries that hosted it, and that many suits against online intermediaries will ultimately fail on the merits. As to the first objection, it is worth emphasizing that the nature of online communications makes it challenging and often impossible for plaintiffs to discover the iden-tity of the person who has most directly wronged them, often because the intermediary protects their anonymity. What is more, it is well-recognized that third parties who have contributed or

profited from wrongdoing are often appropriate targets of suit. As
to the second objection, it is always indeterminate whether a plaintiff's claim will ultimately succeed in any given case. The value of
the right to bring a claim is not contingent on or reducible to
whether the claim is vindicated in the end. "Even when a plaintiff's
case fails on the merits," writes Yale Law School professor Douglas
A. Kysar in "The Public Life of Private Law," "judicial engagement
with the details of her claim helps to frame her suffering as a legible
subject of public attention and governance."[141] Moreover, in many
cases, the discovery process will provide significant value, not just
to the plaintiff in the case at hand but also to legislators, regulators,
future plaintiffs, and the public. As Michael L. Rustad and Thomas
H. Koenig explain in "Rebooting Cybertort Law," "Prolonged discovery . . . will enable plaintiffs to uncover more information about
the nature, nexus, and extent of prior crimes and torts on websites.
Plaintiffs could use the locomotive of discovery to unearth aggra-
vating factors, such as whether the ISP [internet service provider]
profited by being too closely connected to fraudulent schemes that
injured consumers. Discovery in these cases might even result in
ISPs or websites being stripped of their immunity as primary publishers because of a close connection to the creators of illegal
content."[142]

Given that the costs of online injuries so often fall disproportionately on marginalized populations, the ability to hold online
intermediaries responsible is also key to protecting "cyber civil
rights,"[143] a phrase coined by Citron in 2009.[144] The anonymity,
amplification, and aggregation possibilities offered by the internet
have allowed private actors to discriminate, harass, and threaten
vulnerable groups on a massive, unprecedented scale. As the internet has multiplied the possibilities of expression, it has also multiplied the possibilities of repression, facilitating a censorious
backlash against women and minorities. The internet lowers the
costs of abuse by providing abusers with anonymity and social validation while offering new ways to increase the range and impact of
that abuse. Abundant empirical evidence demonstrates that online
abuse further chills the intimate, artistic, and professional

expression of individuals whose rights were already under assault offline.[145]

In bestowing a right of recklessness upon the tech industry and preempting the right of injured individuals to sue for online harms, Section 230(c)(1) has contributed to a truly dystopian state of affairs where expressive, economic, and information inequalities divide our society; where global corporations can extract astronomical profits from exploiting private data; where women and minorities are silenced by online mobs; and where massive disinformation and misinformation campaigns can micro-target populations to create public health crises, foment armed rebellions, and undermine democracy itself.

5

The Promise of Fearless Speech

SOPHIE SCHOLL WAS BORN IN 1921 INTO A MIDDLE-CLASS GERMAN family. As a child, she joined the girls' branch of the Hitler Youth. While a college student at the University of Munich, however, she became a member of the White Rose, a secret group of university students who, between 1942 and 1943, distributed pamphlets highlighting and denouncing Nazi atrocities. One of these pamphlets emphasized that "since the conquest of Poland *three hundred thousand* Jews have been murdered" and asked, "Why are the German people so apathetic in the face of all these abominable crimes?"[1] Another leaflet vowed that the group "will not be silent. We are your bad conscience. The White Rose will not leave you in peace!"[2]

On February 18, 1943, Scholl and her brother, Hans, brought a suitcase full of pamphlets to the University of Munich campus. Jakob Schmidt, a university janitor and member of the Nazi Party, observed Scholl throwing copies of the pamphlet from a balcony overlooking a courtyard where students were walking. He reported the siblings to the Gestapo, and they were arrested and taken into custody that day.

Over several days of interrogation, Scholl was offered the chance to save her life in exchange for implicating her brother and pledging allegiance to Adolf Hitler. Scholl refused.[3] After four days in custody, Scholl, her brother, and a third member of the White Rose, Christoph Probst, appeared in the so-called People's Court for trial. They were not given an opportunity to speak, but Scholl interrupted Judge Roland Freisler anyway, shouting, "Somebody, after all, had to make a start. What we wrote and said is also believed by many others. They just don't dare express themselves as we did."[4]

Freisler sentenced all three members of the White Rose to be executed via guillotine the same day. Scholl's cellmate recorded what many believe to be her last words: "How can we expect right-eousness to prevail when there is hardly anyone willing to give himself up individually to a righteous cause? Such a fine, sunny day, and I have to go, but what does my death matter, if through us, thousands of people are awakened and stirred to action?"[5] Even in the face of death, Scholl expressed no fear, serene in the knowledge that she had used her voice to fight for justice.

Scholl's speech is the epitome of parrhesia, of complete fearless-ness in pursuing truth.[6] Her courageous exercise of speech, casting off the safety and privilege of her race and background to give voice to Nazi atrocities, provides the most dramatic contrast possible to the cowardly spectacle of reckless speakers like Frank Collin demanding the right to dress up in Nazi uniforms to intimidate Holocaust survivors.

The ancient Greeks recognized two different conceptions of freedom of speech—*isegoria* and *parrhesia*.[7] Both were rights pro-tected by the Athenian constitution and both are often translated as "free speech," but the two concepts differ in significant ways. "In ancient Athens," writes political theorist Teresa Bejan, "*iseogria* described the equal right of citizens to participate in public debate in the democratic assembly," whereas *parrhesia* is "the license to say what one pleased, how and when one pleased, and to whom."[8] While isegoria, according to classics scholar Dana Fields, "did not necessarily extend to everyone and thus had more oligarchic poten-tial,"[9] parrhesia "described the freedom to speak one's mind frankly and with complete openness, to say the whole truth as one under-stands the truth. The truth-telling prescribed by parrhēsia typically had a confrontative, critical bite."[10]

The French philosopher Michel Foucault was so intrigued by the interplay of power and risk inherent in the concept of parrhesia that he devoted a series of lectures to the concept in the 1980s at the University of Berkeley. In his account, parrhesia is

> a kind of verbal activity where the speaker has a specific rela-
> tion to truth through frankness, a certain relationship to his
> own life through danger, a certain type of relation to himself
> or other people through criticism (self-criticism or criticism
> of other people), and a specific relation to moral law through
> freedom and duty. More precisely, parrhesia is a verbal activ-
> ity in which a speaker expresses his personal relationship to
> truth, and risks his life because he recognizes truth-telling as
> a duty to improve or help other people (as well as himself).
> In parrhesia, the speaker uses his freedom and chooses
> frankness instead of persuasion, truth instead of falsehood or
> silence, the risk of death instead of life and security, criticism
> instead of flattery, and moral duty instead of self-interest and
> moral apathy.[11]

While Foucault clarified that parrhesia did not always involve the risk of death, it always involved risk of some kind and required "courage in the face of danger: it demands the courage to speak the truth in spite of some danger."[12] According to legal scholar Jona-than Simon, parrhesia raises complex questions about power and truth, including, "Who is able to tell the truth? What are the moral, the ethical, and the spiritual conditions which entitle some-one to present himself as, and to be considered as, a truth-teller? About what topics is it important to tell the truth? . . . What are the consequences of telling the truth? What are the anticipated posi-tive effects for the city, for the city's rulers, for the individual?, etc. And finally: What is the relation between the activity of truth-tell-ing and the exercise of power?"[13]

Fearless speech, unlike mere free speech, has three substantive characteristics: it is candid, it is critical, and it is courageous. In contrast to the reckless speaker, the fearless speaker takes ownership of her positions and communicates them straightforwardly to her audience; her speech seeks to hold those in power accountable; and she is undeterred by the risk of harm to herself that her speech creates. Where reckless speakers use speech to pursue self-interest and to expand the influence of the powerful, fearless speakers use speech to challenge power and vindicate the rights of the oppressed. In contrast to a reckless speech culture that fetishizes speakers who endanger others for selfish ends, a fearless speech culture valorizes speakers who risk their own welfare for the collective good.

Foucault distinguishes parrhesia's direct and transparent nature from speech that relies on rhetorical manipulation. This feature can be described as frankness or candor, as the speaker reveals "everything he has in mind: he does not hide anything, but opens his heart and mind completely to other people."[14] The fearless speaker takes full ownership and responsibility for what is expressed, "mak[ing] it manifestly clear and obvious that what he says is his own opinion"[15] without the disclaimer of ironic distance or devil's-advocate posturing.

But candor alone is not sufficient for speech to qualify as fearless. Fearless speech must address topics of significant public importance, and it must take positions that are critical of existing power. "What makes parrhesia dangerous," writes Simon, "is that it is likely to be critical. It is not parrhesia to praise the sovereign or flatter one's friends, even if one believes what one says."[16]

Crucially, however, while fearless speech is always critical, not all critical speech is fearless. The fearless speakers address one of two targets—themselves or someone with more power:

Parrhesia is a form of criticism, either towards another or towards oneself, but always in a situation where the speaker or confessor is in a position of inferiority with respect to the interlocutor. The parrhesiastes is always less powerful than the one with whom he or she speaks. The parrhesia comes from "below," as it were, and is directed towards "above." This is why an ancient Greek would not say that a teacher or father who criticizes a child uses parrhesia. But when a philosopher criticizes a tyrant, when a citizen criticizes the majority, when a pupil criticizes his or her teacher, then such speakers may be using parrhesia.[17]

The three key elements of fearless speech are intertwined: "If there is a kind of 'proof' of the sincerity of the parrhesiastes, it is his courage. The fact that a speaker says something dangerous—different from what the majority believes—is a strong indication that he is a parrhesiastes."[18] A speaker's courage in engaging in dangerous critique proves his candor.

The risk of danger, it is important to emphasize, is always directed inward, not outward. The fearless speaker "says something which is dangerous *to himself* and thus involves a risk,"[19] including, in the most extreme cases, a risk of death. This is the most significant distinction between reckless speakers and fearless speakers.

In the age of the internet, however, virtually any speech act can draw criticism from some quarter, especially if the speaker is high profile. This creates the possibility that a very broad range of speakers may attempt to cast themselves as engaged in parrhesia, pointing to the negative consequences engendered by their controversial opinions. Indeed, a key tactic of the reactionary right is to engage in offensive and outlandish speech in the hopes of provoking violent backlash, which is then offered as proof of the speaker's courage. This is the modus operandi of right-wing provocateurs who present themselves as speakers with ideas so dangerous they are constantly being suppressed by "leftists," the "establishment," "mainstream media," and the like.

In describing the concept of frankness, Fields notes that there can be "great reputational advantages to be gained from presenting oneself as a teller of uncomfortable truths, especially when doing so entailed a personal risk," and "presenting oneself as a frank speaker (as distinct from simply telling the truth) is clearly a rhetorical act and part of a larger rhetorical strategy to gain the trust of one's audience(s) through the establishment of one's character (ethos). As such, any claim to frankness is open to suspicion of artifice and deception."[20]

But such speakers can be distinguished from truly fearless speakers through a careful evaluation of their speech in terms of their candor and their relationship to power. Many self-styled provocateurs, such as Alex Jones, admit that much of what they say is a performance calculated to inflame their supporters' prejudices, not to arrive at truth or serve the common good. This kind of performative distance is fundamentally incompatible with parrhesia. Constitutional law scholar Keith Werhan clarifies the distinction: "The brave and honest parrhesiast, devoted to enhancing the welfare of the polis rather than his own power and prestige, would never stoop to ingratiating himself with his audience. He would neither flatter his listeners nor appeal to their prejudices. To do so would constitute an abuse rather than an exercise of parrhēsia, because such a speaker would have focused on pleasing his audience rather than on confronting it with the truth."[21]

What is more, the risk in parrhesia depends on the relationship of the speaker to power. A powerful person criticizing a less powerful person is not engaging in parrhesia, although this speech may be valuable in other ways. It simply does not involve the kind of risk, and thus the kind of courage, entailed by fearless speech. Parrhesia is determined, as Fields says, by "the good intentions of the speaker and a power differential between him and the recipient of his advice."[22]

Foucault specifies that "because the parrhesiastes must take a risk in speaking the truth . . . the king or tyrant generally cannot use parrhesia; for he risks nothing."[23] A president who uses speech to attack a citizen, for example, as Trump did repeatedly while president, is not engaged in fearless speech. Powerful figures who use speech to attack less powerful figures are often instead engaging in reckless speech, creating a substantial and unjustified risk of harm to the person they target.

The positive form of parrhesia can be contrasted with the pejorative sense of parrhesia (negative parrhesia), which "consists in saying any or everything one has in mind without qualification."[24] Negative parrhesia results when "everyone has the right to address himself to his fellow citizens and to tell them anything—even the most stupid or dangerous things for the city."[25] The exercise of positive parrhesia requires a minimal level of competence and knowledge.

———

In his lectures, Foucault illustrates the concept of fearless speech through Greek philosophy, mythology, and tragic plays. Socrates is perhaps the quintessential parrhesiastes: In his famous dialogues, Socrates questioned and critiqued the values of the Athenian elite. He undertook this speech for the greater good—namely, to help his fellow Greeks understand themselves more deeply and to live more fulfilled lives—even though it meant incurring the wrath of the Athenian government. Indeed, Socrates's speech so angered the powerful majority that he was ultimately sentenced to death for it, a fate that he declined to escape despite having the opportunity to do so.

Foucault unearths other examples of parrhesia in his close readings of ancient Greek plays. One of the most compelling emerges in his analysis of Euripides's tragedy *Ion*, which tells the story of a woman named Creusa who is raped and impregnated by the god Apollo when she is a girl. She hides in a cave to give birth alone. Full of shame and fearful that her parents will learn what has happened, Creusa abandons her newborn son to exposure and wild animals. Unbeknownst to her, Apollo sends his brother Hermes to take the child to his temple, the oracle at Delphi. The boy, Ion, is raised as a servant, and his identity as Apollo's son is known only to Apollo.

Creusa marries a foreigner named Xuthus, but the couple struggles to conceive a child. They decide to travel to the oracle at Delphi, where mortals could seek answers from the gods, to ask if they will ever have children. Xuthus's question to the oracle is straightforward; he only wants to know if he and Creusa will ever have children. Creusa, however, has a different, secret question; she wants to know if the son she had with Apollo is dead or alive.

When they arrive at the temple, they are met by Apollo's servant, Ion, but neither he, Xuthus, nor Creusa knows the truth of his parentage. Creusa is ashamed of her story, so she tells Ion that she is consulting the oracle for a friend who was raped by Apollo. She asks Ion if he thinks Apollo will admit his wrongdoing and answer the question about the fate of the child. Ion, a faithful servant to Apollo, warns Creusa that if Apollo has done what she describes, there would be dangerous consequences for exposing it:

ION: Is Apollo to reveal what he intends should remain a mystery?
CREUSA: Surely his oracle is open for every Greek to question?
ION: No. His honor is involved; you must respect his feelings.
CREUSA: What of his victim's feelings? What does this involve for her?
ION: There is no one who will ask this question for you. Suppose it were proved in Apollo's own temple that he had behaved so badly, he would be justified in making your interpreter suffer for it. My lady, let the matter drop. We must not accuse Apollo in his own court. That is what our folly would amount to, if we try to force a reluctant god to speak, to give signs in sacrifice or the flight of birds. Those ends we pursue against the gods' will can do us little good when we gain them.[26]

When Creusa's husband Xuthus asks Apollo if he will have a child, Apollo lies to him and tells him that his servant Ion is actually Xuthus's child. When Creusa is told that Apollo has given her husband a son, she flies into a rage; not only will Apollo not admit to his offense, nor tell her whether her child is alive, but he also (so it appears) gives her husband a son who is a stranger to her. In her anger and despair, she speaks the truth about what Apollo has done: "Clinging to my pale wrists as I cried for my mother's help you led me to bed in a cave, a god and my lover, with no shame, submitting to the Cyprian's will. In misery I bore you a son, whom in fear of my mother I placed in that bed where you cruelly forced me."[27]

As Foucault describes it, "Creusa's tirade against Apollo is that form of parrhesia where someone publicly accuses another of a crime, or of a fault, or of an injustice that has been committed. And this accusation is an instance of parrhesia insofar as the one who is accused is more powerful than the one who accuses. For there is the danger that because of the accusation made, the accused may retaliate in some way against his or her accuser."[28]

According to Simon, parrhesia is rare in modern society, though "not, however, wholly absent from contemporary political life. The western tradition of critical parrhesiastic speech by intellectuals, a recognizable genealogy that stretches from Socrates through Emile Zola to Daniel Ellsberg, remains alive today but only episodically."[29]

Simon makes the intriguing argument that "today, crime victims have emerged as perhaps the most important source of parrhesia."[30] The victim who speaks takes a risk in two ways: "First, the reprocessing of the traumatic experiences that underlie parrhesiastic truth may do damage to the speaker through his own circuits of memory and emotion. Second, the truth spoken may offend powerful members of the audience who may seek to retaliate. 'In parrhesia the danger always comes from the fact that the said truth is capable of hurting or angering the interlocutor.' In both senses, parrhesiastic speech is fearless speech because it knowingly embraces risk."[31]

In July 2018, after Judge Brett Kavanaugh of the United States Court of Appeals for the DC Circuit was rumored to be on Trump's shortlist of nominees for the Supreme Court to replace retiring Justice Anthony M. Kennedy, Dr. Christine Blasey Ford reached out to her congressional representative, Anna Eshoo, and the *Washington Post*. On Eshoo's advice, she sent a letter to Senator Dianne Feinstein, the ranking Democrat on the Judiciary Committee, describing a sexual assault incident involving Ford and Kavanaugh when both were teenagers. Ford asked Feinstein to keep the letter confidential and did not go on the record with the *Washington Post*, "as she grappled with concerns about what going public would mean for her and her family—and what she said was her duty as a citizen to tell the story."[32]

Ford hired lawyer Debra Katz, an expert in sexual harassment cases, who advised her to take a polygraph test to preempt accusations that she was lying. Katz provided the results of the test, which indicated that Ford was telling the truth about her allegation, to the *Post*. Ford decided in August not to go public with her accusation, believing that it would "upend her life" and likely have no effect on Kavanaugh's nomination, which seemed to be a foregone conclusion. "Why suffer through the annihilation if it's not going to matter?" Ford told the *Post*.[33]

Having promised to keep the letter confidential, Feinstein did not mention the allegation during Kavanaugh's initial confirmation hearings. *The Intercept* learned from other Democratic members of the Judiciary Committee that Feinstein was in possession of a document relating to Kavanaugh and reported this claim on September 12 without naming Ford. At that point, Feinstein sent Ford's letter to the FBI, which sent the letter to the White House with Ford's name redacted. The White House in turn sent the letter to the full Senate Judiciary Committee.

On September 16, 2018, Ford went public as the author of the allegations. She told the *Washington Post* on the record that in 1982, when she was fifteen years old, Kavanaugh had sexually assaulted her at a party. According to her account, Ford was pushed into a bedroom where rock music was playing loudly. An intoxicated seventeen-year-old Kavanaugh held her down on a bed, tried to pull her clothes off, and covered her mouth with his hand to stifle her screams. She managed to escape when Kavanaugh's friend Mark Judge, who was watching the incident, fell on top of them. She fled to a bathroom and locked herself in, waiting until she heard the two teenagers going down the stairs before leaving the house.

According to Ford, she told no one what had happened at the time, terrified that her parents would discover that she had attended a party where teenagers were drinking. In addition to the polygraph results, Ford gave the *Post* therapist session notes from 2012 that recount the assault. Kavanaugh's name is not mentioned in the notes, but they include the details of Ford's attack by students "from an elitist boys' school" who went on to become "highly respected and high-ranking members of society in Washington."[34] Ford's husband has stated that Ford had identified Kavanaugh as her attacker when she told him of the attack in 2012.

After Ford went public, her home address was posted online, her email was hacked, and she received death threats that forced her and her husband and sons to leave their home.[35] Her credibility and character were attacked by multiple Republican members of Congress and by then-President Trump. On September 21, 2018, Trump, who had by that time himself been accused of sexual misconduct by more than fifteen women, stated in a Twitter post that "I have no doubt that, if the attack on Dr. Ford was as bad as she says, charges would have been immediately filed with local Law Enforcement Authorities [*sic*] by either her or her loving parents. I ask that she bring those filings forward so that we can learn date, time, and place!"[36]

According to a statement issued by her lawyers on September 23, "Despite actual threats to her safety and her life, Dr. Ford believes it is important for senators to hear directly from her about the sexual assault committed against her."[37] Ford testified in an open Senate hearing on September 27, 2018, about her allegations.

Ford's speech exhibits the three key hallmarks of parrhesia: sincerity, criticism, and courage. Her story is a direct account of her experience with Kavanaugh. Her letter detailing the assault describes the event as she remembers it, free of rhetorical manipulation or embellishment. Commentators noted that her story has the ring of authenticity because it contains awkward details that a fraudulent account would not, such as the presence of a third party and the admission of imperfect memory. The speech is critical, constituting a very serious attack on Kavanaugh's character and fitness as a judge, especially as he was being considered for a lifetime appointment on the nation's highest court. Her speech is courageous because she risked the wrath not only of a man more powerful than she is but also of his extremely powerful supporters, including multiple high-ranking members of Congress and the president of the United States. Nearly as soon as she went public with her story, Ford faced serious attacks on her safety and well-being in the form of death threats and harassment. Ford nonetheless voluntarily chose to continue her speech act by testifying before Congress, exposing herself to the hostility of Kavanaugh's Republican supporters as well as to the judgment and scrutiny of the world at large. Ford's speech highlights the risky nature of sexual misconduct allegations generally, especially against powerful men.

As the #MeToo movement has demonstrated, women who accuse men of sexual assault routinely face malicious and misogynistic scrutiny by the public, the press, and social media, as well as threats to their physical safety, their families, their employment, and their property. Before "Me Too" went viral as #MeToo, it was a phrase used by Tarana Burke, an American social activist and community organizer. Around 2006, Burke began using the phrase on the social network MySpace as part of a campaign to promote "empowerment through empathy" among victims of sexual abuse, especially women of color within underprivileged communities.[38]

Following the disclosure of multiple sexual abuse allegations against Hollywood producer Harvey Weinstein in October 2017, the actress Alyssa Milano encouraged Twitter users to reply with the hashtag #MeToo if they had also experienced sexual harassment or abuse. Within a few hours of her original post, the phrase had been used more than two hundred thousand times and tweeted more than half a million times by the following day. On Facebook, the hashtag was used more than 4.7 million times in over twelve million posts during the first twenty-four hours. Thousands of individuals, mostly women, shared #MeToo stories, including many celebrities.

Ford's testimony was reminiscent of a historic pre-#MeToo moment, when Anita Hill testified before a hostile Senate in 1991 about sexual harassment allegations against then-judicial nominee Clarence Thomas. Hill, the first African American professor to receive tenure at Oklahoma University (OU), was deluged by bomb threats, hate mail, and prank calls to her home following her testimony. While a group of supporters raised $250,000 to endow a professorship in her name at the Oklahoma University College of Law, conservative Oklahoma state legislators led by Representative Leonard E. Sullivan attempted to block matching state funds for the chair and even introduced legislation to shut down the law school altogether. Sullivan called Hill a "cancerous growth" on the law school and compared her to serial killer Jeffrey Dahmer.[39] State Representative Tim Pope compared Hill to Hitler and viciously attacked her credentials, claiming that she had received special treatment from the law school: "She didn't have the published works and papers everyone else had to have. Her only claim to fame was that she lied to a U.S. Senate committee. Our people in Oklahoma do not believe Anita Hill for the most part and they don't want her name forever memorialized as someone who actually accomplished something."[40] The attacks led Hill to resign from OU in 1996; she later became a professor at Brandeis University.

As discussed in chapter 2, attempts to suppress women's speech about male violence has a long history in the United States. In her acceptance speech for the 2018 Cecil B. DeMille Award at the Golden Globes ceremony, Oprah Winfrey told the story of Recy Taylor, a young black wife and mother who, in 1944, was gang raped by six armed white men who threatened to kill her if she told anyone what they had done. But Taylor told someone anyway—Rosa Parks, who at the time was working as an investigator for the NAACP. Despite Parks's valiant efforts to secure justice for Taylor, the case was dismissed by an all-white grand jury. While Parks and others brought national attention to her case, Taylor's home was firebombed, and she and her family were terrorized by death threats for months. The national outcry over her case led to the convening of a second grand jury, but this jury also failed to produce any indictments. Taylor continued to be subjected to threats and harassment until she left Alabama, and the men who raped her were never prosecuted. "For too long," Winfrey concluded,

women have not been heard or believed if they dared to speak their truth to the power of those men. But their time is up. Their time is up. Your time is up. And I just hope, I just hope that Recy Taylor died knowing that her truth, like the truth of so many other women who were tormented in those years and even now tormented, goes marching on. It was somewhere in Rosa Parks's heart almost 11 years later when she made the decision to stay seated on that bus in Montgomery. And it's here with every women [*sic*] who chooses to say "Me too."[41]

Fearless speakers like Scholl, Ford, Hill, Burke, and Taylor should be protected and praised. But no one should have to be a martyr for their speech. A truly democratic society must not only honor fearless speech but also strive to correct the injustices that make it necessary.

6

Profiles in Fearless Speech

THE CONCEPT OF FEARLESS SPEECH IS BEST ILLUSTRATED THROUGH speakers who exemplify it. Some of the individuals profiled in this chapter are well known, but not particularly for their contributions as courageous speakers. Others are more obscure. What they all have in common is that they have at least once in their lives practiced parrhesia, "saying everything" in the sense of "telling the truth without concealment, reserve, empty manner of speech, or rhetorical ornament which might encode or hide it."[1] This distinguishes these speakers from the conventional free speech canon, which is dominated by those who "say everything" in a reckless sense, saying "anything that comes to mind, anything that serves the cause one is defending, anything that serves the passion or interest driving the person who is speaking."[2]

These profiles are not intended to be hagiographies; the fearless speakers featured in this chapter are full of complexity and contradiction that brief profiles cannot fully capture. Some of them practiced fearless speech consistently throughout their lives, others engaged in fearless speech only intermittently, and still others spoke fearlessly at some points in their lives and recklessly at others. But each of these speakers endangered themselves at some point in order to speak the truth: "For there to be parrhesia, in speaking the truth one must open up, establish, and confront the risk of offending the other person, of irritating him, of making him angry and provoking him to conduct which may even be extremely violent. So it is the truth subject to risk of violence."[3]

The seven profiles offered here, while drawn from a range of backgrounds, geographical locations, and historical periods, can of course represent only a small fraction of fearless speakers throughout the world and throughout history. But each one provides a glimpse into the truly revolutionary possibilities of speech.

Elizabeth Freeman (1744–1829)

Elizabeth Freeman could not read or write, but her fearless speech not only freed her from slavery but also helped end slavery throughout Massachusetts. Freeman, known throughout most of her life as "Betty," "Mumbet," or simply "Bet," had been enslaved since childhood along with her younger sister, Lizzy, in the household of Colonel John Ashley. Ashley was a prominent figure in Sheffield, Massachusetts—a much-admired judge with a benevolent personality. His wife, Hannah, by contrast, was notorious for her cruelty toward enslaved people. On one occasion, Hannah discovered Lizzy eating scrapings left over from the household bread making. Enraged, she went to strike Lizzy with a red-hot kitchen shovel that had just been used to clean the oven, but Bet intervened: "Bet interposed her brawny arm, and took the blow. It cut quite across the arm to the bone."[4] The wound left a terrible scar, and when Bet was asked the cause of it, she would respond, "ask missis!"[5] According to Bet, "Madam never again laid her hand on Lizzy. I had a bad arm all winter, but Madam had the worst of it." Bet's equanimity led the chronicler of this incident to ask, with obvious admiration, "Which was the slave and which was the real mistress?"[6]

One of Bet's tasks was to serve refreshments when Ashley hosted gatherings of the town's influential citizens in his home.[7] That is what she was doing in the Ashleys' second-floor study during a meeting in early 1773, when eleven of the town elders were drawing up a version of a landmark document that would later become known as the Sheffield Declaration of Independence. The draft was committed to paper by a young up-and-coming lawyer named Thomas Sedgwick. The declaration, considered by some historians to be "the colonies' first formal declaration of independence from England,"[8] included the resolution that "Mankind in a State of Nature are equal, free and independent of each other, and have a right to the undisturbed Enjoyment of their lives, their Liberty and Property."[9] Overhearing this discussion of freedom, equality, and natural rights left a strong impression on Bet.

Shortly after, the declaration was read at a town meeting and adopted as law in Sheffield; later, its principles were incorporated into the Massachusetts Constitution,[10] which was finally ratified in 1780, five years into the Revolutionary War. Bet was also present in the central square of Sheffield when the new constitution—including the words from the first article of its Declaration of Rights—was read out loud: "All men are born free and equal, and have certain natural, essential, and inalienable rights."[11] Bet recalled the meeting of the town elders in Ashley's study in 1773 and sought out the lawyer who had served as the committee's clerk. Standing before Sedgwick in his office, Bet asked, "I heard the words read on the steps of the town hall about all men being free and equal. I am not a dumb critter, won't the law give me my freedom?"[12]

In some ways, it was understandable that Bet decided to bring her case to Sedgwick; he was a broad-minded, skilled attorney who would later go on to serve as a state senator, the Speaker of the House, and a judge on the Massachusetts Supreme Court. But he was also a friend of Ashley's and a former slave owner, and he did not immediately agree to take Bet's case. Sedgwick first asked Bet how she had come by "the doctrine and facts on which she proceeded." Bet responded that she had done so by "'keepin' still and mindin' things,'" including, "for instance, when she was waiting at table, she heard gentlemen talking over the Bill of Rights and the new constitution of Massachusetts; and in all they said she never heard but that all people were born free and equal, and she thought long about it, and resolved she would try whether she did not come in among them."[13]

Ultimately, Sedgwick was convinced and enlisted the help of his mentor, Tapping Reeve, to prepare Bet's suit. Underscoring the challenges raised not only by Bet's race but also her gender, the team decided to add an enslaved man to the suit out of concern that a suit brought only on behalf of a woman might not be recognized in a court of law.[14]

Though there is no transcript of the argument that Sedgwick and Reeve made in court, the account recorded by the Duc de la Rochefoucauld-Liancourt in his *Travels Through the United States of North America* (1799) suggests that it was, in effect, Bet's: that even if the law of Massachusetts had ever sanctioned slavery, "it was obviated by the Constitution of 1780, which held that all men are free and equal. Thus any laws enacted prior to this new document were to be considered null and void."[15] The all-male, all-white jury[16] agreed that Ashley did not own Bet. In addition, the court ordered that Ashley pay Bet damages and court costs.[17]

After winning her freedom, Bet adopted the name of Elizabeth Freeman. Her case, along with a contemporaneous case brought by a slave named Quok Walker, helped abolish slavery throughout Massachusetts. Bet went to work in the household of Sedgwick, who joined the Pennsylvania Abolition Society in 1785.[18] She was so beloved by the Sedgwick family that when she died at eighty-five, having accumulated considerable property as well as renown as a healer and midwife, she was buried in the Sedgwick family plot in Stockbridge Cemetery. The inscription on her headstone, written by one of Sedgwick's sons, reads, "She could neither read nor write, yet in her own sphere, she had no superior or equal. She neither wasted time nor property. She never violated a trust, nor failed to perform a duty. In every situation of domestic trial she was the most efficient helper and the tenderest friend. Good mother, farewell."[19]

At a time when enslaved people could be beaten or killed for the most minor of indiscretions, when women had virtually no recognized rights, Freeman heard the revolutionary call for freedom and equality and demanded, no matter the consequences, that it apply to her as much as anyone else. As she would later recount to the novelist Catharine Sedgwick, Sedgwick's daughter and Freeman's close friend, "Any time, any time while I was a slave, if one minute's freedom had been offered to me, and I had been told I must die at the end of that minute, I would have taken it. Just to stand one minute on God's *airth* a free woman—I would."[20]

―――

Dorothy Thompson (1893–1961)

As one of the most famous and influential journalists of her time— "the undisputed queen of the overseas press corps, the first woman to head a foreign news bureau of any importance"[21]—Dorothy Thompson understood the importance of free speech better than most. Thompson served as the chief of the Central European Bureau for the *New York Evening Post* and *Philadelphia Public Ledger* during the late 1920s and early 1930s. She was one of the first journalists to warn of the rising tide of fascism sweeping Germany, describing National Socialism as "placing will above reason; the ideal over reality; appealing, unremittingly, to totem and taboo; elevating tribal fetishes; subjugating and destroying the common sense that grows out of human experience; of an oceanic boundlessness" and "the enemy of whatever is sunny, reasonable, pragmatic, common-sense, freedom-loving, life-affirming, form-seeking and conscious of tradition."[22]

Thompson interviewed Adolf Hitler in 1931, describing him as "inconsequent and voluble, ill poised and insecure . . . the very prototype of the little man" and *Mein Kampf* as "eight hundred pages of Gothic script, pathetic gestures, inaccurate German, and unlimited self-satisfaction."[23] Within a month of Hitler installing himself as Führer in 1934, Thompson was expelled from Germany, an unprecedented act that demonstrated the new regime's intolerance of political dissent.

On November 7, 1938, a Jewish teenager named Herschel Grynszpan killed a German diplomat in Paris. Herschel's parents had sent him to live with an uncle in France, where he was struggling to find work when the Nazis deported his family, along with twelve thousand other Polish Jews, from Germany. They were transported to the Polish border and left stranded when Poland refused to allow them entry. After his sister wrote to him describing their plight and pleading for help, Herschel entered the German embassy and asked to see the German ambassador. He was instead shown into the office of Ernst vom Rath, an embassy official, whom he shot and killed. Herschel was arrested with a postcard to his family in his pocket that asked for their forgiveness: "My dear parents, I could not do otherwise, may God forgive me, the heart bleeds when I hear of your tragedy and that of the 12,000 Jews. I must protest so that the whole world hears my protest, and that I will do. Forgive me."[24]

Two days later, the Nazis used the assassination as a pretext for a violent assault against Jewish communities throughout Germany that became known as Kristallnacht ("Crystal Night"). Paramilitary forces burned down hundreds of synagogues, looted and destroyed Jewish businesses, and arrested, beat, and deported thousands of Jewish men. Thompson was horrified by the escalating violence and implored her American audience to understand the significance of what was unfolding in Germany. On November 14, she wrote in her column, On the Record, "I beg you to regard this horror as not more personal to you than it is to me, and to all the millions of others on this soil. . . . The crisis is not a Jewish crisis. It is a human crisis. . . . I would beg you not to isolate yourself in a fierce and bitter pride, but to have the courage to continue in the common front with which your life and your actions have allied you—the front of human decency."[25] Thompson also addressed Herschel's trial for murder in her radio broadcasts, asking, "Who is on trial in this case? . . . I say we are all on trial. I say the Christian world is on trial. I say the men of Munich are on trial, who signed a pact without one word of protection for helpless minorities. . . . We who are not Jews must speak, speak our sorrow and indignation and disgust in so many voices that they will be heard."[26]

Though Thompson had only asked her audience for their attention and their solidarity, her appeals were so eloquent that listeners sent in thousands of dollars, enough for her to start an international defense fund for Grynszpan. But her advocacy also led to a vicious backlash: "Her mail began to fill with racist diatribes, death threats, and the kind of incoherent cursing that American bigots had developed practically into an art. Why didn't the Jews go 'back where they came from,' one of Dorothy's antagonists asked—why didn't they go back 'in leaky boats?' 'You are Jewry's protégée'. . . 'Alleged Gentiles' of Dorothy's stripe—anyone who spoke as loudly as she did in defense of 'foul, Christ-killing Jews'—was probably a Christ-killer herself, a 'refu-Jew,' in racist slang."[27]

The vitriol was reflective of rising anti-Semitic and xenophobic sentiment in the United States, fueled by figures such as Father Charles Coughlin, whose wildly popular radio programs and magazines echoed Nazi propaganda and blamed "international bankers" for American economic troubles.[28] Coughlin republished portions of the infamous anti-Semitic hoax, *The Protocols of the Elders of Zion*, in his magazine and defended Kristallnacht as justifiable retaliation for Jewish persecution of Christians.[29]

Thompson was deeply disturbed by the rhetoric and tactics of Coughlin and other outspoken anti-Semites, especially Fritz Lieber Kuhn, a naturalized German citizen who founded an organization called the German-American Bund in 1936. Thompson immediately recognized the similarities between the Bund's activities in America and the early efforts by the Nazis to establish their ideology in Germany—the youth camps promoting "nationalism" and "patriotism," the physically intimidating security guards wearing matching uniforms, the swastika armbands and banners.

On February 20, 1939, the Bund held a rally in Madison Square Garden that was attended by more than twenty thousand people. The police presence was massive and held back the approximately one hundred thousand protesters attempting to demonstrate against the event. Thompson, armed with her press pass, managed to make it through the blockade. What she saw and heard inside horrified her. "On the eve of George Washington's birthday, twenty-two thousand Nazi sympathizers, having first pledged allegiance to the flag of the United States, sat beneath gigantic swastikas and portraits of Adolf Hitler and roared their approval while the Bund's orators warned them about the 'invisible government,' 'the Hidden

Hand of International Jewry,' and the socialist plots of President
'Franklin D. Rosenfeld.' Banners hung from the walls next to
mounted basketball schedules and advertisements for beer: 'Wake
Up America—Smash Jewish Communists!'"[30]

In what her biographer, Peter Kurth, describes as perhaps her
"finest moment—the indelible dramatization of her promise to
Hitler that she would not be muzzled by thugs," Thompson, dressed
in a regal evening gown, "took her seat in the front row of the press
gallery and commenced to interrupt the speakers with strident
gales of raucous laughter, humiliating and infuriating the pride of
American Nazism so deeply that after about ten minutes of this,
while the Bundists shouted 'Throw her out!,' she was actually sur-
rounded by a unit of Fritz Kuhn's 'Storm Troopers' and muscled
out the door."[31] Even as she was being shoved out of the auditorium, Thompson refused to be silent, shouting "Bunk, bunk, bunk!
Mein Kampf, word for word!"[32]

The mayor of New York, Fiorello LaGuardia, had rejected multiple appeals to deny the Bund's permit for the gathering: "If we are
for free speech, we have to be for free speech for everybody, and
that includes Nazis."[33] Thompson, having personally experienced
Nazi mobs in both Germany and in New York, eloquently countered this glib civil libertarianism in a column published the day
after the rally. She offered an extended explanation of why she had
attended the event and how her experience illustrated the tension
between fascism and free speech.

Thompson described the rally as an "exact duplicate" of a Nazi
rally she had witnessed in Germany in 1931: "That meeting was
also 'protected' by the police of the German Republic. Three years
later the people who had been in charge of that meeting were in
charge of the Government of Germany, and the German citizens
against whom, in 1931, exactly the same statements had been made
as were made by Mr. Kunze, were being beaten, expropriated and
murdered. . . . Every word that he said was made in Germany by
the Nazis, who are openly and avowedly engaged in making a
world-wide counter-revolution against republican and democratic
government."[34]

She had laughed, Thompson said, not only at the preposterousness of Kunze invoking the Golden Rule even as he asserted the supremacy of the white race but also "for a purpose": "I laughed because I wanted to demonstrate how perfectly absurd all this defense of 'free speech' is, in connection with movements and organizations like this one."[35] The thousands of Nazi supporters at the gathering were allowed to applaud and shout their praise of the anti-Semitic speeches, she wrote, but when she instead laughed in contempt, she was immediately seized by police officers and removed from the premises. Is the rule of free assembly, Thompson asked, "that everybody in a public meeting must either applaud the speaker or be silent"? She continued, "As a matter of fact, it is no laughing matter. If this democracy allows a movement, the whole organization and pattern of which is made by a government openly hostile to the American democracy, to organize, set up a private army and propagandize on this soil, we are plain saps. If it mobilizes the police to protect this movement against the opposition of American citizens who believe in the Declaration of Independence, it is committing a crime against itself and paving the way for disaster."[36] The entire purpose of the Nazi movement, Thompson pointed out, is to secure rights for white people while denying them to everyone else—a goal that is fundamentally incompatible with democracy and with the promise of freedom of speech for all. In words that carry particular resonance for our current historic moment, Thompson wrote that the public promotion of fascist expression is a conspiracy to deprive nonwhites of their freedom of speech and other constitutional rights, a conspiracy "protected, heaven help us, by the American Civil Liberties Union."[37]

Daisy Bates (1914–1999)

"No." Sometimes the most fearless act of speech is the refusal to speak.

Daisy Bates spoke, wrote, and published many compelling and courageous words during her long career as a civil rights activist, journalist, and newspaper publisher. These included articles highlighting police brutality and racial injustice in the *Arkansas State Press*, the newspaper she founded in 1941 with her husband, Lucius Christopher ("L. C.") Bates. Her criticism of a powerful local judge in one of these articles led to the two of them being arrested and thrown into jail by that very judge. Their convictions were later thrown out by the Arkansas Supreme Court, which invoked the "inviolate" liberty of the press and held that the article did not present a "clear and present danger."[38] But in some ways, it was what Bates refused to say that most powerfully demonstrated her fearless commitment to justice.

Daisy Lee Gaston grew up in Huttig, Arkansas, a small town a few miles away from the Louisiana border. She learned that she was adopted when she was eight years old; her birth mother had been raped and murdered by three white men, and her father had abandoned her.[39] In her memoir, Bates writes that she was never the same after this discovery: "So happy once, now I was like a sapling which, after a violent storm, puts out only gnarled and twisted branches."[40] But as she grew older, she decided to take to heart the words her beloved adoptive father had told her on his deathbed: "Hate can destroy you, Daisy. Don't hate white people just because they're white. If you hate, make it count for something. Hate the humiliations we are living under in the South. Hate the discrimination that eats away at the soul of every black man and woman. Hate the insults hurled at us by white scum—and then try to do something about it, or your hate won't spell a thing."[41]

When the Supreme Court delivered its momentous decision in *Brown v. Board of Education of Topeka* in 1954, declaring racial segregation in public schools to be incompatible with the Constitution, Bates and her husband began advocating for immediate desegregation in their newspaper. Invoking the service of black soldiers in World War II, they wrote, "It is the belief of this paper that since the Negro's loyalty to America has forced him to shed blood on foreign battle fields against enemies, to safeguard constitutional rights, he is in no mood to sacrifice these rights for peace and harmony at home."[42]

Bates, who served as the president of the Arkansas chapter of the NAACP, became a mentor for the Little Rock 9, the first black students selected to attend the previously all-white Little Rock Central High School. The students were scheduled to start classes in the fall of 1957. On the evening of August 22, 1957, a rock was thrown through the window of the Bates home, showering Daisy with broken glass. The note tied to the rock read "STONE THIS TIME. DYNAMITE NEXT."[43]

On September 2, Arkansas governor Orval Faubus announced that he was calling out the state National Guard out of concern for violence and warned that "'blood will run in the streets' if Negro pupils should attempt to enter Central High School."[44] On September 3, Bates consulted with parents of the black students and local community leaders on a plan to have the nine walk in together. However, one of the students, Elizabeth Eckford, was not informed about the plan; her family did not have a telephone, and Bates forgot to deliver the message to her before the morning of September 4. As documented in now-famous photographs, Elizabeth faced a screaming white mob and a line of armed guards completely alone. The mob hurled racial slurs, profanity, and threats of lynching at the fifteen-year-old girl, who finally escaped to a bus stop flanked by a Jewish *New York Times* reporter and a white female teacher. Bates was stricken with remorse for failing to inform Elizabeth of the changed plans, especially when the girl would wake up screaming from nightmares when she stayed at the Bates house.

Days of unrest and violence against black residents followed the confrontation at Little Rock Central. Friends of the Bateses began taking turns guarding their house at night. The Little Rock City Council passed ordinances targeting organizations that supported integration, most notably the NAACP, requiring them to publicly disclose the names of their members and donors. Bates, the custodian of those records for the Little Rock NAACP, refused to comply. "It is our good faith and belief," she argued, "that the public disclosure of the names of our members and contributors might lead to their harassment, economic reprisals, and even bodily harm."[45] Bates was arrested and convicted for violating the ordinance, and this time, the Arkansas Supreme Court did not come to Bates's aid. The case eventually made its way to the Supreme Court, which ruled that the ordinance violated the First Amendment.[46]

A few days after the failed attempt to escort the Little Rock 9 into the school, Bates received a visit from a white woman who claimed to represent a group of "Southern Christian women" in Little Rock.[47] The woman told Bates that the community clearly needed more time to adjust to integration and appealed to Bates to use her influence to help it do so; specifically, she asked Bates to call a press conference and ask the black students to withdraw their applications from Little Rock Central. The woman assured Bates that she would have the support of the Southern Christian women. After a long conversation, Bates asked, "'You told me what would happen if I withdrew my support from the students. What would happen if I didn't?' She looked me straight in the eye. 'You'll be destroyed—you, your newspaper, your reputation.' Looking around the living-room, she added, 'Everything!'"[48] The woman told Bates she had until 9:00 a.m. the next day to give her answer.

In her memoir, Bates describes her sleepless night following this visit. At dawn, Bates told the neighbor keeping guard outside her house that she would take over. As she sat on her porch with a gun in her lap and her dog at her feet, her mind turned to Elizabeth: "I thought about this tragic youngster who, at age fifteen, had shown more courage than I could possibly muster at this moment."[49] And then Bates made another notable decision to refuse to speak: "I began to think that in the struggle for freedom there could be no turning back, no strategic withdrawals, subterfuges or compromises. What I was going to tell my 'Southern Christian' friend was now perfectly clear. . . . My answer, I told her, was 'No!'"[50]

In the months that followed, as Bates steadfastly supported the Little Rock 9 and the *State Press* continued to advocate for immediate integration, her home was subjected to gunfire, incendiary devices, and burning crosses that nearly set the house on fire. Bates was hanged in effigy, and an organization calling itself the "Save

Our Schools Committee" compared the NAACP to Hitler and Hirohito.[51] One by one, the *State Press*'s advertisers withdrew, many under threats of violence. On October 29, 1959, Bates writes, "the door was closed on the *State Press* and on eighteen years of our lives. No last good-byes, no final editorials. The break had to be clean and sharp, for the pain was too deep. At exactly 5pm, the *State Press* had breathed its last word."[52]

Modern scholars have noted that women's participation in the civil rights movement is all too often relegated to the sidelines. As Willard B. Gatewood Jr. writes in the foreword to the Arkansas edition of Bates's memoir, Bates, "like other black women who took part in this long struggle, bore a double burden: not only were they considered members of an 'inferior' race but also as the 'inferior' sex of that race."[53] Bates was a rare figure who "spoke out at a time when women were supposed to be seen and not heard";[54] just as importantly, she refused to speak when doing so would harm others or endanger the cause of justice.

————

William Baird (1932–)

How controversial would a speaker have to be for the ACLU to withdraw its promise to represent him? As controversial as William Baird, apparently. In 1967, a Boston University student invited Baird, a reproductive rights advocate, to speak on campus. The plan was for Baird to distribute condoms and contraceptive foam to undergraduates as part of the lecture in the hopes of challenging a Massachusetts law that prohibited the distribution of contraceptives to unmarried people. The ACLU had agreed beforehand that they would represent Baird if he were arrested, which he promptly was following the lecture.[55] But only a few weeks later, the ACLU dropped Baird as a client.[56] According to Baird, the ACLU informed him that they would only represent him if he "remained silent" during his appeals; "I couldn't agree to do it . . . the public must be educated during my trial, and I can't compromise my principles."[57]

Baird faced up to ten years for violating the Massachusetts chastity law. In addition to being abandoned by the ACLU, he was publicly criticized by Planned Parenthood, who called him an "embarrassment" and asserted that there was "nothing to be gained"[58] by his case. He was sentenced to three months in the notorious Charles Street Jail, which was overrun by lice and rats and where he was threatened with rape and other violence.[59] In journal entries from this period, he writes of being "panic-stricken" about the fate of his wife and his children, who had been receiving death threats: "Do I have the right to expose my family to violent abuse and depravity?"[60]

Baird was finally vindicated in the 1972 Supreme Court case *Eisenstadt v. Baird*, a landmark case establishing that unmarried individuals have the same right to contraceptive access as married couples. Justice William J. Brennan's famous declaration in *Eisenstadt*—"If the right of privacy means anything, it is the right of the individual, married or single, to be free from unwarranted governmental intrusion into matters so fundamentally affecting a person as the decision whether to bear or beget a child"[61]—set the stage for the Supreme Court to rule a year later that the right to an abortion was protected by the Constitution. The decision also served as a foundation for the protection of other privacy rights, including the right to same-sex marriage established in *Obergefell v. Hodges* (2015).

But for all of *Eisenstadt v. Baird*'s impact as a right to privacy case, the majority opinion made no reference to the free speech implications of Baird's arrest and imprisonment. Only Justice William O. Douglas, concurring in the opinion, maintained that *Eisenstadt* was "a simple First Amendment case."[62] Douglas cited the court's recent decision in *Brandenburg v. Ohio* (1969), which held that the First Amendment protected a KKK leader who called for violence against nonwhite individuals, noting that Baird had done nothing nearly as extreme. He had only given a lecture on birth control and overpopulation that encouraged the audience to petition their government officials to change restrictive laws on contraceptives, which was clearly protected First Amendment activity. Including samples of various birth control products that audience members could take was "merely a projection of the visual aid and should be a permissible adjunct of free speech."[63] In Douglas's view, "The teachings of Baird and those of Galileo might be of a different order; but the suppression of either is equally repugnant."[64]

Regardless, many forces have attempted to suppress Baird's speech over the years: government officials, religious fanatics, and domestic terrorists. "Although our nation prides itself in allowing freedom of speech," Baird wrote in 1993, "I have been jailed eight times in five states in the 1960's and 1970's for merely speaking about reproductive freedom. . . . I've been shot at, firebombed, punched, kicked, spat upon."[65] His commitment to the cause of reproductive rights also took a toll on Baird's employment prospects, his family relationships, and his health.

Baird began his controversial advocacy for women's reproductive rights in 1963, after witnessing a horrifying scene in a New York hospital. At the time, Baird was the clinical director of EMKO Pharmaceuticals, a birth control manufacturer. During a research visit to Harlem Hospital, Baird writes, "I heard the frightening screams of agony of a woman. Racing to the hallway I saw a young, black woman stagger into the corridor. She was covered with blood from the waist down, as if someone had splattered a can of red paint on her. An eight-inch piece of wire coat hanger was embedded in her uterus. In a desperate effort to self-abort, she perforated her uterus with a coat hanger. She died."[66] The incident deeply impacted Baird, who started compiling a network of reputable abortion providers and distributing information and contraceptives directly to impoverished communities from a truck he called the "Plan Van." These activities led to his first arrest in 1965 for violating New York's restrictive birth control laws. Though the charges were later dropped, the arrest led to his termination from EMKO.[67]

After abortion was legalized in 1973, Baird opened three nonprofit abortion clinics and continued to engage in confrontational protests against antiabortion activists, including by picketing pro-life conventions with "an eight-foot cross emblazoned with the message: 'FREE WOMEN FROM THE CROSS OF OPPRESSION. KEEP ABORTION LEGAL.'"[68]

On February 15, 1979, a twenty-one-year-old man firebombed Baird's Hempstead clinic with a two-foot torch and a can of gasoline. All fifty patients and staff members who were inside escaped without injury, perhaps as a result of the safety training drills Baird had insisted on conducting in the clinic.[69] The incident prompted Baird to develop the first US self-defense manual for abortion clinics. Another of his clinics was attacked with chemical agents and later flooded with fire hoses.[70] At one point, a bullet was fired into Baird's living room.

Baird saw a clear line between the violence and the dehumanizing, inflammatory rhetoric deployed by antiabortion activists. The day after his Hempstead clinic was firebombed, Baird told the *New York Times* that the Catholic Church and the National Right to Life Committee were responsible for the attack: "What can you expect? This kind of thing is bound to happen and I am calling on them to stop using the rhetoric which calls us murderers and baby killers, which I believe are the sorts of hateful words which cause just this kind of thing."[71] Baird also felt that religious antiabortion speech had cost him his relationship with his first wife and children: "I lost them all. The kids grew up in a Catholic community. My granddaughter says I murder babies."[72] Baird worked with prominent antiabortion opponents, including Father Frank Pavone of Priests for Life, to produce a joint statement on nonviolence in abortion protests in 2002,[73] although it is clear that the commitment did not hold.

In a 2022 interview following the overturning of *Roe*, Baird bemoaned the complacency of reproductive health activists who failed to realize the threat posed by adherents of "dogmatic religion and fundamentalist belief systems" who call abortion "murder" and "genocide."[74] He has warned for years that the sexism of the antiabortion movement, which tells women "if you play with fire, you should be burned" even though "men are not 'burned,'" is a constant and pernicious threat.[75] And despite everything his uncompromising speech has cost him, despite his feeling that his contribution to women's rights has been underappreciated and erased ("no one knows I exist"[76]), Baird remains steadfast in his commitment to reproductive justice. "I have fought a good battle and will continue as long as I can with the fervent belief that no man is truly free unless women are free."[77]

––––––

Annette Lu Hsiu-lien (1944–)

Before she was Taiwan's first female vice president, before she was a political prisoner sentenced to twelve years for sedition, and before she was a feminist advocate and a champion of Taiwanese independence, Annette Lu Hsiu-lien was a three-year-old child strapped to her mother's back as she walked forty miles from a wedding ceremony to their home in Taoyuan. They made the journey by foot because train and bus services had been suspended in the wake of a mass uprising that had broken out across Taiwan on February 28, 1947. The riots were a product of tensions between Taiwanese civilians and the Chinese Kuomintang Party, also known as the KMT or Nationalist Party, which had taken control of Taiwan in 1945.

Since coming to power, the KMT had banned Taiwanese local languages, severely restricted the expression of Taiwanese art and music, and largely excluded Taiwanese residents from political participation. The KMT massacred between eighteen thousand and twenty-eight thousand in its crackdown against the 1947 revolt. After the KMT was pushed out of mainland China by the Communists in 1949, it instituted a brutal, decades-long regime of political suppression in Taiwan known as the White Terror. Tens of thousands of Taiwanese citizens—lawyers, teachers, artists, anyone suspected of opposing the KMT or supporting the Communists—were surveilled, arrested, tortured, jailed, and murdered.

In the long shadow of the February 28 massacre and in the midst of the White Terror, on December 10, 1979, Lu stood before a massive crowd outside the *Formosa Magazine* headquarters and spoke passionately and provocatively as a member of the *Dangwai*, meaning those who are "outside the party" of the KMT:

My beloved fellow Taiwanese, all of you with a conscience, with compassion, my name is Lu Hsiu-lien. I'm from Taoyuan. Today, December 10, is International Human Rights Day. For hundreds of years, Taiwanese have never had a chance like they have today, a chance to give resounding expression to the appeal of our hearts for justice, to cry out our demand for human rights. . . .[78]

Some people say the Dangwai are savage and violent. Some say Dangwai are separatists. I ask you, why is the Dangwai savage? Where do they disagree with the government? Today, everyone has seen that the drivers of the riot trucks are Taiwanese and ordinary citizens—these people are the real separatists among us. If the Dangwai are savage or forceful in nature, this is because the Nationalists rule without the permission of the Taiwanese and have yet to return authority to the eighteen million people.[79]

Lu's twenty-minute speech led to her being arrested, brutally interrogated, and imprisoned. By the time Lu was granted medical release to receive treatment for thyroid cancer five and a half years after she began her sentence, her mother, who had carried her on her back for forty miles and who had spent her last months bedridden, disoriented, and calling for her daughter, had died.[80]

Long before her arrest, Lu had been subjected to threats, investigations, and harassment for her views. An excellent student, she had studied law at National Taiwan University and then traveled to the United States to undertake graduate legal studies at the University of Illinois at Urbana-Champaign in 1971 and at Harvard in 1978. Her American experiences changed her worldview and her life path in profound ways, challenging the beliefs she had developed through her traditional, patriarchal Confucian upbringing and the Nationalist propaganda she had been fed since she was a child. At the University of Illinois, she encountered and embraced the concept of feminism; at Harvard, she began to seriously develop her advocacy of Taiwanese independence. Sometime in between,

Lu began to view the question of women's equality and the question of democracy as fundamentally interconnected.

After she returned from Illinois, Lu became an outspoken advocate for gender equality. In a speech on Women's Day, March 8, 1972, at her alma mater, Lu publicly challenged the prevailing patriarchal stereotype that men should work outside the home and women should remain inside the home.[81] She became a weekly columnist for the *China Times*, tackling issues of gender equality and violence against women.[82] In one column, Lu lambasted the sexualized vilification of a woman who had been murdered by her husband after she asked for a divorce. Not only did the man receive a light sentence, but he was portrayed by some commentators as the true victim in the case—a victim of his promiscuous wife's infidelity. Lu took particular issue with the circulation of a photo of the woman with her breasts partially exposed. She asked her readers to consider whether they would be equally supportive of murder as a punishment for infidelity when the unfaithful spouse was the husband.[83]

Lu published two books explaining her views on feminism, including one titled *New Feminism*, "an exposition of my feminist beliefs and a critique of male chauvinism rooted in Confucian philosophy."[84] Her opinion that "women have a right to equal participation in all social, political, and economic activities" was "perceived by many in Taiwan as heresy."[85] Lu was accused of encouraging promiscuity, sexual perversion, and hatred of men. According to Lu, the harassing letters ceased after she published a book featuring every reaction that had been expressed about her work, with images of the actual letters and their authors' signatures.[86]

Lu writes that she became more enthusiastic about "the establishment of a democratic and independent Taiwan" when she "realized that democratization and feminist activism are two sides of the same coin."[87] She continues, "To achieve true democracy, all citizens—male and female—must enjoy equal rights. Moreover, women do not win respect, recognition, or support from men if they fight exclusively for women's rights. Women should participate in a wide range of political, economic, and social debates and activities. Similarly, democracy advocates who preach equality but cannot rectify gender biases in their societies fail as champions of democracy."[88]

In 1976, Lu established a telephone hotline to assist victims of rape and domestic violence that was staffed by volunteer social workers, professors, lawyers, and psychologists.[89] She helped social welfare centers provide self-defense classes and other forms of support to rape victims. Her speeches, writing, and advocacy efforts attracted the attention of the KMT, who began to surveil Lu and to infiltrate her organizations.[90] When she was offered the opportunity to leave Taiwan for a fellowship at Harvard in 1977, Lu took it. While at Harvard, Lu began to write *Taiwan: Past and Future*, a history of Taiwan as an independent nation. She later smuggled the draft into Taiwan "by photographing each page and sending the rolls of undeveloped film."[91]

Given the risk of imprisonment or worse that she could face in Taiwan for her subversive ideas, Lu considered staying in the US to continue her graduate work. But while Lu "was tempted to accept a post-graduate fellowship that would have allowed further study and research at Harvard while awaiting the impending upheavals in international relations and Taiwan politics," according to Lu's mentor, Harvard professor Jerome A. Cohen, "she decided instead to plunge into the furnace of history."[92]

For Lu, one of the most painful consequences of her imprisonment was not being present when her mother died and being unable to attend her funeral. Lu describes the experience of being allowed to briefly leave the prison to visit her mother's gravesite a year after her death:

> There I saw Mother's name written on a shiny new tombstone amid the rows of other tombstones stretching toward the horizon. With tears streaming down my cheeks, I knelt, lit incense, and prayed for her spirit. Mother had known little but work, worry, and self-sacrifice in her lifetime. With no education, she had never had the opportunity to rise above the barriers that women of her generation faced. She had

derived meaning from life, not through her own accomplishments, but through the accomplishments of her children. . . .

I stood up, looked at the rows of tombstones and the expanse of the sky, and swore to myself that I would make Mother proud, and in my own way give significance to her life.[93]

On December 10, 1999, fourteen years after she was released from prison, Lu was asked to become presidential candidate Chen Shui-bian's running mate. Lu's acceptance speech was characteristically bold, almost taunting voters with her progressive commitments.

This presidential election is to put an end to government solely by men; it is to usher in an era of gender equality in which women and men administer national affairs together. Throughout history . . . the half of our population that is female has been ruled by men and denied a voice in many of the decisions that affect their lives and well-being. Government has traditionally been of men, by men, for men. By electing Chen Shui-bian and me, Taiwan can move toward real gender equality in society and politics. We can create a government of women, by women, and for women—side by side with men.[94]

On March 18, 2000, twenty years to the day that she had been charged with sedition for her Human Rights Day speech, Lu became the first woman in history to serve as the vice president of Taiwan—one of the many accomplishments that doubtless would have made her mother proud.

———

Marina Ovsyannikova (1978–)

"Of course, I fear for my life. Each time I speak to my friends in Russia, they say 'What do you prefer—Novichok [nerve agent], polonium or a car crash?'"[95] Marina Ovsyannikova is all too aware of the dangers faced by critics and political opponents of Russian President Vladimir Putin. But Ovsyannikova wasn't always a critic of Putin. Indeed, she was a longtime producer for Perivy Kanal (Channel One), a Russian state-controlled television channel, and played an active role in producing propaganda that portrayed Putin and his government in a positive light regardless of the reality. However, after Russia invaded Ukraine on February 24, 2022, this became harder and harder for Ovsyannikova to do.

Since 2003, Ovsyannikova's job had been "to watch Western news streams and press conferences, looking for tidbits that made the West look bad and Russia look good," which meant that she was allowed to freely access worldwide media that the vast majority of Russians were never allowed to see.[96] But from these sources, she learned that the Kremlin was lying to its people, especially about the Ukraine invasion. As the Russian government launched an unprecedented suppression campaign against antiwar protesters, making it illegal to refer to the Ukraine invasion as a "war" and prohibiting "false information" about the military,[97] Ovsyannikova decided that she could no longer remain silent.

On March 13, 2022, Ovsyannikova, whose mother is Russian and whose father is Ukrainian, made a necklace that combined the colors of the Russian and Ukrainian flags and recorded a video of herself making a short speech. She also made a poster that read, in Russian, "Stop the war. Don't believe the propaganda. They are lying to you here," and, in English, "No war" and "Russians against war."[98] The next day, she went to the Channel One newsroom wearing the necklace and with the poster tucked inside her jacket. During a live broadcast of *Vremya*, the most-watched news program in Russia, Ovsyannikova slipped past a distracted security guard and suddenly appeared behind the broadcaster holding her poster and shouting "Stop the war! No to war!" before the cameras cut away.[99]

As the footage of her interruption of the live broadcast went viral, her prerecorded video was shared on social media. In it,

Ovsyannikova, again wearing her Russian-Ukrainian necklace, expressed regret for her role in promoting Kremlin propaganda and encouraged the Russian people to protest the Ukraine war:

> What is happening in Ukraine is a crime. And Russia is the aggressor here. And responsibility for this aggression rests on the conscience of a single man: Vladimir Putin. My father is Ukrainian. My mother is Russian. And they've never been enemies. And this necklace I'm wearing is a symbol of that fact that Russia must immediately end this fratricidal war. And our fraternal peoples will still be able to make peace. Unfortunately, I've spent many of the last few years working for Channel One, doing Kremlin propaganda, and I'm deeply ashamed of this. Ashamed that I allowed lies to come from the TV screen. Ashamed that I allowed the zombification of Russian people. We were silent in 2014 when all this had just started. We didn't protest when the Kremlin poisoned Navalny. We just silently watched this anti-human regime at work. And now the whole world has turned its back on us. And the next 10 generations won't wash away the stain of this fratricidal war. We Russians are thinking and intelligent people. It's in our power alone to stop all this madness. Go protest. Don't be afraid of anything. They can't lock us all away.[100]

Predictably, her actions were denounced by the Kremlin. Ovsyannikova was detained and interrogated for more than fourteen hours without access to legal counsel.[101] But opponents of the Ukraine war and critics of the Russian government were effusive in their praise. "Five seconds of truth can wash away the dirt of weeks of propaganda," opposition politician Lev Shlosberg said of Ovsyannikova's protest, while Ukrainian president Volodymyr Zelenskyy expressed his gratitude "to those Russians who do not stop trying to convey the truth . . . who fight disinformation and tell the truth, real facts to their friends and loved ones . . . who are not afraid to protest," and, in particular, "personally to the woman who entered the studio of Channel One with a poster against the war."[102]

For the statements she made in her prerecorded video, Ovsyannikova was charged with attempting to stage an unlawful protest and fined.[103] She quit her job at Channel One and moved to Berlin but returned to Russia in July 2022 to deal with a dispute with her ex-husband over custody of their daughter.[104] On July 15, she demonstrated alone in front of the Kremlin with a poster that read, "Putin is a murderer. His soldiers are fascists."[105] She was charged with discrediting the military and placed under house arrest in August, but she fled Russia in a dramatic escape to France with her eleven-year-old daughter in October, assisted by the organization Reporters Sans Frontières (Reporters Without Borders).[106] A year later, Ovsyannikova was sentenced in absentia to eight and a half years for the Kremlin demonstration; shortly after, she lost parental custody rights to both of her children "for political reasons" (though her daughter continued to reside with her in Paris).[107]

"If they decide to kill me, it means that we are incredibly strong." Aleksei Navalny, the Russian opposition leader and anticorruption activist Ovsyannikova had named in her video speech, offered these words as closing thoughts in a 2022 documentary about his life.[108] On February 16, 2024, it was announced that Navalny had died while incarcerated in an Arctic prison. Though Russian authorities denied involvement in his death, it is widely believed that he was murdered by the Kremlin, a belief bolstered by reports that Navalny was soon to be released in a prisoner swap.[109] The most important thing to remember, Navalny says in the documentary, is that "you're not allowed to give up." It was a message that he knew Ovsyannikova understood. On March 16, 2022, as he was being tried for fraud in a Moscow courtroom, Navalny highlighted Ovsyannikova's bravery: "If you think I'll get scared, or that you can scare everybody in Russia," he said, you should remember "Marina Ovsyannikova, who didn't just speak up—she recorded a video and told us the most important words: act now."[110]

X González (1999–)

The Nation called it "6 Minutes and 20 Seconds That Could Change the World."[111] X González, eighteen years old and then known as Emma González, stood on a stage in front of a million people in Washington, DC, and described the day that a gunman entered Marjorie Stoneman Douglas High School and killed fourteen of their classmates and three members of the school staff.

> Six minutes and 20 seconds with an AR-15, and my friend Carmen would never complain to me about piano practice. Aaron Feis would never call Kyra "Miss Sunshine," Alex Schachter would never walk into school with his brother Ryan, Scott Beigel would never joke around with Cameron at camp, Helena Ramsay would never hang around after school with Max, Gina Montalto would never wave to her friend Liam at lunch, Joaquin Oliver would never play basketball with Sam or Dylan. Alaina Petty would never, Cara Loughren would never, Chris Hixon would never, Luke Hoyer would never, Martin Duque Anguiano would never, Peter Wang would never, Alyssa Alhadeff would never, Jamie Guttenberg would never, Meadow Pollack would never.[112]

González then stopped speaking and stood silently for nearly four and a half minutes, staring resolutely out into the crowd, not wiping away the tears running down their cheeks. Then, a timer beeped, and González resumed: "Since the time that I came out here, it has been 6 minutes and 20 seconds. The shooter has ceased shooting, and will soon abandon his rifle, blend in with the students as they escape, and walk free for an hour before arrest. Fight for your lives, before it's someone else's job."[113]

It wasn't the first time that González, who now uses they/them pronouns and identifies as nonbinary,[114] had spoken publicly about the massacre that had taken place in Parkland on Valentine's Day 2018. On that day, González had sheltered with hundreds of other students in the high school auditorium for hours, not knowing whether the active shooter alert that had been issued was real or if

anyone was hurt.[115] González, an outgoing and upbeat student who
was president of the school's Gay-Straight Alliance, tried to reassure their terrified classmates: "Listen to me: we are not going to
die. The universe will hear me and we will not die. Not today."[116]
Three days after the shooting, as the extent of the horror began to
sink in, González spoke at a gun control rally in Fort Lauderdale.
González called out the passivity of the government and the mer-
cenary propaganda of the NRA in an impassioned speech that
ended in a poignantly juvenile call-and-response rhythm:

> The people in the government who were voted into power
> are lying to us. And us kids seem to be the only ones who
> notice and are prepared to call BS. Companies [are] trying
> to make caricatures of the teenagers nowadays, saying that
> all we are self-involved and trend-obsessed and they hush us
> into submission when our message doesn't reach the ears of
> the nation, we are prepared to call BS. . . . Politicians who sit
> in their gilded House and Senate seats funded by the NRA
> telling us nothing could have been done to prevent this, we
> call BS. . . . They say tougher guns laws do not decrease gun
> violence. We call BS. They say a good guy with a gun stops a
> bad guy with a gun. We call BS. They say guns are just tools
> like knives and are as dangerous as cars. We call BS. They
> say no laws could have prevented the hundreds of senseless
> tragedies that have occurred. We call BS. That us kids don't
> know what we're talking about, that we're too young to
> understand how the government works. We call BS. If you
> agree, register to vote. Contact your local congresspeople.
> Give them a piece of your mind![117]

González, along with fellow Parkland survivors Jaclyn Corin,
David Hogg, Cameron Kasky, Alex Wind, and Sarah Chadwick,
organized the March for Our Lives protest that became a nationwide movement for gun safety. Beyond raising awareness of gun
violence, the students had specific policy proposals to "digitize
gun-sales records, mandate universal background checks, close

gun-show loopholes and straw-man purchases, ban high-capacity magazines, and push for a comprehensive assault weapons ban with an extensive buyback system."[118] The Parkland students received enormous attention and support—attention that they recognized had been denied to young people from less racially and economically privileged communities who suffered daily from the effects of gun violence. "We Stoneman Douglas students may have woken up only recently from our sheltered lives to fight this fight," wrote González, "but we stand in solidarity with those who have struggled before us, and we will fight alongside them moving forward to enact change and make life survivable for *all* young people."[119] González vowed that "the platform us Parkland Students have established is to be shared with every person, black or white, gay or straight, religious or not, who has experienced gun violence, and hand in hand, side by side, We Will Make This Change Together."[120] True to this vision, the 2018 March for Our Lives rally featured speakers from inner-city communities, including Edna Lizbeth Chávez from south Los Angeles and Zion Kelly from DC, both of whom lost brothers to gun violence.

For their outspoken advocacy, González and other Parkland survivors became the targets of numerous far-right conspiracy theories and vicious personal attacks. Like victims of Sandy Hook and other school shootings, the Parkland students were accused of being "crisis actors."[121] Extremist gun groups on social media forums circulated photos and video that had been manipulated to make it appear that González had torn up a copy of the Constitution; the original images had come from a *Vogue* video shoot in which González tore up a gun range target poster.[122] The comedian Louis C.K. later mocked them in a stand-up routine: "You're not interesting 'cause you went to a high school where kids got shot. Why does that mean I have to listen to you? . . . How does that make you interesting? You didn't get shot. You pushed some fat kid in the way and now I got to listen to you talking?"[123] When the students went on a bus tour around America calling for gun control and encouraging young people to vote, they frequently encountered protesters carrying AR-15s and signs saying "COME AND TAKE IT."

In addition to the vitriol and intimidation was the weight of all the grief—not just for their murdered classmates but for all the victims who reached out to González to tell their stories: "The strangest part of being a survivor was how badly strangers wanted to touch me, like I was a living relic. They'd shake my hand, or hug me, or lean on me to cry. They also wanted to tell me about the tragedies that touched them. So many voices saying how their loved ones had been gruesomely shot and killed."[124]

And despite all that the March for Our Lives movement accomplished over five years, González wrote in 2023, including the passage of hundreds of gun safety laws, "it's hard not to feel like things are pretty much the same."[125] González and the other Parkland activists had vowed that the Stoneman Douglas school shooting would be the last school shooting—but of course it wasn't. "Uvalde. Chesapeake. Colorado Springs. There have been 636 mass shootings in 2022 as I write this, the second-deadliest year on record."[126] While it is eminently understandable that González should feel despair at the world, it is also true that they have already done more in their short life to speak out against violence and injustice than most people will do in a lifetime. Moreover, they have inspired countless others to take up the task they described so eloquently in 2018: "We are speaking up for those who don't have anyone listening to them, for those who can't talk about it just yet, and for those who will never speak again. We are grieving, we are furious, and we are using our words fiercely and desperately because that's the only thing standing between us and this happening again."[127]

7

Fostering Fearless Speech

IF WE WANT TO TRANSFORM OUR RECKLESS SPEECH CULTURE INTO a fearless one, we must identify the institutions and practices that can help correct the distortions of antidemocratic speech. We must think about how law, technology, education, and community spaces could be redesigned to foster equality and individual flourishing.

The key to fostering fearless speech is to focus on vulnerability— not the professed vulnerability of the unpopular or the offensive, but the objective, historical, material conditions of subordination. The principle of "the last girl first," derived from writings by Mahatma Gandhi, can be instructive here: it calls us to look to the most exploited members of a community to guide our legal and social choices. In doing so, we will learn not only how to most effectively address the multiple injustices that imperil vulnerable groups but also how to restructure legal systems so that they benefit the general welfare and encourage fearless speech.

Among the notes Gandhi left behind after his death in 1948 was a "talisman" about the "the poorest and weakest member of society," the "daridranarayan":[1]

Whenever you are in doubt, or when the self becomes too much with you, apply the following test. Recall the face of the poorest and the weakest person whom you have seen, and ask yourself if the next step you contemplate is going to be of any use to that person. Will that person gain anything by it? Will it restore that person to a control over his or her own life and destiny? In other words, will it lead to freedom for the hungry and spiritually starving millions? Then you will find your doubts and your self melting away.[2]

The particular gloss of the "last *girl*" was added by human rights scholars to highlight the particular vulnerabilities of girls and women, especially in terms of social devaluation and sexual exploitation.[3] The concept embodies the insights of intersectionality theory in recognizing that the forces of marginalization and discrimination, whether related to poverty, race, or gender, do not exist in isolation from each other. Kimberlé Crenshaw coined the term *intersectionality* to describe the multidimensionality of lived subordination, echoing Pauli Murray's earlier insights about "overlapping and interconnected forms of inequality."[4] To illustrate how individuals may face discrimination from multiple sources and on multiple levels, Crenshaw used the analogy of traffic at a four-way intersection: "Discrimination, like traffic through an intersection, may flow in one direction, and it may flow in another. If an accident happens at an intersection, it can be caused by cars traveling from any number of directions, and, sometimes, from all of them."[5] If we want to build truly just and equal systems, writes Crenshaw, we should build them around the "multiply-burdened" subject. This is not only a matter of justice for the exploited subject; it will also have the effect of improving outcomes for all people.

As a matter of individual justice, the concept of the last girl echoes both John Rawls's difference principle ("Social and economic inequalities are to be arranged so that they are to the greatest benefit of the least advantaged"[6]) and liberation theology's "preferential option for the poor." It is reminiscent of Jesus's admonition in Matthew 25:40–45:

> [40] "Truly I tell you, whatever you did for one of the least of these brothers and sisters of mine, you did for me."

⁴¹ Then he will say to those on his left, "Depart from me, you
who are cursed, into the eternal fire prepared for the devil
and his angels.⁴² For I was hungry and you gave me nothing to eat, I was thirsty and you gave me nothing to
drink,⁴³ I was a stranger and you did not invite me in, I
needed clothes and you did not clothe me, I was sick and
in prison and you did not look after me."
⁴⁴ They also will answer, "Lord, when did we see you hungry
or thirsty or a stranger or needing clothes or sick or in
prison, and did not help you?"
⁴⁵ He will reply, "Truly I tell you, whatever you did not do for
one of the least of these, you did not do for me."[7]

Looking to the last girl can be justified on the grounds that it is
the morally appropriate response to suffering. But there is another
pragmatic reason to adopt the principle of the last girl—namely,
because it is socially as well as individually beneficial.

To understand how looking to the last girl—the subject of multiple, intersecting systems of subordination—benefits the general
welfare, we must take seriously the idea of vulnerability as an ines-
capable fact of the human condition. In her work on vulnerability
and equality, feminist legal theorist and political philosopher Martha Fineman describes vulnerability as the "state of constant possibility of harm."[8] These understandings of vulnerability emphasize
its universal dimension; the potential to be harmed is a fundamental feature of humanity. But, as Fineman observes, vulnerability is
also very particular: "While all human beings stand in a position of
constant vulnerability, we are individually positioned differently.
We have different forms of embodiment and also are differently
situated within webs of economic and institutional relationships.
As a result, our vulnerabilities range in magnitude and potential at
the individual level. Vulnerability, therefore, is both universal and
particular; it is experienced uniquely by each of us. Important in
regard to this particularity point is the fact that our individual
experience of vulnerability varies according to the quality and
quantity of resources we possess or can command."[9]

Fineman further observes that society plays an important role in addressing individual vulnerability: "While society cannot eradicate our vulnerability, it can and does mediate, compensate, and lessen our vulnerability through programs, institutions, and structures."[10] Thus, vulnerability must be assessed at least in part according to the way that it is addressed by existing social and legal structures. Inequalities of vulnerability can be exacerbated by institutional preferences: "Within the various systems for conferring assets, individuals are often positioned differently from one another; some are more privileged, while others are relatively disadvantaged. Important to the consideration of privilege is the fact that these systems interact in ways that further affect these inequalities. Privileges and disadvantages accumulate across systems and can combine to create effects that are more devastating or more beneficial than the weight of each separate part. Sometimes privileges conferred within certain systems can mediate or even cancel out disadvantages conferred in others."[11]

Focusing on the last girl—on the most vulnerable individuals—also serves the interests of those who are relatively more privileged. Crenshaw explains, "If we began with addressing the needs and problems of those who are most disadvantaged and with restructuring and remaking the world where necessary, then others who are singularly disadvantaged would also benefit . . . placing those who currently are marginalized in the center is the most effective way to resist efforts to compartmentalize experiences and undermine potential collective action."[12]

In this sense, intersectionality is the inverse of interest convergence: it is driven by the revolutionary drive for equality rather than the regressive preservation of privilege and urges the convergence of the interests of the powerful with those of the vulnerable rather than the other way around. Instead of "free speech for the white man," which does nothing more than replicate the status quo, we should strive for "free speech for the last girl."

A practical operation of the last girl principle can be observed in universal-design theory, in particular the "curb-cut effect."[13] The idea of the curb-cut effect is simple: the adoption of measures designed to accommodate people with particular needs or vulnerabilities ends up benefiting everyone. As the story goes, one evening in the 1970s in Berkeley, a group of disability advocates poured cement on a sidewalk to make a ramp so that people in wheelchairs could more easily navigate the daunting gap between the sidewalk and the street. This was a makeshift "curb cut," one of the environmental accommodations mandated by the 1990 Americans with Disabilities Act.

Angela Blackwell describes the "magnificent and unexpected thing" that happened when the "wall of exclusion came down" through curb cuts: "Everybody benefitted—not only people in wheelchairs. Parents pushing strollers headed straight for curb cuts. So did workers pushing heavy carts, business travelers wheeling luggage, even runners and skateboarders. . . . Nine out of 10 'unencumbered pedestrians' go out of their way to use a curb cut."[14] The curb-cut effect demonstrates that accommodation is not a zero-sum game: "When we create the circumstances that allow those who have been left behind to participate and contribute fully—everyone wins."[15]

Applying these insights of universal-design theory to law, educational institutions, and private spaces requires first admitting that there is no such thing as a neutral design. In the words of writer and documentarian Astra Taylor, "If equity is something we value, we have to build it into the system, developing structures that encourage fairness, serendipity, deliberation, and diversity through a process of trial and error. . . . No doubt, some will find the idea of engineering platforms to promote diversity or adapting laws to curb online harassment unsettling and paternalistic, but such criticism ignores the ways online spaces are already contrived with specific outcomes in mind: they are designed to serve Silicon Valley venture capitalists, who want a return on investment, and advertisers, who want to sell us things."[16]

Designing for democracy requires explicitly acknowledging existing injustice and inequality and making intentional efforts to change them, guided by the experiences of the most vulnerable members of society. This is the principle that underpins the reforms and recommendations that follow.

Redesigning Law

Reform Reckless Technology

As detailed in chapter 4, the tech industry drives attention and energy away from meaningful expressive pursuits and toward an endless loop of conflict and "engagement," rendering society vulnerable to the forces of extremism. The January 6, 2021, insurrection was not the first or last violent illustration of the threat that an individualist, acquisitive, reckless view of free speech poses to democracy, and the tech industry's role in accelerating violence must be addressed. Achieving tech industry accountability will require scaling back current platform immunity.

Reform of tech industry immunity should include greater regulation of the tech industry by the Federal Trade Commission, especially with regard to the illusion of "free" services. The interests of social media companies that rely on an advertising business model will never align with the public's interests. Of necessity, the goal of that model is to keep individuals in a perpetually "engaged" state, directing their attention and their energy toward activities that can be harvested for profitable data. This goal is deliberately obscured by the illusion that the services provided by social media and search companies are "free." Given that such services allow companies to harvest user data for profit, the FTC could treat the offer of free services as a "deceptive and unfair act and practice" and require tech companies to charge fees for their services in order to make the transactional nature of these services clear. These fees could help offset some of the damage that the internet has inflicted upon traditional media outlets that have been unable to compete with "free." The fees could also be used to subsidize public resources in a variety of spaces and complement meaningful investments in journalism, public education, universities, community centers, and small businesses to allow them to return to being or to become alternate sites of free expression and informed debate. The goal should be to ensure that no one host or forum, or even one medium, dominates the shaping of public opinion or the boundaries of free speech.

But the most crucial reform essential in achieving tech industry accountability is reform of Section 230 of the 1996 Communications Decency Act, the federal law that grants broad immunity to tech companies, discussed in chapter 4. Congress should amend Section 230 to ensure that people who have been injured by online harms can have their day in court. Unless the harmful content or conduct in question is speech protected by the First Amendment, plaintiffs should not be barred from suing online intermediaries, and online intermediaries that demonstrate deliberate indifference to harmful content unprotected by the First Amendment should not be able to take advantage of Section 230's protections.

First, Section 230 should be amended to make clear that its protections apply only to speech, not to the entire range of online conduct. If the broad immunity afforded online intermediaries is justified on First Amendment principles, then it should apply only with regard to online activity that can plausibly be characterized as speech protected by the First Amendment. Second, the legal protections offered by Section 230 should only extend to third-party protected speech for which platforms serve as true intermediaries, not speech that the platform itself creates, controls, or profits from.[17]

Third, the "Good Samaritan" immunity provided by Section 230 should be limited, as it is in the offline world, to those who choose to assist others despite having no preexisting duty to do so. It should not be extended to those who do not provide assistance, were responsible in some way for creating the situation requiring assistance, or exploited the situation for their own personal gain. Online intermediaries who do not voluntarily intervene to prevent or alleviate harm inflicted by another person are in no sense Good Samaritans. They are at best passive bystanders who do nothing to intervene against harm, and at worst, they are accomplices who encourage and profit from harm. Section 230 (c)(1) should accordingly be amended to make clear that providers or users of interactive computer services will not receive immunity when they intentionally encourage, solicit, or generate revenue from the speech of others or demonstrate deliberate indifference to harm caused by that speech.

Some Section 230 defenders equate limiting the Section 230 immunity of intermediaries with imposing liability on them for the actions of third parties (often imprecisely referred to as "user-generated content"). But the removal of immunity is not the imposition of liability. Most people and most industries, most of the time, do not enjoy preemptive legal immunity for actions they take that might harm other people, but that does not make them automatically liable for those actions. A complex set of facts and relationships must be established before any entity can be held legally accountable for harm to another entity. Plaintiffs must, at a minimum, need to demonstrate basic elements of concrete harm and causation—high bars to clear with regard to speech.

A slightly more sophisticated version of this objection maintains that the risk of liability—the *possibility* of being sued—will incentivize tech companies to take down any third-party content that could be controversial, resulting in the loss of valuable First Amendment–protected expression. That is, the specter of potential liability may lead platforms to remove content that seems even remotely controversial, including speech by women, minorities, and other historically marginalized groups. This is a legitimate concern, but not one that overrides the need for reform.

It must first be noted that whether an online platform leaves content up or takes it down, it makes a choice—there is no neutral position. Platforms *already* make choices about whether to leave content up or take it down, and they make that choice primarily based on their corporate bottom line. Right now, the tech industry's calculus for making choices about potentially harmful content is very simple: there is virtually no downside to leaving up even egregiously harmful content. Such content generates engagement, which in turn generates profit. It may also draw some bad press, but even that isn't necessarily a negative consequence from a financial perspective. Without any credible fear of liability, there is simply no real incentive for social media companies to do anything other than leave content up unless it drives down user engagement.

If Section 230 immunity were limited in the ways recommended here, it would complicate this calculus. Would it mean that valuable speech would disappear? Possibly, although this is by no means inevitable. The imposition of a modest restriction on the extravagant immunity currently enjoyed by the tech industry would not suddenly make social media companies automatically liable for user content, no matter how controversial. And any risk of liability for not taking content down would still need to be weighed against the potential benefit of keeping it up. Controversial speech would still generally mean more engagement, and engagement would still generally mean more profit.

Again, every industry (with the noted possible exception of the firearms industry) has to contend with the risk of liability. There is no reason to think that allowing people to sue when they are harmed by a product means that the product will cease to exist in any meaningful sense. Indeed, the potential for litigation is often a powerful motivator for industries to become safer, more efficient, and more innovative. Cigarette companies were sued for concealing known risks that smokers get cancer, and while cigarettes keep being sold, less toxic e-cigarettes are being sold as well, and lung cancer deaths attributable to smoking continue to decline.

Some Section 230 defenders counter that the tech industry isn't like other industries—the internet is about speech, and speech is special, and therefore special rules should apply. There are two points to note in response to this. First, as previously discussed, the way that Section 230 is currently interpreted protects far more—everything from defamation to credit card transactions to sales of illegal firearms—than First Amendment–protected speech. The text of Section 230 allows intermediaries to be immunized not only for the *speech* provided by others but also for "information" provided by others. This has allowed tech platforms to use Section 230 to absolve themselves of responsibility for virtually everything individuals do online—a protection that goes far beyond anything the First Amendment would or should protect.

Second, the tech industry is not the only speech-focused industry. Speech is the core business of newspapers, radio stations, television companies, and book publishers and distributors. Speech is integral to many workplaces, schools, and universities. And yet, all of these entities can be held liable when they cause or promote—and even in some cases when they fail to prevent—harm. None of these industries or entities enjoys anything like the sweeping immunity granted to the tech industry. The potential to be held responsible for harm has not driven any of these industries into the ground or eradicated free expression in those enterprises, and there is no reason that the tech industry should be granted such an undeserved competitive advantage over them.

Some also argue that any reform of Section 230 jeopardizes free speech in a larger sense, even if not strictly in the sense of violating the First Amendment. Of course, free speech is a cultural as well as a constitutional matter. It is shaped by nonlegal as well as legal norms, and tech companies play an outsized role in establishing those norms. There is indeed good reason to be concerned about the influence of tech companies and other powerful private actors over the ability of individuals to express themselves. This is an observation scholars and advocates who work on online abuse issues have been making for years—that some of the most serious threats to free speech come not from the government but from nonstate actors. Marginalized groups in particular, including women and racial minorities, have long battled with private censorial forces as well as governmental ones.

But the unregulated tech industry—or rather, the selectively regulated tech industry—makes this problem worse, not better. Granting sweeping protections to the industry has not prevented a handful of multibillion-dollar corporations from taking over the online world; it has helped make it possible. And those corporations are not invested in amplifying vulnerable voices or encouraging democratic participation or providing responsible platforms for meaningful public discourse. Their priority is profit, and abuse is nothing if not profitable. Unchecked online abuse does not just inflict economic, physical, and psychological harms on victims; it also silences them. Targeted individuals shut down social media profiles and withdraw from public discourse. Those with political ambitions are deterred from running for office. Journalists refrain from reporting on controversial topics. While the current model shielding the tech industry from liability may ensure free speech for the privileged few, protecting free speech for all requires legal reform.

Under the status quo, certain forms of valuable speech are never able to flourish. When platforms are overrun by death threats, rape threats, harassment campaigns, and the exposure of private information, many people—especially women, minorities, and other marginalized and vulnerable groups—go silent. They exit. Their valuable speech goes missing from those platforms.

This is also why Congress should reject attempts to characterize new and highly destructive forms of technology-facilitated abuse—especially those disproportionately targeted at vulnerable groups—as free speech and enact legislation to prohibit them. These abuses include nonconsensually distributed intimate imagery ("revenge porn"), sexual extortion (also called "sextortion," a form of blackmail in which sexual information or images are used to coerce the victim into doing something against their will), doxing, and digital forgeries ("deepfakes"), which have all proven particularly destructive to victims' privacy and freedom of expression.[18]

Redesigning Education

Develop a Fearless Speech College Curriculum

Educational institutions can play a vital role in highlighting the antidemocratic distortions that result from privileging reckless speech. They can provide students with accurate and comprehensive information about the complexities and limitations of First Amendment doctrine, highlight misinformation and disinformation about free speech law and its consequences, and acknowledge the nonlegal dimensions of freedom of expression. This should include not only rejecting false equivalences between government censorship and private choices but also emphasizing that the right *not* to speak and *not* to associate are themselves valuable exercises of the First Amendment, whether the entity in question is an individual or a private business.

These lessons could be developed as a Fearless Speech Curriculum to help institutions recognize the ideology of reckless speech and provide counter-examples of fearless speech. For higher education, this curriculum could include principles and protocols for handling outside speaker invitations and student protests. A version of these resources could also be directed at media institutions to raise awareness about the distorting effects of granting disproportionate space to "controversial" and antidemocratic views with little or no grounding in facts or science. These resources could highlight the inappropriateness of "both sides" rhetoric when one party or ideology is clearly the dominant force in a conflict (e.g., the current GOP-driven attack on the freedom and credibility of educators and educational institutions).

The curriculum should take as its starting point the speech that is currently under fiercest attack in educational institutions—namely, the recognition of the extent of racial, sexual, and economic inequality in America. One of the vital functions of a university education, and one vital to the preservation of true democracy, is teaching students to think critically about what they are told and sold. This includes what they may have been taught in grade school and high school survey courses in American history as well as received wisdom from other sources in a culture dominated by white, male, Christian perspectives. Critical evaluation of the history and evolution of the Constitution generally and the First Amendment in particular, rather than the pseudo-patriotic censorship now championed by Republican governors and reactionary school boards, is essential to the preservation of a functional democracy.

Prioritize Teaching First Amendment Principles in Law Schools

Law schools in particular should be well positioned to help with the current tangle of competing and inconsistent free speech claims, as legal education emphasizes the importance of defining issues, identifying rules, and applying them to specific facts. What is more, given the extent to which freedom of expression is intertwined with legal doctrine, law students have unique opportunities to develop professional expertise in the complex law of the First Amendment and free speech.

Accordingly, law schools should prioritize the teaching of First Amendment principles, not only in specialized classes but also through more general integration into the student experience. Arming students with accurate information about settled free speech doctrine and highlighting areas of uncertainty and challenge will help elevate the state of free speech discourse.

This includes confronting the reality of how First Amendment doctrine has historically been applied, especially when it has tended to serve the interests of the powerful and the privileged. Law schools should encourage critical reflection about this fact and encourage students to explore alternatives to prevailing orthodoxy about free speech law and practice. As they do with other legal doctrines and questions, students should be urged to consider free speech issues not only in the abstract but also in the context of specific facts, empirical and historical evidence, and evolving standards of justice, fairness, and equality.

One of the great gifts of legal education is the opportunity to wrestle seriously with the concept of harm, including the concept of reckless harm. In many areas of the law, recklessness is viewed in a negative light; it is considered not only a legally culpable state of mind in many situations but also a morally culpable one. As discussed throughout this book, however, in First Amendment law, recklessness is often treated as a virtue rather than a vice. The most commonly taught First Amendment cases involve speech that serves the speaker's own self-interest while creating risks of harm to others—KKK members burning crosses, neo-Nazis brandishing swastikas, and corporations producing violent, misogynist pornography. In the prevailing First Amendment orthodoxy, recklessness tends to be privileged rather than punished.

Law schools could deliberately seek to provide, through classroom instruction, extracurricular events, and invited speakers, examples of fearless speech, bearing in mind that the most consequential characteristic of fearless speech is the critique of power. While reckless speech that promotes hierarchies of race, gender, class, orientation, religion, or other arbitrary classifications might be *protected* under the First Amendment, it does not follow that such speech must be *promoted*. If a law school truly wishes to inspire courage and open-mindedness, it should give preference where possible to the exploration of speech that challenges, or at least does not simply defer to, long-standing power asymmetries.

Law schools could also provide processes for student organizations and the student body as a whole to come together and share information in advance about outside speaker invitations and protocols, providing students with meaningful opportunities to understand how institutional resources are allocated and to express concerns or questions about those allocations. Providing a forum for such conversations could help administrators identify and address potential conflicts before the fact, enabling them to avoid media spectacles that rarely serve the interests of anyone within the educational institution.

Law schools could also strive to provide more opportunities to explore how the much-touted value of "objectivity" in the face of prejudice or hatred might be a luxury more accessible to some students than others. It is all too easy for law professors to forget (or never consider) how their students' lives might be precarious in ways that make it difficult for them to leave their personal experiences at the classroom door. Directly addressing those experiences can be a valuable exercise, particularly in the context of First Amendment law, to test how abstract legal principles actually work in practice.

Redesigning Public Squares

Create Multiple Counterpublics

As we saw in chapter 4, the amorphous and ambiguous concept of the public square has for too long served as the dominant model for tech platforms. The claim that social media platforms are or should be modern "public squares" is often used to justify a superficially laissez-faire approach to speech that perpetuates an elitist status quo.[19]

The traditional public square is an idealized myth that ignores how access to and expression in public spaces have always been heavily mediated by gender, race, and class and that the online public square suffers from the same problems. Confident assertions that sidewalks and public parks have always been places where people can speak freely (see, for example, in *McCullen v. Coakley* [2014], where this claim was used to justify the harassment of women outside abortion clinics as a form of protected speech) are undercut by the historical reality of formal and informal regulations—including street harassment, police harassment, stop-and-frisk practices, and laws against prostitution, panhandling, vagrancy, and loitering—that have operated to exclude women, people of color, people experiencing homelessness, dissidents, and other vulnerable groups.

The domination of corporate-owned social media has impoverished the concept of the public square. There is a reason that billionaires like Musk insist that social media platforms like X are, or should be, the public square. This identification erases the most obvious distinction between the public square and a social media site: social media sites are owned and operated by private enterprises, not the government. Individuals are not permitted to use a social media site at will; they may only use it at the discretion of the site's owner, as many discovered for the first time when they were removed from X for criticizing or mocking Musk.

More fundamentally, the idealized vision of the public square as a democratic space dedicated to the free exchange of ideas could not be more different from profit-oriented sites such as X or Facebook. Social media corporations are not interested in democratic exchange or the substance of individual expression; they are interested in speech only insofar as it keeps users engaged enough to expose increasingly detailed information about themselves that can be extracted and sold to data brokers. Developing true public squares will require investment in public universities, traditional media, libraries, and other non–social media avenues of expression and information.

Tech platforms have tremendous power to regulate online harassment and abuse. For many years, however, they did not make much effort to do so. In the last decade, tech industry leaders have finally begun to take some of these issues seriously. Tech companies have developed tools and policies to address nonconsensually distributed intimate imagery, racist message boards, mug-shot sites, fake news, and terrorist propaganda.

Tech innovations to curb abuse on these platforms have not only reduced harassment and hateful speech but also fostered more speech by more diverse groups. Their efforts do not implicate the First Amendment or involve any powers of the state. Tech platforms, as nonstate actors that are not restrained by current First Amendment doctrine and arguably exert more influence on public discourse than state actors, have a unique opportunity to develop and model this standard of fearless speech. They can encourage fearless speech by exercising their right to moderate or prohibit violent or false content, especially when that content comes from popular or powerful sources.

Those who wish to create spaces of true democratic deliberation should abandon the false position of neutrality and fully embrace the role of curator. Those who want the spaces they control to become sites of democratic deliberation should embrace more creative and innovative models for encouraging free expression and critical thinking.

If we want online spaces that do not merely replicate existing hierarchies and reinforce radically unequal distributions of social, economic, cultural, and political power, we must move beyond the simplistic and corrosive cliché of the unregulated public square and commit to the hard work of designing for democracy. Once we acknowledge that no truly inclusive, democratic, and free arena for public discourse has ever existed in the United States, either online or off, we can acknowledge that no single space is likely to achieve all of these ends simultaneously. Instead of an idealized public square, we can envision the flourishing of multiple spaces—online and off, public and private—that provide the conditions necessary for free expression and democratic deliberation.

Questions then arise: What lessons can be learned from the failures of the physical public square? What is the theory of the public square that provides a way to normatively assess current structures and approaches to public interaction? What are the salient differences between offline and online discourse that might provide paths forward to greater democracy and free speech? What are the thoughtful, intentional design choices or commitments that can be made to create true sites of public discourse and rational deliberation?

Part of the problem with the concept of the public square is that it is invoked in imprecise and undertheorized ways. It is often used to describe places or activities in which contentious speech takes place, even though contentious speech alone is not a marker of democratic deliberation. For a more sophisticated view, we can look to the philosopher Jürgen Habermas, who offers an influential and comprehensive description and theory of the public sphere. For Habermas, the public sphere must be distinct from the state; it must be a "site for the production and circulation of discourses that can in principle be critical of the state."[20] It must also be distinct from the market and instead be "a theater for debating and deliberating rather than for buying and selling."[21] The public sphere is a place accessible to all private citizens, where they can discuss matters of common interest in an unrestricted manner.[22]

Habermas's theory of the public sphere is useful in many respects. It demonstrates how social media forums cannot constitute a public sphere because they are not truly distinct from either the state or the market. Powerful government figures wield tremendous influence in social media forums, and the forums themselves are for-profit operations of private enterprises.

But Habermas's theory also replicates the false claims of more popular views of the public square. As Douglas Kellner writes, "while the concept of the public sphere and democracy assume a liberal and populist celebration of diversity, tolerance, debate, and consensus, in actuality, the bourgeois public sphere was dominated by white, property-owning males."[23]

One of Habermas's most trenchant critics, Nancy Fraser, directly addressed limitations of the concept of the public sphere, given its elitist and exclusionary history: "Should we conclude that

the very concept of the public sphere is a piece of bourgeois mascu-
linist ideology, so thoroughly compromised that it can shed no genuinely critical light on the limits of actually existing democracy?
Or, should we conclude, rather, that the public sphere was a good
idea that unfortunately was not realized in practice but that retains
some emancipatory force? In short, is the idea of the public sphere
an instrument of domination or a utopian ideal? Well, perhaps
both. But actually neither."[24]

Fraser emphasizes that one of the greatest flaws in the theory of
the public sphere is its unitary focus. Given how the public sphere
reinforces existing power structures, "where there is only a single,
comprehensive public sphere . . . members of subordinated groups
would have no arenas for deliberation among themselves about
their needs, objectives, and strategies."[25] Instead, society should be
arranged so as to "accommodate contestation among a plurality of
competing publics" in order to "better promote the ideal of partici-
patory parity."[26] As an example, Fraser points to what she refers to
as the "U.S. feminist subaltern counterpublic, with its variegated
array of journals, bookstores, publishing companies, film and video
distribution networks, lecture series, research centers, academic
programs, conferences, conventions, festivals, and local meeting
places."[27] Jane Mansbridge suggests adding factories, which "unex-
pectedly brought workers together to share their experiences, and
black colleges that initiated the sit-ins of the civil rights movement."[28] These counterpublics "have deliberative uses even for
members of dominant majorities, but are crucial for the marginalized as a protection against hegemonic discourse."[29]

One model for counterpublics to consider instead of the abstract
public square is the academy, with its emphasis on scholarship, rigor,
and norms of civil interaction.[30] In its most noble form, the project
of higher learning encourages critical reflection and intellectual
evolution. Such a project requires discernment and evaluation, not
the simplistic embrace of "both sides." As Justice Felix Frankfurter
wrote in *Wieman v. Updegraff* (1952), democracy is built on "disci-
plined and responsible" public opinion, and "it is the special task of
teachers to foster those habits of open-mindedness and critical

inquiry which alone make for responsible citizens, who, in turn, make possible an enlightened and effective public opinion."[31]

Another potential model is the Enlightenment-era European salon. While the salon (like the academy) was by no means free of the trappings of wealth and privilege, the ideals it promoted were egalitarian, democratic, and revolutionary for their time. According to historian Dena Goodman, the salon played a key role in the development of the concept of the public sphere.[32] Unlike the historical public sphere, however, salons were ruled by women. Known as *salonières*, these women created spaces in their homes for people of diverse backgrounds to debate politics, art, and culture in a safe and respectful setting.[33] Salonières were influential Enlightenment figures who demonstrated "a respect for all opinions, a refusal to prejudge, and a distaste for orthodoxies of all kinds."[34] They invited a wide variety of individuals to participate in interactive, informal education outside of elite institutions:

> Those participating in a salon understood that they were entering a space in which typical forms of valorization such as wealth, social status, or family lineage were not prioritized, or to a far lesser extent than in other forms of social interaction. What mattered most were the ideas and knowledge that could be gained from contemplation that benefited the collective. Erudition, wit, inventiveness, the ability to poetically capture an idea or elegantly communicate a concept, these were the cardinal virtues of the salon. Equally, the manner in which ideas were pursued was of great importance. Self-love and arrogance were discouraged for they signaled the wrong motivation for participation.[35]

A third potential model is the library. Libraries have long provided vital resources—intellectual, literary, historical, educational—to the public for free. They have served as inclusive and accessible sites of knowledge and community and have often been frontline defenders of the right to information and the right of free speech.

It is worth imagining what social media platforms might look like if they were modeled on the ideals of the academy, the salon, or the library rather than on the public square: a variety of semiprivate, secure spaces where members of the public could explore and discuss politics, art, and culture in safety and mutual respect.

They might look something like MetaFilter, a once-iconic weblog that has existed since 1999. On its "About" page, MetaFilter (MeFi for short) states: "Here you can expect thoughtful and varied discussions. Since 1999, we've been focused on fulfilling the web's potential to bring people together and create genuine, vibrant, good-hearted community spaces."[36] The site features a diverse array of content, ranging from news to art to politics, and a question-and-answer subsite called Ask MeFi.[37] Unlike most social media forums, MetaFilter restricts participation on the site in several ways.[38] First, while anyone can view content on the site, individuals must register in order to post content. They must also pay a one-time five-dollar fee to participate in the forum.[39] Participants are also subjected to mandatory waiting periods between posts.[40] In naming MetaFilter one of the "50 Best Websites" of 2009, *Time Magazine* wrote that the subscription fee "ends up feeling like a feature rather than an impediment, because it manages to keep the site remarkably free of trolls, griefers and other anonymous jerks," and that the site "has the public-spirited flavor of a small town or good university."[41]

MetaFilter is much less well known today. Its decline in prominence can be traced to 2012, when MetaFilter experienced a dramatic drop-off in traffic following the "Panda" update to Google's indexing algorithm. The update was intended to promote high-quality content and downrank sites using search-optimization techniques or spam. But there was already a consensus that MetaFilter *was* a high-quality site. Therefore, it should not have suffered negative consequences from the update, raising the suspicion that Google was using its black-box powers to crush small communities.[42]

MetaFilter's decline raised other, deeper issues about the changing nature of what we see and how we connect online. As Caitlin Dewey wrote in the *Washington Post*, "the most striking, prescient takeaway from the whole MetaFilter episode" is "the extent to which the modern Web does not incentivize quality."[43] Sites that deliberately set standards to encourage thoughtfulness, reflection, and consideration of community norms constantly lose out to sites that reward impulsivity, provocation, and narcissism.

But it does not have to be this way. Instead of funneling humanity into a handful of corporate-owned, cacophonous spaces, the internet could provide pathways into a multitude of settings designed to serve a diverse array of personal, cultural, and intellectual interests. As the late congressman John Lewis wrote, democracy is not a state, but an act.[44] It requires deliberate design and constant commitment, in online spaces as well as off.

Cyndi Suarez writes that "the history of democracy is about the fight for the public square—who speaks and who doesn't, whose issues matter and whose are marginalized, who can congregate and who is intimidated." She asks, "What happens when the government does not step in to ensure peace and order, and may even instead stoke chaos and entropy? Can we rely on public opinion and counter-demonstrations, using constructive, unifying speech to counter destructive, segregating speech?"[45] In the United States, calls to protect the public square, whether physical or virtual, are often efforts to maintain its status quo domination by the white, wealthy, and male. Rather than function as a site of free expression and democratic deliberation, the public square excludes and exploits women, nonwhite men, and other vulnerable groups.

A truly democratic society should provide myriad possibilities to develop free speech. We can build a multitude of spaces designed for reflection instead of performativity; accessibility instead of exclusion; intellectual curiosity, humility, and empathy instead of ignorance, arrogance, and cruelty; fearless instead of reckless speech. We can construct multiple spaces—online and off, public and private—designed to provide the conditions necessary for free expression and democratic deliberation for different groups with different needs.[46] We can be fearless in our designs for democracy.

CONCLUSION

"I Choose My Own Way to Burn"

PLAYWRIGHT LILLIAN GARRETT-GROAG'S FATHER FLED AUSTRIA in 1938 to escape Nazi persecution. He settled in Argentina, where Garrett-Groag was born, only to be confronted with an outbreak of anti-Semitic violence under Juan Perón's dictatorship in the 1950s. Garrett-Groag recalls that her parents shielded her from the reality of the rising danger by telling her that the signs going up around Buenos Aires calling for the death of Jews and the man they saw gunned down by soldiers were all just scenes from movies being filmed in the city.[1] It was partly this background that led Garrett-Groag to write a play about Sophie Scholl and the White Rose movement, which she called "possibly the most spectacular moment of resistance" of the twentieth century.[2]

Garrett-Groag was particularly interested in accounts that Robert Mohr, the Gestapo specialist who interrogated the White Rose activists, had been sympathetic to Scholl and attempted to spare her from execution. Mohr claimed to Scholl's father that he had tried to save her life by encouraging her to testify that she only participated in the group's activities due to the influence of her brother, Hans. In her play *The White Rose* (1993), Garrett-Groag imagines the interrogation sessions between Scholl and Mohr. Mohr pleads with Scholl to take advantage of her respectable and comfortable position as a girl from a middle-class German family, to just "go along" with the tide of prevailing sentiment so that she can survive. In the play's most compelling scene, Scholl responds:

> The real damage is done by those millions who want to "survive." Those honest men who just want to be left in peace; who don't want their little lives disturbed by anything bigger than themselves. Those with no sides, and no causes. . . . Those who live small, mate small and die small. . . . And it's an illusion, because they die too, those people who rolled up their spirits into tiny little balls to hide them under their puny lives to be safe. Safe?! From what? Life is always on the edge of death. Narrow streets lead to the same place as the big, wide avenues, and the little candles burn themselves out just like the flaming torch. I choose my own way to burn.[3]

In her foreword to the play, Garrett-Groag marvels, "All these young people had to do to save their lives," she writes, "was to keep their mouths shut." They could have said nothing and simply given themselves over to "the gradual, imperceptible sliding into the moral chaos responsible for great communal disasters."[4] Instead, like the abolitionists, the suffragists, the civil rights advocates, and the other truth tellers whose stories are recounted in this book, they chose to burn, to risk everything—their comfort, their privilege, their very lives—to speak out against injustice.

As fearless speakers demonstrate, the power and potential of speech is vast. The First Amendment, by contrast, is very, very small. It has had little to no relevance for the most courageous speech acts in America's history. Enslaved people who were discovered secretly learning to read could not invoke the First Amendment to avoid being lashed; women who were physically prevented from speaking in public could not protest that their First Amendment rights were being violated. The First Amendment did not stop abolitionists from being lynched or black-owned presses from being destroyed, and it did not halt book burnings or the imprisonment of political dissidents. Nor does the First Amendment today stop abusive men from silencing their victims with defamation lawsuits or police officers from beating students protesting the state-sponsored murders of women and children.

And yet the First Amendment continues to be treated as the lodestar for free expression, offered as the model for universities and social media platforms and other public conversations. As if there were no other way to envision the richness and diversity of human interaction than through the lens of a narrow legal rule. As if identifying the speech the government cannot punish is somehow determinative of the speech our society should promote. As if we have no ability and no obligation to distinguish between reckless and fearless speech, between speech that seeks to challenge power and speech that seeks to conserve it, between speech that advances democracy and speech that destroys it.

Just a little over a century after an enraged mob tried to silence Angelina Grimké Weld's powerful antislavery speech in Pennsylvania Hall, an angry crowd surged outside of a Chicago auditorium where the Reverend Arthur W. Terminiello was speaking. Terminiello, a rabid Christian Nationalist, repeatedly referred to Jewish people as "scum" and "bedbugs" that needed to be removed from the country; members of his audience responded with shouts such as "Yes, send the Jews back to Russia. Kill the Jews." Terminiello was convicted for breach of the peace. He challenged his conviction on First Amendment grounds, and in 1949, the Supreme Court ruled in his favor. Justice Douglas wrote the majority opinion, holding that "a function of free speech under our system of government is to invite dispute. It may indeed best serve its high purpose when it induces a condition of unrest, creates dissatisfaction with conditions as they are, or even stirs people to anger."[5]

Justice Robert H. Jackson issued a fiery dissent that was clearly informed by his recent experiences as chief US prosecutor at the Nuremberg war crimes trials. "There are many appeals these days to liberty," he wrote, "often by those who are working for an opportunity to taunt democracy with its stupidity in furnishing them the weapons to destroy it."[6] He offered as a pointed example the Nazi propagandist Joseph Goebbels, who observed, "We National Socialists never asserted that we represented a democratic point of

view, but we have declared openly that we used democratic methods only in order to gain the power and that, after assuming the
power, we would deny to our adversaries without any consideration
of the means which were granted to us in times of (our) opposition."[7] There is a distinction, Jackson maintained, between the
exercise of a liberty and the abuse of it. If we abdicate our responsibility to distinguish between those, we "will convert the constitutional Bill of Rights into a suicide pact."[8]

As the January 6, 2021, insurrection demonstrated, we are per-
ilously close to democratic suicide. At 3:41 a.m. on January 7, 2021,
closing the joint session of Congress that finally and formally recognized the democratic transfer of presidential power, Senate
chaplain Barry Black led the legislative body in prayer: "These tragedies have reminded us that words matter . . . and that the power of
life and death is in the tongue."[9] It is a lesson that no democracy can
afford to forget, and one that fearless speech impels us to remember.

Epilogue

"And a little child shall lead them"
— Isaiah 11:6, New King James Version

ONE HUNDRED STATUES, TWO FROM EVERY US STATE, ARE HOUSED in the National Statuary Hall Collection in the US Capitol. As of January 2024, one is missing. An empty plinth marks the spot where, from 1909 to 2020, a statue of Robert E. Lee had stood next to Virginia's other representative, George Washington. Lee's statute was removed during the wave of protests that swept the US following the brutal 2020 murder of George Floyd by Minneapolis police officers.

In December 2020, the Virginia Commission for Historical Statues in the US Capitol determined that Lee's statue will be replaced by a statue of African American civil rights activist Barbara Rose Johns.[1] It will feature Johns at age sixteen, holding a book aloft in her right hand while her left hand rests on a podium. The statue evokes the day in April 1951 when she stood before the entire student body of Robert Russa Moton High School in Prince Edward County, Virginia, and led them in a walkout to protest substandard conditions of their segregated school.

More than 450 students had been crowding into the school building built to house 180, and tarpaper shacks had been hastily constructed around it to absorb the overflow. Students shivered through freezing winter days and had to open umbrellas inside if it rained. The school had no cafeteria, no lockers, and no gym. Just minutes away in Farmville, by contrast, students at an all-white school enjoyed "spacious classrooms, modern heating, and a real cafeteria."[2] For months, Johns had been attending school board meetings with the student body president and vice president to demand renovations, but nothing had been done. "We wanted so much here and had so little," Johns would say later. "And we had talents and abilities here that weren't really being realized." Johns decided that they needed to take more dramatic action.

As John Bubar described it in the *New York Times*, "Barbara organized a group of juniors and seniors to help her execute her plan. On April 23, they lured their principal, M. Boyd Jones, out of school by making up a story about some students who were getting in trouble with the police downtown. When Principal Jones rushed to check on the phony situation, the group passed around notes, calling for an assembly in the auditorium."[3]

The notes were signed "B.J.," which just happened to be both Johns's and the principal's initials. When teachers and students arrived in the auditorium, the curtain was pulled back to reveal Johns onstage at the podium. "There wasn't any fear," she would later write. "I just thought this is your moment—seize it!"[4]

Johns told all the teachers to leave and then asked the students, "Are we just going to accept these conditions, or are we going to do something about it?" The students then walked out en masse.[5] After Johns contacted NAACP lawyers Oliver Hill Sr. and Spottswood Robinson to assist them in their fight for equal school conditions, their case was joined with *Brown v. Board of Education*. Before the Supreme Court issued its landmark ruling in 1954, Johns was subjected to death threats and a cross was burned in her yard. Her family moved her out of state to Alabama to finish high school. Later, her family home was set on fire and burned to the ground.[6] And instead of complying with the Supreme Court's command to integrate, Prince Edward County officials closed all the public schools in the county for five years.

A "Light of Reconciliation" has shined from the Prince Edward County courthouse bell tower every evening since 2008, the year that county supervisors officially apologized for those five years of vengeful defiance. A historical marker in front of the courthouse reads, "We grieve for the way lives were forever changed, for the pain that was caused, and for how those locked doors shuttered opportunities and barricaded the dreams our children had for their own lifetimes."[7]

"Freedom of speech plays a critical role in contemporary democracy," laments Jonathan Simon, "but fearless speech does not."[8] But this can change. We can give fearless speech pride of place in our law and our society. We can shift our resources and veneration away from the reckless, cowardly speech of the privileged and powerful toward the speech of the sincere, critical, and brave—of speakers like Barbara Johns.

It is truly fitting that a statue of Johns, a symbol of fearless speech and the demand for racial justice, will replace the statue of Robert E. Lee, a symbol of craven propaganda and racial patriarchy, in the nation's capital. It is an inspiring illustration of how white male supremacy *will* be replaced by democracy—in the halls of our government, in the public square, and in our words.

Acknowledgments

I am grateful to the Knight Foundation for the generous grant that made much of the research for this book possible. I also want to acknowledge the support, patience, and brilliant insights of so many dear friends, colleagues, and family members—including (but not limited to) Belle Torek, Jason Walta, Danielle Keats Citron, Susan Brison, Dan Solove, Ariana Aboulafia, Michelle Gonzalez, Gordon Hull, David Franks, Matthew Franks, and my mother, Dolores Kang Franks—how I wish she had lived to read it and circle all the typos. Many thanks also to the U. S. Holocaust Memorial Museum for assisting my research into the writings of Sophie Scholl, to my agent, Andrew Wylie, and to Geoffrey Shandler, Lisa Kaufman, Amy Azmoun, and Allison Gudenau for their thoughtful and lighting-fast editing. And thank you, Jeffrey Kusama-Hinte, for keeping faith in this project even when I lost it.

Endnotes

Prologue

1 Boston College Libraries, "White Rose: Student Resistance to Hitler (1942–43)," accessed April 24, 2024, https://library.bc.edu/exhibits/2017/02/white-rose/.

Introduction: When Free Speech Burned

1 Ida B. Wells, *Southern Horrors and Other Writings: Anti-Lynching Campaign of Ida B. Wells, 1892–1900*, ed. Jacqueline Jones Royster (Boston: Bedford/St. Martin's Press, 1997), 52.

2 Wells, *Southern Horrors*, 52.

3 Robin Hardin and Marcie Hinton, "The Squelching of Free Speech in Memphis: The Life of a Black Post-Reconstruction Newspaper," *Race, Gender & Class* 8, no. 4 (2001): 78–95, http://www.jstor.org/stable/41674996.

4 Paula J. Giddings, *Ida: A Sword Among Lions* (New York: Amistad, 2008), 212.

5 Giddings, *Ida*, 213.

6 Mark I. Pinksy, "Maligned in Black and White," *Poynter*, September 1, 2020, https://www.poynter.org/maligned-in-black-white/.

7 Giddings, *Ida*, 213.

8 Lee C. Bollinger and Geoffrey R. Stone, *The Free Speech Century* (New York: Oxford University Press, 2019), 1.

9 Anthony Lewis, *Freedom for the Thought That We Hate: A Biography of the First Amendment* (New York: Basic Books, 2007), ix.

10 Mary Anne Franks, *The Cult of the Constitution: Our Deadly Devotion to Guns and Free Speech* (Stanford, CA: Stanford University Press, 2019), 23-34.

11 Arthur Holmes, *Parties and Their Principles* (New York: D. Appleton, 1859), 188–189.

12 Quoted in Merriam H. Allen, "Elijah Lovejoy and Free Speech," paper, Annual Meeting of the Speech Communication Association, Boston, MA, November 1987.

13 William Dorsey to the Pennsylvania Hall Association, May 14, 1838, in *History of Pennsylvania Hall*, ed. Samuel Webb (New York: Merrihew and Gunn, 1838), https://books.google.com/books?id=cTUWAAAAYAAJ.

14 John Quincy Adams to the Committee of the Pennsylvania Hall Association, January 19, 1838, quoted in *History of Pennsylvania Hall*, 12.

15 E. C. Pritchett, "Speech on May 17, 1838, Philadelphia, PA," quoted in *History of Pennsylvania Hall*, 97.

16 Beverly C. Tomek, *Pennsylvania Hall: A "Legal Lynching" in the Shadow of the Liberty Bell* (New York: Oxford University Press, 2014), 107.

17 Quoted in Tomek, *Pennsylvania Hall*, 107.

18 Angelina E. Grimké Weld, "Speech, May 17, 1838, Philadelphia, PA," quoted in *History of Pennsylvania Hall*, 124–125.

19 Weld, "Speech," quoted in *History of Pennsylvania Hall*, 125.

20 Quoted in *History of Pennsylvania Hall*, 127.

21 Weld, "Speech," quoted in *History of Pennsylvania Hall*, 127.

22 Quoted in Tomek, *Pennsylvania Hall*, 132.

23 Quoted in Tomek, *Pennsylvania Hall*, 132.

24 *Richmond Whig and Public Advertiser*, May 22, 1838, 2, quoted in Michael Kent Curtis, "The 1837 Killing of Elijah Lovejoy by an Anti-Abolution Mob: Free Speech, Mobs, Republican Government, and the Privileges of American Citizens," *UCLA Law Review* 44, no. 4 (1996–1997), 1109.

25 J. A. Holman, "Mrs. Felton Speaks," *Weekly Star*, August 26, 1898.

26 Act for the Suppression of Trade in, and Circulation of, Obscene Literature and Articles of Immoral Use, 18 U.S. Code § 1461–63 (1873).

27 Annalee Newitz, "The 19th-Century Troll Who Hated Dirty Postcards and Sex Toys," *New York Times*, September 20, 2019, https://www.nytimes.com/2019/09/20/opinion/sunday/mens-rights-activists-comstock.html.

28 The Sedition Act of 1918, from the United States Statutes at Large, V. 40 (April 1917–March 1919), https://www.thirteen.org/wnet/supremecourt/capitalism/sources_document1.html.

29 *Debs v. United States*, 249 U.S. 211, 214 (1919).

30 Alan Taylor, "Photos: The Battle for Women's Suffrage in the U.S.," *Atlantic*, June 6, 2019, photo 16, https://www.theatlantic.com/photo/2019/06/the-battle-for-womens-suffrage-in-photos/591103/#img16.

31 Dale Mineshima-Lowe, "Criminal Syndicalism Laws," Free Speech Center, January 1, 2009, https://firstamendment.mtsu.edu/article/criminal-syndicalism-laws/.

32 David Skover and Ronald Collins, "A Curious Concurrence: Justice Brandeis' Vote in *Whitney v. California*, 2005 Sup. Ct. Rev. 333," *Digital Commons* (2005), https://digitalcommons.law.seattleu.edu/faculty/583.

33 Charlotte Anne Whitney, "Speech at the Women's Civic Center of Oakland, Oakland, CA, November 28, 1919," quoted in Skover and Collins, "A Curious Concurrence."

34 "Woman Syndicalist Will Not Seek Pardon," *New York Times*, October 22, 1925.

35 Tim Arango, "Films Revisit Overlooked Shootings on a Black Campus," *New York Times*, April 16, 2008, https://www.nytimes.com/2008/04/16/arts/16oran.html.

36 Samuel B. Hoff and Carlos Holmes, "Kent State and Jackson State: Remembering the Age of Student Protests: 1968 to 1970," *USA Today*, May 10, 2020.

37 *Whitney*, 274 U.S. at 376.

38 *Brandenburg v. Ohio*, 395 U.S. 446 (1969).

39 *Brandenburg*, 395 U.S. at 457.

40 *Brandenburg*, 395 U.S. at 447.

41 Ohio Rev. Code Ann. § 2923.13.

42 *W. Virginia State Bd. of Educ. v. Barnette*, 319 U.S. 624 (1943), 642.

43 *Cohen v. California*, 403 U.S. 25 (1971).

Chapter 1: Burning Crosses

1 David Wark Griffith, *The Rise and Fall of Free Speech in America* (Los Angeles, 1916), https://books.google.com/books?id=XCQNAAAAIAAJ.

2 Griffith, *Rise and Fall of Free Speech.*

3 Griffith, *Rise and Fall of Free Speech.*

4 Griffith, *Rise and Fall of Free Speech.*

5 Griffith, *Rise and Fall of Free Speech.*

6 Griffith, *Rise and Fall of Free Speech.*

7 Roger N. Baldwin, "Letters from Readers," *The Crisis*, August 1940, 268–269, https://books.google.com/books?id=9FoEAAAAMBAJ.

8 Baldwin, "Letters from Readers."

9 Baldwin, "Letters from Readers."

10 Quoted in Dorian Lynskey, "Public Menace: How the Fight to Ban *The Birth of a Nation* Shaped the Nascent Civil Rights Movement," *Slate*, March 31, 2015, https://slate.com/culture/2015/03/the-birth-of-a-nation-how-the-fight-to-censor-d-w-griffiths-film-shaped-american-history.html.

11 Lynskey, "Public Menace."

12 Mary Child Nerney, quoted in Lynskey, "Public Menace."

13 Both the white costumes and the ritual of the burning cross were Dixon's inventions, introduced in his 1905 novel, *The Clansman: A Historical Romance of the Ku Klux Klan*, which served as the basis for his play *The Clansman*, which in turn served as the basis for *Birth of a Nation*.

14 Desmond Ang, "The Birth of a Nation: Media and Racial Hate," *American Economic Review* 113, no. 6 (June 2023), 1427.

15 Kevin Sack and Alan Blinder, "Jurors Hear Dylann Roof Explain Shooting in Video: 'I Had to Do It,'" *New York Times*, December 9, 2016, https://www.ny

times.com/2016/12/09/us/dylann-roof-shooting-charleston-south-carolina
-church-video.html.

16 "Jeffries Won't Fight Johnson," *Philadelphia Inquirer,* February 6, 1904, quoted
    in Barak Y. Orbach, "The Johnson-Jeffries Fight 100 Years Thence: The Johnson-
    Jeffries Fight and Censorship of Black Supremacy," *New York University Jour-
    nal of Law and Liberty* 5, no. 2 (July 2010): 270–346.

17 "Jack London Describes the Fight and Jack Johnson's Golden Smile," *San Francisco
    Caller,* December 27, 1908, 1, quoted in Orbach, "The Johnson-Jeffries Fight," 289.

18 Michael Walsh, "A Year of Hope for Joplin and Johnson," *Smithsonian Maga-
    zine,* May 31, 2010, https://www.smithsonianmag.com/history/a-year-of-hope
    -for-joplin-and-johnson-123024/.

19 Walsh, "A Year of Hope."

20 Orbach, "The Johnson-Jeffries Fight," 313.

21 In a rare illustration of true "bad precedent" theory, when Johnson was finally
    defeated in 1915 by a white fighter, Jess Willard, white audiences called for
    "rejiggering" the Sims Act so that this fight film could be easily distributed
    among the states. Lee Grieveson, "Fighting Films: Race, Morality, and the
    Governing of Cinema, 1912–1915," *Cinema Journal* 38, no. 1 (1998): 41.

22 Grieveson, "Fighting Films," 58.

23 Modupe Labode, "'Defend Your Manhood and Womanhood Rights': *The
    Birth of a Nation,* Race, and the Politics of Respectability in Early Twentieth-
    Century Denver, Colorado." *Pacific Historical Review* 84, no. 2 (2015): 181.

24 Labode, "Defend Your Manhood,"181.

25 *Mutual Film Corporation v. Industrial Commission of Ohio,* 236 U.S. 230 (1915).

26 Al-Tony Gilmore, "Jack Johnson and White Women: The National Impact,"
    Journal of Negro History 58, no. 1 (1973): 32.

27 As I described the concept in *The Cult of the Constitution,* "victim-claiming" is
    a "common corollary of victim-blaming, which attempts to deprive victims of
    sympathy" that "attempts to garner sympathy for non-victims, to allow power-
    ful groups to occupy the space of the vulnerable." Mary Anne Franks, *The Cult
    of the Constitution: Our Deadly Devotion to Guns and Free Speech* (Stanford, CA:
    Stanford University Press, 2019), xiii.

28 See Mary Anne Franks, "Beyond 'Free Speech for the White Man': Feminism
    and the First Amendment," in *Research Handbook on Feminist Jurisprudence*
    (Cheltenham: Edward Elgar Publishing, 2019), 366.

29 *Cohen,* 403 U.S. at 15.

30 *Cohen,* 403 U.S. at 15, quoted in *Village of Skokie v. Nat'l Socialist Party of America,*
    373 N.E. 2d 21 (U.S. 1978).

31 David Gutman quoted in Mark A. Rabinowitz, "Nazis in Skokie: Fighting
    Words or Heckler's Veto?," *DePaul Law Review* 28, no. 2 (Winter 1979): 281–282.

32 "Guardians of Freedom," ACLU, accessed April 25, 2024, https://www.aclu.
    org/guardians-freedom.

33 Aryeh Neier, "Lessons in Free Speech 40 Years After Nazis Planned Skokie
    March," *Chicago Sun Times,* April 25, 2017, https://chicago.suntimes.com/2017

/4/25/18363965/lessons-in-free-speech-40-years-after-nazis-planned-skokie-march.

34 Jessica Owley and Jess Phelps, "The Life and Death of Confederate Monuments," *Buffalo Law Review* 68, no. 5 (December 17, 2020): 1406.

35 David A. Graham, "The United States of Confederate America," *Atlantic*, October 4, 2022, https://www.theatlantic.com/ideas/archive/2022/10/confederate-monuments-survey-race-religion-education-divide/671639/.

36 Complaint for Declaratory and Injunctive Relief and Damages at 4, *Kessler v. Charlottesville*, 441 F. Supp. 3d 277 (W.D. Va. 2020) (no. 3:17-cv-00056), https://storage.courtlistener.com/recap/gov.uscourts.vawd.108351.1.0.pdf.

37 Politico staff, "Full text: Trump's Comments on White Supremacists, 'Alt-Left' in Charlottesville," *Politico*, August 15, 2017, https://www.politico.com/story/2017/08/15/full-text-trump-comments-white-supremacists-alt-left-transcript-241662.

38 "Neo-Confederate, The Extremist Files," Southern Poverty Law Center, accessed April 25, 2024, https://www.splcenter.org/fighting-hate/extremist-files/ideology/neo-confederate.

39 Gregory S. Schneider, Laura Vozzella, Patricia Sullivan, and Michael E. Miller, "Weapons, Flags, No Violence: Mass Pro-Gun Rally in Virginia Capital," *Washington Post*, January 20, 2020, https://www.washingtonpost.com/local/virginia-politics/2020/01/20/4b36852c-3baa-11ea-8872-5df698785a4e_story.html.

40 Ryan Saavedra, "The Rebellion Explodes: 22,000+ Pro-Gun Activists Flood Virginia's Capital to Push Back on Democrat Extremism," *Daily Wire*, January 20, 2020; and Ann Coulter, "Fully Automatic Media," *Breitbart*, January 29, 2020.

41 Luke Mogelson, "Among the Insurrectionists," *New Yorker*, January 15, 2021, https://www.newyorker.com/magazine/2021/01/25/among-the-insurrectionists.

42 Chris Cameron, "These Are the People Who Died in Connection With the Capitol Riot," *New York Times*, January 5, 2022, https://www.nytimes.com/2022/01/05/us/politics/jan-6-capitol-deaths.html.

43 Marcia Cramer, "Confederate Flag an Unnerving Sight in Capitol," *New York Times*, January 9, 2021, https://www.nytimes.com/2021/01/09/us/politics/confederate-flag-capitol.html.

44 David A. Graham, "The New Lost Cause," *Atlantic*, October 18, 2021, https://www.theatlantic.com/ideas/archive/2021/10/donald-trumps-new-lost-cause-centers-january-6/620407/.

45 Melissa Smislova, Acting Under Secretary Office of Intelligence and Analysis, U.S. Department of Homeland Security, "Statement," Examining the January 6 Attack on the U.S. Capitol, Before the United States Senate Committee on Homeland Security and Governmental Affairs and Committee on Rules and Administration, 117th Cong. (2021), 31.

46 Aaron C. Davis, "Red Flags," *Washington Post*, October 31, 2021, https://www.washingtonpost.com/politics/interactive/2021/warnings-jan-6-insurrection/.

47 Davis, "Red Flags."

48 "Resolution to Formally Censure Liz Cheney and Adam Kinzinger and to No Longer Support Them as Members of the Republican Party," Republican National Committee, February 4, 2022, https://prod-static.gop.com/media/2-RESO LUTION-TO-FORMALLY-CENSURE-LIZ-CHENEY-AND-ADAM -KINZINGER.pdf.

Chapter 2: Burning Women

1 *Whitney*, 274 U.S. at 376.

2 Amanda Foreman, "Why I'm Shouting about the 4,000 Year Campaign to Gag Women in Our History Books," *Telegraph*, September 1, 2015, https://www .telegraph.co.uk/women/womens-life/11837025/BBC-documentary-Amanda -Foreman-on-silent-womens-history.html.

3 Foreman, "Why I'm Shouting."

4 Mary Beard, "The Public Voice of Women," *London Review of Books* 36, no. 6 (March 20, 2014), https://www.lrb.co.uk/the-paper/v36/n06/mary-beard/the -public-voice-of-women.

5 Beard, "The Public Voice of Women."

6 Beard, "The Public Voice of Women."

7 Mary Beard, *Women & Power: A Manifesto* (New York: Liveright, 2017), preface.

8 Roberta Magnani, "Powerful Men Have Tried to Silence Abused Women since Medieval Times," *Conversation*, October 27, 2017, https://theconversation .com/powerful-men-have-tried-to-silence-abused-women-since-medieval -times-86117.

9 1 Timothy 2:12 (King James Version).

10 William Blackstone, *Commentaries on the Laws of England*, vol. 4, ed. Wilfred Prest (New York: Oxford University Press, 2016), 123.

11 Stacy Schiff, "The Witches of Salem," *New Yorker*, August 31, 2015, https:// www.newyorker.com/magazine/2015/09/07/the-witches-of-salem.

12 Schiff, "The Witches of Salem."

13 Mary Anne Franks, "Witch Hunts: Free Speech, #MeToo, and the Fear of Women's Words," *University of Chicago Legal Forum* (2019).

14 Amber Heard, "I Spoke Up Against Sexual Violence—and Faced Our Cul- ture's Wrath. That Has to Change," *Washington Post*, December 18, 2018, https://www.washingtonpost.com/opinions/ive-seen-how-institutions-protect -men-accused-of-abuse-heres-what-we-can-do/2018/12/18/71fd876a-02ed -11e9-b5df-5d3874f1ac36_story.html.

15 *Depp v. News Group Newspapers Ltd.* (2020) EWHC 2911 (QB), https://www .bailii.org/ew/cases/EWHC/QB/2020/2911.html.

16 Heard, "I Spoke Up."

17 Plaintiff's Complaint, *Depp v. Heard* 19-CV2911.

18 Defendants Counterclaim, *Depp v. Heard* 19-CV2911.

19 Defendants Counterclaim, *Depp v. Heard* 19-CV2911.

20   Lara Bazelon, "The ACLU Has Lost Its Way," *Atlantic*, May 10, 2022, https:// www.theatlantic.com/ideas/archive/2022/05/aclu-johnny-depp-amber -heard-trial/629808/.

21   David Cole, "The ACLU Never Stopped Defending Free Speech," *Nation*, May 31, 2022, https://www.thenation.com/article/activism/aclu-free-speech/.

22   "What You Need to Know About ACLU Artist Ambassadors, Including Amber Heard," ACLU, May 18, 2022, https://www.aclu.org/news/civil-liber- ties/what-you-need-to-know-about-aclu-ambassadors-including-amber- heard.

23   One commentator characterized the ACLU's involvement with Heard's op-ed as evidence that it had "abandoned its celebrated legacy as a fearless organiza- tion fighting for civil liberties and individual rights." Jonathan Turley, "The Depp Trial and the Demise of the ACLU: How a Celebrity Trial Exposed the Collapse of a Once Celebrated Group," June 2, 2022, https://jonathanturley .org/2022/06/02/the-depp-trial-and-the-demise-of-the-aclu-how-a- celebrity-trial-exposed-the-collapse-of-a-celebrated-civil-liberties- group/.

24   Cole, "The ACLU Never Stopped Defending Free Speech."

25   Amber Heard (@AmberHeard), Instagram post, December 19, 2022, https:// www.instagram.com/p/CmWiuanLXPT/?hl=en&img_index.

26   Moira Donegan, "The Amber Heard-Johnny Depp Trial Was an Orgy of Misogyny," *Guardian*, June 1, 2022, https://www.theguardian.com/commen tisfree/2022/jun/01/amber-heard-johnny-depp-trial-metoo-backlash.

27   Moira Donegan, "I Started the Media Men List," *Cut*, January 10, 2018, https://www.thecut.com/2018/01/moira-donegan-i-started-the-media-men -list.html.

28   Donegan, "I Started the Media Men List."

29   April Rubin, "Taylor Swift Fake Nudes Show This Harassment Could Hap- pen to Anyone," *Axios*, February 3, 2024, https://www.axios.com/2024/02/03 /taylor-swift-deepfake-ai-image-protection.

30   Noah Rothman, "Explicit Image of S. E. Cupp (It's a Fake) in *Hustler* Maga- zine Sparks Outrage," Mediaite, May 23, 2012, https://www.mediaite.com /online/explicit-image-of-s-e-cupp-its-a-fake-in-hustler-magazine-sparks -outrage/.

31   PR Newswire, "Larry Flynt Defends Ad Parody Featuring S. E. Cupp," press release by *Hustler*, May 24, 2012, https://www.prnewswire.com/news-releases /larry-flynt-defends-ad-parody-featuring-se-cupp-153816605.html.

32   *Jerry Faldwell v. Larry Flynt*, 797 F.2d 1270 (1986).

33   Isabel Jones, "Aristotle Onassis Allegedly 'Arranged for' the Paparazzi to Take Nude Photos of Jackie Kennedy," *InStyle*, July 26, 2019, https://www.instyle .com/news/jackie-kennedy-aristotle-onassis-paparazzi-nude-photos-americas -reluctant-prince-book.

34   Johann Hari, "Larry Flynt: Freedom Fighter, Pornographer, Monster?," *Inde- pendent*, May 27, 2011, https://www.independent.co.uk/news/people/profiles /larry-flynt-freedom-fighter-pornographer-monster-2289592.html.

35 Cheryl Lavin, "The Redemption of Larry Flynt, *Chicago Tribune*, December 27, 1996, https://www.chicagotribune.com/news/ct-xpm-1996-12-27-9612270 302-story.html.

36 Hari, "Larry Flynt."

37 Hari, "Larry Flynt."

38 *Hustler v. Falwell*, 485 U.S. 46 (1988).

39 Hari, "Larry Flynt."

40 Lavin, "The Redemption."

41 Mary Ellen Gale and Nadine Strossen, "The Real ACLU," *Yale Journal of Law and Feminism* 5 (1989): 161.

42 Gale and Strossen, "The Real ACLU," 180.

43 *Dworkin v. Hustler Magazine, Inc.*, 634 F. Supp. 727, 731 (D. Wyo. 1986).

44 "Awards History: Past Judges & Winners," Hugh M. Hefner Foundation, https://www.hmhfoundation.org/awards-history-past-judges-winners/.

45 Leigh Ann Wheeler, *How Sex Became a Civil Liberty* (New York: Oxford University Press, 2012), 135.

46 Hefner to A. C. Spectorsky, memorandum, January 6, 1970, ACS Papers, quoted in Wheeler, *How Sex Became a Civil Liberty*, 135.

47 Morton Hunt, "Up Against the Wall, Male Chauvinist Pig!," *Playboy*, May 1970.

48 Crystal Harris (@CrystalHefner), "I found thousands of those disposable camera photos you are talking about @hollymadison. I immediately ripped them up and destroyed every single one of them for you and the countless other women in them. They're gone," Twitter, January 4, 2022, https://twitter .com/crystalhefner/status/1485828161614974976.

49 *Secrets of Playboy*, A&E video, quoted in Clémence Michallon, "The Secrets of Hugh Hefner and His Playboy Mansion," *Independent*, February 1, 2022, https://www.independent.co.uk/news/world/americas/hugh-hefner-playboy -mansion-documentary-b2005451.html.

50 *Secrets of Playboy*, directed by Arlene Nelson, featuring Miki Garcia, quoted in Lanford Beard, "Hugh Hefner Was Allegedly '*Playboy*'s 'Predator Number One,'" *People*, March 21, 2022, https://people.com/crime/secrets-of-playboy -hugh-hefner-predator-number-one/.

51 Derrick A. Bell Jr., "*Brown v. Board of Education* and the Interest-Convergence Dilemma," *Harvard Law Review* 93, no. 3 (January 1980): 518, 523.

52 Bell Jr., "*Brown v. Board of Education*." But see Justin Driver, "Rethinking the Interest-Convergence Thesis," 105 *Northwestern University Law Review* 149 (2015).

53 Wheeler, *How Sex Became a Civil Liberty*, 135.

54 *American Booksellers Association v. Hudnut*, 771 F.2d 323, 329 (7th Cir. 1985), aff'd, 475 U.S. 1001 (1986), 324.

55 *American Booksellers Association v. Hudnut*, 771 F.2d 323, 329 (7th Cir. 1985), aff'd, 475 U.S. 1001 (1986).

56 *Hudnut v. Am. Booksellers Ass'n, Inc.*, 475 U.S. 1001 (1986).

57 *American Booksellers Association*, 771 F.2d at 329.

58 *American Booksellers Association*, 771 F.2d at 329.

59 *American Booksellers Association*, 771 F.2d at 329.

60 *American Booksellers Association*, 771 F.2d at 330.

61 *American Booksellers Association*, 771 F.2d at 330.

62 *Miller v. California*, 413 U.S. 15, 24 (1973).

63 *Miller*, 413 U.S. at 24.

64 *Miller*, 413 U.S. at 324–325.

65 Catharine A. MacKinnon, "Not a Moral Issue," *Yale Law and Policy Review* 2, no. 2 (Spring 1984): 321.

66 Catharine A. MacKinnon, *Feminism Unmodified: Discourses on Life and Law* (Cambridge, MA: Harvard University Press, 1987), 152.

67 MacKinnon, *Feminism Unmodified*, 203.

68 Ann Scales, "Feminist Legal Method: Not So Scary," *UCLA Women's Law Journal*, 2(0) (1992): 22. Scales quotes Mari J. Matsuda, who states that to recognize the harm of "lies spread about one's professional competency . . . yet fail to see that [similar psychic harms] happen to the victims of racist speech, is selective vision" ("Public Response to Racist Speech: Considering the Victim's Story," *Michigan Law Review* [1989]: 2387).

69 *Chaplinsky v. New Hampshire*, 315 U.S. 568, 573 (1942).

70 *Chaplinsky*, 315 U.S. at 573.

71 Cynthia Grant Bowman, "Street Harassment and the Informal Ghettoization of Women," *Harvard Law Review* 106, no. 3 (January 1993): 517–563. But *Cf. Lewis v. City of New Orleans* (1974).

72 *Counterman v. Colorado*, 600 U.S. 66.

73 Anna Nasset, "Stalking: Slow Motion Homicide—Anna Nasset," in *HUSH No More*, podcast, https://podcasters.spotify.com/pod/show/hushnomore/episodes /Stalking-Slow-Motion-Homicide-Anna-Nasset-eojrvt.

74 *Counterman v. Colorado*, 143 S.Ct. 2106 (U.S. 2023).

75 Kyle Wagner, "U.S. Supreme Court Will Hear Colorado Social Media Stalking Case Involving Musician," *Westword*, January 25, 2023, https://www.west word.com/news/supreme-court-colorado-social-media-case-bill-counterman -coles-whalen-16009703.

76 Colo. Rev. Stat. §18–3–602(1)(c) (2022).

77 *Counterman*, 143 S.Ct. at 2110.

78 Jonathon W. Penney, "Understanding Chilling Effects," *Minnesota Law Review* 106 (2022): 1451.

79 "Prosecutors Guide to Stalking," *Stalking Prevention, Awareness and Resource Center*, accessed April 25, 2024, https://www.stalkingawareness.org/wp-content/ uploads/2020/01/SPA-19.005-Prosecutors-Guide-to-Stalking-00000002.pdf.

80 Mary Anne Franks, "Chief Justice John Roberts' Mockery of Stalking Victims Points to a Deeper Problem," *Slate*, April 21, 2023, https://slate.com/news-and -politics/2023/04/counterman-colorado-supreme-court-threats-stalking.html.

81 *Dobbs v. Jackson Women's Health Organization*, 142 S. Ct. 2325 (2022).

82 *Dobbs*, 142 S. Ct. 2318.

83 "ACLU Commends Supreme Court Decision to Protect Free Speech in Case Defining True Threats," ACLU press release, June 27, 2023, https://www.aclu .org/press-releases/aclu-commends-supreme-court-decision-to-protect-free -speech-in-case-defining-true-threats.

84 Jay Diaz, "FIRE statement on the Supreme Court decision in *Counterman v. Colorado*," Foundation for Individual Rights and Expression, June 27, 2023, https://www.thefire.org/news/fire-statement-supreme-court-decision-counter man-v-colorado.

85 MacKinnon, *Feminism Unmodified*, 204–205.

86 *Chaplinsky*, 315 U.S. at 571–572 (1942) quoted in *United States v. Stevens*, 559 U.S. 460, 468–69 (2010).

87 *United States v. Stevens*, 559 U.S. 460, 471–472 (2022).

88 Ronald K. L. Collins, "Exceptional Freedom—The Roberts Court, the First Amendment, and the New Absolutism," *Albany Law Review* 76 (2013): 417–418.

89 See Steven H. Shiffrin, "The Dark Side of the First Amendment," *UCLA Law Review* 61 (2014): 1490–1491. "The historical test imagines that the Framers were intent on freezing the set of then-unprotected categories. If the Framers thought that certain categories of speech should not be protected under the First Amendment, however, presumably they would not have wanted similar categories to be protected. The old categories developed under a common law process; there is little reason to believe that the Framers would have wanted the common law process to be abandoned. Indeed, given that, there is good reason to believe that the supposedly historical approach is unhistorical. . . . It leaves the law in a chaotic state in which some categories are protected for no better reason than that the technology giving rise to them was not in existence at an earlier point in our history."

90 *Stevens*, 559 U.S. at 470.

91 *Chaplinsky*, 315 U.S. at 572. References footnote 5, Chafee, Free Speech in the United States (1941), 149 (emphasis added).

92 Lucinda M. Finley, "Breaking Women's Silence in Law: The Dilemma of the Gendered Nature of Legal Reasoning," *Notre Dame Law Review* 64, no. 886 (1989): 893.

93 Finley, "Breaking Women's Silence," 898.

94 Mary Anne Franks, "*The Criminalization of Non-consensual Pornography in the U.S.*" in *Criminalising Intimate Image Abuse*, ed. Gian Marco Caletti and Kolis Summerer (Oxford: Oxford University Press, 2024), 169–171.

95 Gale and Strossen, "The Real ACLU," 180–181.

96 Gale and Strossen, "The Real ACLU," 187.

Chapter 3: Burning Books

1 "Governor Ron DeSantis Signs Legislation to Strengthen Florida's Position as National Leader in Higher Education," press release from the office of Florida State Governor Ron DeSantis, May 15, 2023, https://www.flgov.com /2023/05/15/governor-ron-desantis-signs-legislation-to-strengthen-floridas -position-as-national-leader-in-higher-education/.

2   Ron DeSantis, press conference, Florida State University, April 15, 2019, Tallahassee, FL, quoted in Jenni Fink, "Florida Governor: Some Universities Seek to Impose 'Orthodoxy,' Echoes Trump's Call for College Commitment to Free Speech," *Newsweek*, April 15, 2019, https://www.newsweek.com/florida -governor-ron-desantis-backs-trump-campus-free-speech-says-some -1397270.

3   Geoffrey R. Stone et al., "Report of the Committee on Freedom of Expression," Huffington Post, January 6, 2015, https://www.huffpost.com/entry/free -speech-on-campus_b_6426082.

4   The organization is now known as the Foundation for Individual Rights and Expression (FIRE).

5   Mary Griffin, "Florida Public Universities to Adopt 'Chicago Statement' Following Governor's Announcement," FIRE, April 17, 2019, https://www.the fire.org/news/florida-public-universities-adopt-chicago-statement-following -governors-announcement.

6   DeSantis, press conference, Florida State University, April 15, 2019, Tallahassee, FL, quoted in Emily L. Mahoney, "Ron DeSantis Seeks Free Speech Resolution Allowing Controversial Speakers at Florida Universities," *Tampa Bay Times*, April 15, 2019, https://www.tampabay.com/florida-politics/2019/04 /15/ron-desantis-seeks-free-speech-policy-allowing-controversial-speakers -at-florida-universities.

7   Richard Corcoran, "Education Is Freedom," Hillsdale College, May 14, 2021, YouTube video, 00:38:19, https://www.youtube.com/watch?v=HVujpIator0 &t=2299s.

8   Corcoran, "Education Is Freedom," 00:38:37.

9   Bobby Caina Calvan, "Florida Bans 'Critical Race Theory' from Its Classrooms," Associated Press, June 10, 2021, https://apnews.com/article/florida -race-and-ethnicity-government-and-politics-education-74d0af6c52c0009ec 3fa3ee9955b0a8d.

10 Jason Delgado, "State Lawmaker, Lobbyist Skirmish over KKK Remarks, Free Speech Issues during Hearing," Florida Politics, February 19, 2021, https:// floridapolitics.com/archives/405164-state-lawmaker-lobbyist-skirmish-over -kkk-remarks-free-speech-issues-during-hearing/.

11 Paul Blest, "Florida Just Passed Its 'Stop WOKE' Anti-CRT Bill," VICE, March 11, 2022, https://www.vice.com/en/article/wxdbwb/stope-woke-act -florida-crt-bill.

12 Daniel Conrad, "Florida Anti-Riot Law Struck Down as Unconstitutional to Protesters," *Courthouse News*, September 9, 2011, https://www.courthouse news.com/florida-anti-riot-law-chills-protestors-speech-finds-federal-judge/.

13 Amelia Nierenberg, "What Does 'Don't Say Gay' Actually Say?," *New York Times*, March 23, 2022, https://www.nytimes.com/2022/03/23/us/what-does -dont-say-gay-actually-say.html.

14 Christina Pushaw (@ChristinaPushaw), "If you're against the Anti-Grooming Bill, you are probably a groomer or at least you don't denounce the grooming of 4–8 year old children. Silence is complicity. This is how it works, Democrats, and I didn't make the rules," Twitter, March 4, 2022, https://

twitter.com/ChristinaPushaw/status/1499890719691051008. Also reported in Ben Mathis-Lilley, "How One Florida Woman With Twitter Problems Plunged Us Into a Nightmarish National Conversation About 'Grooming,'" *Slate*, April 21, 2022, https://slate.com/news-and-politics/2022/04/christina-pushaw-ron-desantis-libsoftiktok-groomer.html.

15 Anthony Izaguirre, "DeSantis Takes Over Disney District, Punishing Company," Associated Press, February 27, 2023, https://apnews.com/article/ron-desantis-politics-florida-state-government-36ec16b56ac6e72b9efcce26def dd0d8.

16 Herb Scribner, "DeSantis Violated First Amendment by Removing Elected Official, Judge Rules," *Axios*, January 21, 2023, https://www.axios.com/2023/01/21/ron-desantis-first-amendment-andrew-warren-ruling.

17 *Times Co. v. Sullivan*, 376 U.S. 254 (1964).

18 H.B. 951, 125th Leg. Reg. Sess. (Florida 2023).

19 Colin Kalmbacher, "First Amendment Attorney Attacks Florida Effort to Roll Back Protections in Defamation Law, Calling It Unconstitutional," *Law & Crime*, February 20, 2023, https://lawandcrime.com/first-amendment/first-amendment-attorney-attacks-florida-effort-to-roll-back-protections-in-defamation-law-calling-it-unconstitutional.

20 Jeremy C. Young and Jonathan Friedman, "America's Censored Classrooms," PEN America, August 17, 2022, https://pen.org/report/americas-censored-classrooms.

21 Young and Friedman, "America's Censored Classrooms."

22 Young and Friedman, "America's Censored Classrooms."

23 Brennan Suen and Ari Drennen, "The Real Victims in the 'Libs of TikTok' Discourse Are the Teachers and LGBTQ People Harassed Because of the Account," Media Matters for America, April 19, 2022, https://www.mediamatters.org/twitter/real-victims-libs-tiktok-discourse-are-teachers-and-lgbtq-people-harassed-because-account.

24 Benjamin Wallace-Wells, "How a Conservative Activist Invented the Conflict Over Critical Race Theory," *New Yorker*, June 18, 2021, https://www.newyorker.com/news/annals-of-inquiry/how-a-conservative-activist-invented-the-conflict-over-critical-race-theory.

25 Wallace-Wells, "How a Conservative Activist Invented."

26 Donald J. Trump, "Executive Order on Combating Race and Sex Stereotyping," White House Archives, September 22, 2020, https://trumpwhitehouse.archives.gov/presidential-actions/executive-order-combating-race-sex-stereotyping/.

27 Trump, "Executive Order on Combating Race and Sex Stereotyping."

28 Trump, "Executive Order on Combating Race and Sex Stereotyping."

29 Jeffrey Sachs, Jeremy C. Young, and Jonathan Friedman, "For Educational Gag Orders, the Vagueness Is the Point," PEN America, April 28, 2022, https://pen.org/for-educational-gag-orders-the-vagueness-is-the-point/.

30 "PEN America Index of Educational Gag Orders," PEN America, accessed March 3, 2024, https://airtable.com/appg59iDuPhlLPPFp/shrtwubfBUo2tu HyO/tbl49yod7l01o0TCk/viw6VOxb6SUYd5nXM?blocks=hide.

31   "PEN America Index of Educational Gag Orders."

32   Jordan Williams, "20 State AGs Tell Education Dept They Oppose Teaching Critical Race Theory," *The Hill*, May 20, 2021, https://thehill.com/homenews /state-watch/554650-20-state-ags-tell-education-department-they-oppose -teaching-critical/.

33   Sachs, Young, and Friedman, "For Educational Gag Orders."

34   Vimal Patel, "Utah Bans D.E.I. Programs, Joining Other States," *New York Times*, February 1, 2024, https://www.nytimes.com/2024/02/01/us/states-anti -dei-laws-utah.html.

35   Matt Krupnick, "Restrictions on Tenure and Academic Freedom Have College Professors Eyeing the Exits," *USA Today*, December 19, 2023.

36   *Students for Fair Admissions, Inc. v. President and Fellows of Harvard College*, 142 S. Ct. 895 (U.S. 2022).

37   Peter Greene, "Teacher Anti-CRT Bills Coast to Coast: A State by State Guide," *Forbes*, February 16, 2022, https://www.forbes.com/sites/petergreene /2022/02/16/teacher-anti-crt-bills-coast-to-coast-a-state-by-state-guide/?sh =23fe4d554ff6.

38   Theresa Vargas, "Youngkin's Tell-on-a-Teacher Tip Line Drew Jokes, but Behind the Laughter Is a Serious Concern," *Washington Post*, January 26, 2022, https://www.washingtonpost.com/dc-md-va/2022/01/26/tip-line-teachers -jokes-concern/.

39   Greg Childress, "National Watchlist for 'Radical Left' Policies Includes 5 North Carolina School Boards," NC Policy Watch, September 7, 2021, https://pulse.ncpolicywatch.org/2021/09/07/national-watchlist-for-radical -left-policies-includes-5-north-carolina-school-boards/.

40   Daniel Villarreal, "Death Threats and Fights Over Critical Race Theory Have Driven at Least Six Educators to Resign," *Newsweek*, July 14, 2021, https:// www.newsweek.com/death-threats-fights-over-critical-race-theory-have -driven-least-six-educators-resign-1609461.

41   Claire Woodstock, "Oklahoma Threatens Librarians: 'Don't Use the Word Abortion,'" VICE, July 21, 2022, https://www.vice.com/en/article/4axwqw /oklahoma-threatens-librarians-dont-use-the-word-abortion.

42   Jennifer D. Jenkins, "I'm a Florida School Board Member. This Is How Protesters Come After Me," *Washington Post*, October 20, 2011, https://www .washingtonpost.com/outlook/2021/10/20/jennifer-jenkins-brevard-school -board-masks-threats/.

43   Jenkins, "I'm a Florida School Board Member."

44   Jenkins, "I'm a Florida School Board Member."

45   Ligaya Mishan, "The Long and Tortured History of Cancel Culture," *New York Times*, December 3, 2020, https://www.nytimes.com/2020/12/03/t-magazine /cancel-culture-history.html.

46   Sophia A. McClennen, "The Conservative Urge to Be a Victim: Why Right-Wing Victimhood Is Spreading So Fast," *Salon*, December 27, 2021, https:// www.salon.com/2021/12/27/the-conservative-urge-to-be-a-victim-why -right-wing-victimhood-is-spreading-so-fast/.

47   Robert Jay Lifton, *Thought Reform and the Psychology of Totalism* (Chapel Hill: University of North Carolina Press, 1963), 429. The term can be used to describe how "the most far-reaching and complex of human problems are compressed into brief, highly reductive, definitive-sounding phrases, easily memorized and easily expressed."

48   Jake Lahut, "Fox News Is Betting Big on the 'Cancel Culture' Wars Post-Trump," Business Insider, April 6, 2021, https://www.businessinsider.com /fox-news-cancel-culture-tucker-carlson-gutfeld-new-show-2021-4.

49   Joshua Katz, "Princeton Fed Me to the Cancel Culture Mob," *Wall Street Journal*, May 24, 2022, https://www.wsj.com/articles/joshua-katz-princeton-campus -cancel-culture-woke-mob-11653350161.

50   Daniel Politi, "Trump Decries 'Cancel Culture,' Calls on Republicans to Boycott More Companies," *Slate*, April 4, 2021, https://slate.com/news-and -politics/2021/04/trump-decries-cancel-culture-calls-boycott-georgia-law .html.

51   "President Trump's Full Speech at Mount Rushmore," *USA Today*, July 4, 2020, YouTube video, 00:07:26, https://www.youtube.com/watch?v=mXD4z PY4Ai0.

52   Trump, "Trump's Acceptance Speech for the GOP Nomination," *U.S. News*, August 27, 2020, https://www.usnews.com/news/elections/articles/2020-08 -27/read-donald-trumps-republican-convention-acceptance-speech.

53   *Encyclopedia Britannica*, s.v. "cup and balls trick," accessed April 1, 2024, https://www.britannica.com/art/cups-and-balls-trick.

54   Doug Shadel, "Confessions of a Con Artist," AARP, September 27, 2012, https://www.aarp.org/money/scams-fraud/info-09-2012/confessions-of-a -con-artist.html.

55   Richard Feloni, "Psychologist: Being Smart Could Make You More Prone to Fall for a Con Artist's Lies," Business Insider, March 24, 2016, https://www .businessinsider.com/why-you-cant-be-too-smart-for-a-con-artist-2016-3.

56   Emma Camp, "I Came to College Eager to Debate. I Found Self-Censorship Instead," *New York Times*, March 7, 2022, https://www.nytimes.com/2022 /03/07/opinion/campus-speech-cancel-culture.html.

57   Zack Beauchamp, "The 'Free Speech Debate' Isn't Really About Free Speech," *Vox*, July 22, 2020, https://www.vox.com/policy-and-politics/2020/7/22/2132 5942/free-speech-harpers-letter-bari-weiss-andrew-sullivan. "'Cancel culture' . . . is a notoriously fuzzy concept. It is often taken to refer to all of the following things at once: allegedly widespread self-censorship in elite intellectual institutions, a rise in vicious social media mobbing, and the firing of non-public figures for allegedly racist or bigoted behavior."

58   Osita Nwanevu, "The 'Cancel Culture' Con," *New Republic*, September 23, 2019, https://newrepublic.com/article/155141/cancel-culture-con-dave-chap pelle-shane-gillis.

59   Mishan, "The Long and Tortured History."

60   Laurence Silberman, "Email," quoted in Mark Joseph Stern, "The Truth About the Yale Law Protest That Prompted a Federal Judge to Threaten a

Clerkship Blacklist," *Slate*, March 18, 2022, https://slate.com/news-and-poli
tics/2022/03/yale-law-school-laurence-silberman-free-speech-blacklist.html.

61 Nate Raymond, "U.S. Supreme Court's Alito Calls Law School Free Speech
'Abysmal,'" Reuters, October 27, 2022, https://www.reuters.com/legal/gov
ernment/us-supreme-courts-alito-calls-law-school-free-speech-abysmal
-2022-10-26.

62 James C. Ho and Elizabeth L. Branch, "Stop the Chaos: Law Schools Need to
Crack Down on Student Disrupters Now," *National Review*, March 15, 2023,
https://nationalreview.com/2023/03/stop-the-chaos-law-schools-need-to
-crack-down-on-student-disrupters-now.

63 Elie Mystal, "Protesting an Anti-Trans Trump Judge Isn't Disrespectful, It's
American," *Nation*, March 15, 2023, https://www.thenation.com/article/politics
/protesting-anti-trans-judge-kyle-duncan-is-american/.

64 Neil Vigdor, "A Law Student Mocked the Federalist Society. It Jeopardized
His Graduation," *New York Times*, June 3, 2021, https://www.nytimes.com
/2021/06/03/us/stanford-federalist-society-nicholas-wallace.html.

65 Trump, campaign speech, Florence Regional Airport, March 12, 2022, Florence, SC, quoted in Bess Levin, "Trump Tells Supporters They Must Fight to
the Death to Stop Schools from Teaching Kids about Systemic Racism," *Vanity Fair*, March 14, 2022, https://www.vanityfair.com/news/2022/03/donald
-trump-critical-race-theory-lay-down-lives.

66 Julia Carrie Wong, "The ACLU on Fighting Critical Race Theory Bans: 'It's
about Our Country Reckoning with Racism,'" *Guardian*, July 1, 2021, https://
www.theguardian.com/us-news/2021/jul/01/aclu-fights-state-bans-teaching
-critical-race-theory.

67 "Fire in the Courts," Foundation for Individual Rights and Expression (FIRE),
accessed April 1, 2024, https://www.thefire.org/cases/litigation-fire-courts/.

68 See Mary Anne Franks, *The Cult of the Constitution: Our Deadly Devotion to
Guns and Free Speech* (Stanford, CA: Stanford University Press, 2019). For
examples of FIRE's promotion of cancel-culture propaganda, see Robert
Shibley and Talia Barnes, "Cancel Culture Empowers the Powerful—at
Everyone Else's Expense," FIRE, July 27, 2022, https://www.thefire.org/can-
cel-culture-empowers-the-powerful-at-everyone-elses-expense/; "National
FIRE Survey: Cancel Culture Widely Viewed as Threat to Democracy, Freedom," FIRE, January 31, 2022, https://www.thefire.org/national-fire-survey-
cancel-culture-widely-viewed-as-threat-to-democracy-freedom/; Greg
Lukianoff, Ryne Weiss, and Adam Goldstein, "Greg's Nowhere Near Defini-
tive Outrage/Call-Out/Cancel Culture Study List," FIRE, July 8, 2020,
https://www.thefire.org/gregs-nowhere-near-definitive-outrage-call-out-
cancel-culture-study-list/; Komi T. German and Lukianoff, "Don't Stop
Using the Term 'Cancel Culture,'" *Daily Beast*, June 12, 2022, https://www.
thedailybeast.com/dont-stop-using-the-term-cancel-culture.

69 Franks, "The Miseducation of Free Speech," *Virginia Law Review* 105 (2019).

70 Elizabeth Nolan Brown, "Facebook Is Right to Let the Lying Trump Ad
About Biden Stand," *Reason*, October 11, 2019, https://reason.com/2019/10
/11/facebook-is-right-to-let-the-lying-trump-ad-about-biden-stand/.

71 Nwanevu, "The 'Cancel Culture' Con."

72 Editorial Board, "America Has a Free Speech Problem," *New York Times*, March 18, 2022, https://www.nytimes.com/2022/03/18/opinion/cancel-culture-free-speech-poll.html.

73 Thomas Zimmer (@tzimmerhistory), "As an institution, the NYT just can't bring itself to ditch the 'neutrality' dogma," Twitter, April 27, 2022, https://twitter.com/tzimmer_history/status/1519367792163762181?s=20&t=1-NO2fhhSLkBsJc8joLSeg.

74 Zimmer (@tzimmerhistory), "The resulting coverage constantly privileges the radicalizing rightwing," Twitter, May 31, 2022, https://twitter.com/tzimmer_history/status/1531709557235494912.

75 Editorial Board, "America Has a Free Speech Problem."

76 Camp, "I Came to College Eager to Debate."

77 See Moira Donegan, "Another Reckoning over Sexual Assault in US Colleges Is Starting. Officials Must Listen," *Guardian*, October 31, 2021, https://www.theguardian.com/commentisfree/2021/oct/31/sexual-assault-us-colleges-officials-must-listen?; Lexi McMenamin, "Harvard's Sexual Harassment Lawsuit Is About Free Speech for Students," *Teen Vogue*, February 11, 2022, https://www.teenvogue.com/story/harvard-comaroff-sexual-harassment-oped.

78 Kristin Lam, "Recruiting Hate: White Supremacist Propaganda Rises for Third Straight Year on College Campuses, ADL Says," *USA Today*, June 28, 2019, https://www.usatoday.com/story/news/nation/2019/06/27/white-supremacist-recruiting-rise-college-campuses-report/1590886001/.

79 Donna St. George, "School Shootings Rose to Highest Number in 20 Years, Federal Data Says," *Washington Post*, June 28, 2022, https://www.washingtonpost.com/education/2022/06/28/school-shootings-crime-report/.

80 Adam Gabbatt, "US Rightwing Group Targets Academics with Professor Watchlist," *Guardian*, September 17, 2021, https://www.theguardian.com/education/2021/sep/17/turning-point-usa-professor-watchlist.

81 Pia Ceres, "Kids Are Back in Classrooms and Laptops Are Still Spying on Them," *Wired*, August 3, 2022, https://www.wired.com/story/student-monitoring-software-privacy-in-schools/.

82 Suzanne Nossel, "Opinion: Ron DeSantis Abandons Former First Amendment Defense," *CNN*, February 23, 2023, https://www.cnn.com/2023/02/23/opinions/ron-desantis-threat-to-first-amendment-nossel/index.html.

83 Nossel, "Ron DeSantis Abandons." (Emphasis added.)

84 Nossel, "Ron DeSantis Abandons."

85 Nossel, "Ron DeSantis Abandons."

86 Mishan, "The Long and Tortured History."

87 See Franks, *Cult of the Constitution*; and Shibley and Barnes, "Cancel Culture Empowers the Powerful."

88 Beauchamp, "The 'Free Speech Debate.'"

89 Nwanevu, "The 'Cancel Culture' Con."

90 Franks, "Speaking of Women: Feminism and Free Speech," *Signs, Journal of Women in Culture and Society* (2022), http://signsjournal.org/franks/.

91 Nwanevu, "The 'Cancel Culture' Con."

92 See Franks, "The Miseducation of Free Speech," for a discussion on the reactions to free speech crises on campuses.

Chapter 4: Burning Down the Public Square

1 Elon Musk (@elonmusk), "Starlink has been told by some governments (not Ukraine) to block Russian news sources," Twitter, March 5, 2022, https://x.com/elonmusk/status/1499976967105433600?s=20.

2 "Elon Musk Talks Twitter, Tesla and How His Brain Works—Live at TED 2022," interview by Chris Anderson, video, recorded April 14, 2022, https://gizmodo.com/elon-musk-free-speech-ted-talk-on-twitter-1848795067.

3 "Elon Musk to Acquire Twitter," Twitter press release, April 25, 2022, https://www.prnewswire.com/news-releases/elon-musk-to-acquire-twitter-301532245.html.

4 Elon Musk (@elonmusk), "By 'free speech,' I simply mean that which matches the law," Twitter, April 22, 2022, https://x.com/elonmusk/status/1519036983137509376?s=20.

5 "Market Capitalization of Largest Companies in S&P 500 Index as of September 24, 2021," Statista, accessed April 1, 2024, https://www.statista.com/statistics/1181188/sandp500-largest-companies-market-cap/; as of April 2022, Facebook had fallen out of the top five and Tesla had entered it.

6 Peter Eavis and Steve Lohr, "Big Tech's Domination of Business Reaches New Heights," *New York Times*, August 19, 2020, https://www.nytimes.com/2020/08/19/technology/big-tech-business-domination.html.

7 Dominic Rushe, "Big Tech's Big Week Raises Fears of 'Blade Runner Future' of Mega-Company Rule," *Guardian*, August 1, 2021, https://www.theguardian.com/technology/2021/aug/01/big-techs-big-week-blade-runner-future-amazon-google-apple-microsoft.

8 Brooke Auxier and Monica Anderson, "Social Media Use in 2021," Pew Research Center, April 7, 2021, https://www.pewresearch.org/internet/2021/04/07/social-media-use-in-2021/.

9 Auxier and Anderson, "Social Media Use in 2021."

10 Emily A. Vogels, "56% of Americans Support More Regulation of Major Technology Companies," Pew Research Center, July 20, 2021, https://www.pewresearch.org/fact-tank/2021/07/20/56-of-americans-support-more-regulation-of-major-technology-companies/.

11 President Joseph Biden, "Executive Order on Promoting Competition in the American Economy," White House Briefing Room, July 9, 2021, https://www.whitehouse.gov/briefing-room/presidential-actions/2021/07/09/executive-order-on-promoting-competition-in-the-american-economy/.

12 Brian Fung, "FTC Files Fresh Antitrust Complaint Seeking to Break Up Facebook," *CNN*, August 19, 2021, https://www.cnn.com/2021/08/19/tech/ftc-facebook-antitrust/index.html.

13 Kiran Jeevanjee et al., "All the Ways Congress Wants to Change Section 230," *Slate*, March 23, 2021, https://slate.com/technology/2021/03/section-230-reform-legislative-tracker.html.

14 Gerrit De Vynck et al., "Big Tech CEOs Face Lawmakers in House Hearing on Social Media's Role in Extremism, Misinformation," *Washington Post*, April 9, 2021, https://www.washingtonpost.com/technology/2021/03/25/facebook-google-twitter-house-hearing-live-updates/.

15 Zamaan Qureshi, "Senators Have Stopped Embarrassing Themselves at Tech Hearings," *Slate*, September 15, 2022, https://slate.com/technology/2022/09/meta-tiktok-youtube-senate-hearing-ron-johnson-josh-hawley-gary-peters.html.

16 Nicholas Thompson, "Mr. Nice Guy," *Wired*, August 14, 2017, https://www.wired.com/2017/08/instagram-kevin-systrom-wants-to-clean-up-the-internet/.

17 See Dawn Carla Nunziato, "The Varieties of Counterspeech and Censorship on Social Media," *UC Davis Law Review* 54 (2021): 2501.

18 John Perry Barlow, "A Declaration of the Independence of Cyberspace," Electronic Frontier Foundation, February 8, 1996, https://www.eff.org/cyberspace-independence.

19 Adrien Chen, "Reddit CEO Speaks Out on Violentacrez in Leaked Memo: 'We Stand for Free Speech,'" *Gawker*, October 16, 2012, https://web.archive.org/web/20180425183517/https://www.gawker.com/5952349/reddit-ceo-speaks-out-on-violentacrez-in-leaked-memo-we-stand-for-free-speech.

20 Patrick Howard O'Neill, "8CHAN, the Central Hive of Gamergate, Is Also an Active Pedophile Network," *Cashmere Magazine*, November 17, 2014, https://cashmeremag.com/8chan-pedophiles-child-porn-gamergate-78109/.

21 "Terms of Service," Gab, April 10, 2020, https://gab.com/about/tos.

22 "Community Guidelines 2/14/2021," Parler, https://web.archive.org/web/20210726022238/https://parler.com/documents/guidelines.pdf.

23 Emily Stewart, "Lawmakers Seem Confused about What Facebook Does—and How to Fix It," *Vox*, April 10, 2018, https://www.vox.com/policy-and-politics/2018/4/10/17222062/mark-zuckerberg-testimony-graham-facebook-regulations.

24 Moran Yemini, "The New Irony of Free Speech," *Science and Technology Law Review* 20, no. 1 (January 2019), https://doi.org/10.7916/stlr.v20i1.4769.

25 See Olivier Sylvain, "Intermediary Design Duties," *Connecticut Law Review* 50 (2018): 207.

26 Lucas Introna and Helen Nissenbaum, "Shaping the Web: Why the Politics of Search Engines Matters," *Information Society* 16, no. 3 (2000): 171, https://doi.org/10.1080/01972240050133634.

27 Astra Taylor, *The People's Platform: Taking Back Power and Culture in the Digital Age* (New York: Henry Holt, 2014), 221.

28 Shoshana Zuboff, *The Age of Surveillance Capitalism: The Fight for a Human Future at the New Frontier of Power* (New York: PublicAffairs, 2019), 514.

29 Jen Schradie, *The Revolution That Wasn't: How Digital Activism Favors Conservatives* (Cambridge, MA: Harvard University Press, 2019).

30 Rumman Chowdhury and Luca Belli, "Examining Algorithmic Amplification of Political Content on Twitter," Twitter blog, October 21, 2021, https://blog.twitter.com/en_us/topics/company/2021/rml-politicalcontent.

31 "YouTube's Filter Bubble Problem Is Worse for Fox News Viewers," Tech Transparency Project, October 24, 2021, https://www.techtransparencyproject.org/articles/youtubes-filter-bubble-problem-worse-fox-news-viewers.

32 "YouTube's Filter Bubble Problem Is Worse for Fox News Viewers."

33 See Henry Farrell, "Blame Fox, not Facebook, for Fake News," *Washington Post*, November 6, 2018, https://www.washingtonpost.com/news/monkey-cage/wp/2018/11/06/blame-fox-not-facebook-for-fake-news/; see also Will Oremus, "Fox News Was the Dominant News Source in the 2016 Election, Survey Shows," *Slate*, January 18, 2017, https://slate.com/business/2017/01/fox-news-was-the-dominant-news-source-in-the-2016-election-pew-survey-finds.html.

34 Deepa Seetharaman and Emily Glazer, "How Mark Zuckerberg Learned Politics," *Wall Street Journal*, October 16, 2020, https://www.wsj.com/articles/how-mark-zuckerberg-learned-politics-11602853200.

35 Keach Hagey and Jeff Horwitz, "The Facebook Files: Facebook's Internal Chat Boards Show Politics Often at Center of Decision Making," *Wall Street Journal*, October 24, 2021, https://www.wsj.com/articles/facebook-politics-decision-making-documents-11635100195.

36 Brandy Zadrozny, "'Carol's Journey': What Facebook Knew About How It Radicalized Users," *NBC News*, October 22, 2021, https://www.nbcnews.com/tech/tech-news/facebook-knew-radicalized-users-rcna3581.

37 Ryan Mac and Sheera Frenkel, "Internal Alarm, Public Shrugs: Facebook's Employees Dissect Its Election Role," *New York Times*, October 22, 2021, https://www.nytimes.com/2021/10/22/technology/facebook-election-misinformation.html.

38 Mike Isaac, "Facebook Wrestles With the Features It Used to Define Social Networking," *New York Times*, October 25, 2021, https://www.nytimes.com/2021/10/25/technology/facebook-like-share-buttons.html.

39 Robert O'Harrow Jr., Andrew Ba Tran, and Derek Hawkins, "The Rise of Domestic Extremism in America," *Washington Post*, April 12, 2021, https://www.washingtonpost.com/investigations/interactive/2021/domestic-terrorism-data/.

40 Tony Romm, "Zuckerberg: Standing for Voice and Free Expression," *Washington Post*, October 17, 2019, https://www.washingtonpost.com/technology/2019/10/17/zuckerberg-standing-voice-free-expression.

41 Chip Berlet, "When Hate Went Online," adapted from a paper presented at the Northeast Sociological Association Spring Conference, Sacred Heart University, Fairfield, CT, April 28, 2001, 3.

42 Wayne King, "Computer Network Links Rightist Groups and Offers 'Enemy' List," *New York Times*, February 15, 1985, https://www.nytimes.com/1985/02/15/us/computer-network-links-rihtist-groups-and-offers-enemy-list.html.

43 King, "Computer Network."

44 King, "Computer Network."

45 J. M. Berger, "The Strategy of Violent White Supremacy Is Evolving," *Atlantic*, August 7, 2019, https://www.theatlantic.com/ideas/archive/2019/08/the-new-strategy-of-violent-white-supremacy/595648/.

46 These tactics were arguably perfected during GamerGate, the widespread online harassment campaign in 2014 against women in the gaming industry. See Kyle Wagner, "The Future of the Culture Wars Is Here, and It's Gamergate," *Deadspin*, October 14, 2014, https://deadspin.com/the-future-of-the-culture-wars-is-here-and-its-gamerga-1646145844.

47 Adam Clark Estes, "How Neo-Nazis Used the Internet to Instigate a Right-Wing Extremist Crisis," *Vox*, February 2, 2021, https://www.vox.com/recode/22256387/facebook-telegram-qanon-proud-boys-alt-right-hate-groups.

48 "Teaching AI to View the World Through Your Eyes," Meta, October 14, 2021, https://about.fb.com/news/2021/10/teaching-ai-to-view-the-world-through-your-eyes/.

49 James Vincent, "Facebook Is Researching AI Systems That See, Hear, and Remember Everything You Do," *Verge*, October 14, 2021, https://www.theverge.com/2021/10/14/22725894/facebook-augmented-reality-ar-glasses-ai-systems-ego4d-research.

50 Adrienne LaFrance, "'History Will Not Judge Us Kindly,'" *Atlantic*, October 25, 2021, https://amp.theatlantic.com/amp/article/620478/.

51 Jeff Horwitz, "Facebook Says Its Rules Apply to All. Company Documents Reveal a Secret Elite That's Exempt," *Wall Street Journal*, September 13, 2021, https://www.wsj.com/articles/facebook-files-xcheck-zuckerberg-elite-rules-11631541353?mod=searchresults_pos1&page=1.

52 Craig Timberg, "New Whistleblower Claims Facebook Allowed Hate, Illegal Activity to Go Unchecked," *Washington Post*, October 22, 2021, https://www.washingtonpost.com/technology/2021/10/22/facebook-new-whistleblower-complaint/.

53 See Mary Anne Franks, *The Cult of the Constitution: Our Deadly Devotion to Guns and Free Speech* (Stanford, CA: Stanford University Press, 2019), 70–100.

54 See, for example, Michael C. Dorf, "Identity Politics and the Second Amendment," *Fordham Law Review* 73(2004): 549.

55 Lois Beckett, "Wayne LaPierre: The Man Who Remade the NRA as the 'Good Guy with a Gun,'" *Guardian*, January 5, 2024, https://www.theguardian.com/us-news/2024/jan/05/wayne-lapierre-nra-resigns-corruption-scandal.

56 Franks, "Not Where Bodies Live: The Abstraction of Internet Expression," in *Free Speech in the Digital Age*, eds. Susan J. Brison and Katharine Gelber (New York: Oxford Academic, 2019), https://doi.org/10.1093/oso/9780190883591.003.0009.

57 Protection of Lawful Commerce in Arms Act (PLCAA), 15 U.S. Code § 7901 (2005).

58 Communications Decency Act, 47 U.S. Code § 230 (a) (1995).

59 *Packingham v. North Carolina*, 137 S. Ct. 1730, 1737 (2017).

60 Tom Wilkinson, "Typology: Public Square," *Architectural Review*, March 2, 2017, https://www.architectural-review.com/essays/typology-public-square.

61 See, for example, Genevieve Lakier and Nelson Tebbe, "After the 'Great Deplatforming': Reconsidering the Shape of the First Amendment," LPE Project, March 1, 2021, https://lpeproject.org/blog/after-the-great-deplatforming-reconsidering-the-shape-of-the-first-amendment; Ryan Lovelace, "ACLU Raises Concerns Amid Trump Twitter Ban," *Washington Times*, January 8, 2021, https://www.washingtontimes.com/news/2021/jan/8/aclu-raises-concerns-amid-trump-twitter-ban.

62 See, for example, Nancy Fraser, "Rethinking the Public Sphere: A Contribution to the Critique of Actually Existing Democracy," *Social Text* 25/26 (1990): 67.

63 Fraser, "Rethinking the Public Sphere," Part II.

64 George Michael Peter, "Public Squares: An Analysis of an Urban Space Form and Its Functional Determinants" (master's thesis, University of British Columbia, 1968), 29, 47, 194, https://open.library.ubc.ca/handle/bitstream/129905/UBC_1968_A8%20P38.pdf; see also Riham Nady, "What Is a Public Plaza?," *Arch20*, https://www.arch2o.com/reshaping-squares, which discusses the background and functions of public squares.

65 Yasmeen Serhan, "A Physical Public Square in the Digital Age," *Atlantic*, September 16, 2018, https://www.theatlantic.com/international/archive/2018/09/speakers-corner-london-freedom-of-speech/568963.

66 Franks, "Unwilling Avatars: Idealism and Discrimination in Cyberspace," *Columbia Journal of Gender and Law* 20 (2011): 257.

67 Franks, "Unwilling Avatars," 255–256.

68 See Jamison Hill, "Dear Anti-Trump Protesters: Don't Forget Those of Us With Disabilities," *Vox*, February 10, 2017, https://www.vox.com/first-person/2017/2/10/14567112/trump-protest-disabilities-inclusivity.

69 See Dan Jasper, "An Organizer's Guide to Protests and Political Change," *Street Civics*, https://streetcivics.com/an-organizers-guide-to-protests-and-political-change.

70 See Gregory H. Shill, "How Vehicular Intimidation Became the Norm," *Atlantic*, November 3, 2020, https://www.theatlantic.com/ideas/archive/2020/11/how-trump-train-trucks-became-a-political-weapon/616979.

71 See Hussein Kesvani, "The Quiet Rise of the 'Shy Radical,'" *Mel Magazine*, 2019, https://melmagazine.com/en-us/story/the-quiet-rise-of-the-shy-radical.

72 John Suler, "The Online Disinhibition Effect," *CyberPsychology and Behavior* 7, no. 3 (June 2004): 321–326.

73 Suler, "The Online Disinhibition Effect," 322.

74   Winhkong Hua, "Cybermobs, Civil Conspiracy, and Tort Liability," *Fordham Urban Law Journal* 44, no. 4 (2017): 1228–1229.

75   Franks, "Unwilling Avatars," 255–256.

76   Franks, "Unwilling Avatars," 255–256.

77   Hua, "Cybermobs," 1227, quoting Nancy S. Kim, "Web Site Proprietorship and Online Harassment," *Utah Law Review* (2009): 1010, https://doi.org/10.1089/1094931041291295.

78   Franks, "Unwilling Avatars," 256.

79   David M. Douglas, "Doxing: A Conceptual Analysis," *Ethics and Information Technology* 18 (June 2016): 199–200.

80   Danielle Keats Citron, *Hate Crimes in Cyberspace* (United Kingdom: Harvard University Press, 2014), 4.

81   See, for example, Kashmir Hill, "Our Digital Pasts Weren't Supposed to Be Weaponized Like This," *New York Times*, August 3, 2021, https://www.nytimes.com/2021/05/29/technology/emily-wilder-firing-ap.html.

82   Franks, "Unwilling Avatars," 255–256.

83   Nancy Fraser, "Rethinking the Public Sphere: A Contribution to the Critique of Actually Existing Democracy," 25/26 Soc. Text 56, 63 (1990); Wilkinson, "Typology."

84   See Risa Goluboff, *Vagrant Nation: Police Power, Constitutional Change, and The Making Of The 1960s* (New York: Oxford University Press, 2016), 116–117.

85   See Franks, "Democratic Surveillance," *Harvard Journal of Law and Technology* 30 (2017): 443.

86   See Goluboff, *Vagrant Nation*.

87   See Janet L. Yellen, "The History of Women's Work and Wages and How It Has Created Success for Us All," Brookings Institute (May 2020), https://www.brookings.edu/essay/the-history-of-womens-work-and-wages-and-how-it-has-created-success-for-us-all.

88   See Barbara Matthews, "Women, Education and History," *Theory Into Practice* 15 (1976): 47–48.

89   Goluboff, *Vagrant Nation*, 150–151.

90   See Cynthia Grant Bowman, "Street Harassment and the Informal Ghettoization of Women," *Harvard Law Review* 106 (1993): 519, 522–534 (describing "the very real harms of th[e] widespread social phenomenon" of street harassment).

91   See Goluboff, *Vagrant Nation*, 2–3 ("Officials employed vagrancy laws for a breath-taking array of purposes: to force the local poor to work or suffer for their support; to keep out poor or suspicious strangers.").

92   See Winnie Hu, "'Hostile Architecture': How Public Spaces Keep the Public Out," *New York Times*, November 14, 2019, https://www.nytimes.com/2019/11/08/nyregion/hostile-architecture-nyc.html.

93   German Lopez, "The Battle Over Confederate Statues, Explained," *Vox*, August 23, 2017, https://www.vox.com/identities/2017/8/16/16151252/confederate-statues-white-supremacists.

94 Adam Clark Estes, "How Neo-Nazis Used the Internet to Instigate a Right-Wing Extremist Crisis," *Vox*, February 2, 2021, https://www.vox.com/recode/22256387/facebook-telegram-qanon-proud-boys-alt-right-hate-groups.

95 Danielle Citron and Franks, "Cyber Civil Rights in the Time of COVID-19," *Harvard Law Review* (blog), May 14, 2020, https://blog.harvardlawreview.org/cyber-civil-rights-in-the-time-of-covid-19.

96 Mathew Ingram, "Unlike Everyone Else, Twitter Still Sees Itself as a Champion of Free Speech," *Columbia Journalism Review*, August 8, 2018, https://www.cjr.org/the_new_gatekeepers/twitter-alex-jones-free-speech.php.

97 Elizabeth Dwoskin and Nitasha Tiku, "How Twitter, on the Front Lines of History, Finally Decided to Ban Trump," *Washington Post*, January 16, 2021, https://www.washingtonpost.com/technology/2021/01/16/how-twitter-banned-trump/.

98 Travis Caldwell, "Trump's 'We Love You' to Capitol Rioters Is More of the Same," *CNN*, January 7, 2021, https://www.cnn.com/2021/01/07/politics/trump-history-comments-trnd/index.html.

99 Adi Robertson, "Twitter Says Trump's Account Is Locked, and He's Facing a Ban," *Verge*, January 6, 2021, https://www.theverge.com/2021/1/6/22217686/trump-twitter-account-locked-capitol-hill-riot-tweets-policy-violations.

100 "Permanent Suspension of @realDonaldTrump," Twitter blog, January 8, 2021, https://blog.twitter.com/en_us/topics/company/2020/suspension.html.

101 Tony Romm and Elizabeth Dwoskin, "Trump Banned from Facebook Indefinitely, CEO Mark Zuckerberg Says," *Washington Post*, January 7, 2021, https://www.washingtonpost.com/technology/2021/01/07/trump-twitter-ban/.

102 Robertson, "Twitter Bans QAnon Supporters, Including Former National Security Adviser Michael Flynn," *Verge*, January 8, 2021, https://www.theverge.com/2021/1/8/22221332/twitter-ban-qanon-accounts-michael-flynn-sidney-powell-ron-watkins.

103 Jack Nicas and Davey Alba, "Amazon, Apple and Google Cut Off Parler, an App That Drew Trump Supporters," *New York Times*, January 9, 2021, https://www.nytimes.com/2021/01/09/technology/apple-google-parler.html.

104 Lexi Lonas, "Pompeo, Cruz and Other Trump Allies Condemn Twitter's Ban on President," *The Hill*, January 9, 2021, https://thehill.com/policy/technology/533486-pompeo-cruz-and-other-trump-allies-condemn-twitters-ban-on-president.

105 Mike Pompeo (@MikePompeo), "Silencing speech is dangerous," Twitter, January 9, 2021, https://twitter.com/mikepompeo/status/1347938581424312331.

106 Trump (@DonaldTrumpJr), "Free Speech Is Under Attack!," Twitter, January 28, 2021, https://twitter.com/DonaldJTrumpJr/status/1347724256323497989?lang=en.

107 Lauren Giella, "Fact Check: Did Twitter Violate President Trump's First Amendment Rights?," *Newsweek*, January 11, 2021, https://www.newsweek.com/fact-check-did-twitter-violate-president-trumps-first-amendment-rights-1560673.

108 Matt Gaetz (@RepMattGaetz), "We cannot live in a world," Twitter, January 11, 2021, https://twitter.com/RepMattGaetz/status/1348648248903405571.

109 Sarah Huckabee Sanders (@SarahHuckabee), "I've lost 50k+ followers this week," Twitter, January 9, 2021, https://twitter.com/SarahHuckabee/status/1347990928984842245.

110 Alex Hern and Kari Paul, "Donald Trump Suspended From Facebook Indefinitely, Says Mark Zuckerberg," *Guardian*, January 7, 2021, https://www.theguardian.com/us-news/2021/jan/07/donald-trump-twitter-ban-comes-to-end-amid-calls-for-tougher-action.

111 Corynne McSherry, "EFF's Response to Social Media Companies' Decisions to Block President Trump's Accounts," Electronic Frontier Foundation, January 7, 2021, https://www.eff.org/deeplinks/2021/01/eff-response-social-media-companies-decision-block-president-trumps-accounts.

112 Natalie Colarossi, "ACLU Counsel Warns of 'Unchecked Power' of Twitter, Facebook After Trump Suspension," *Newsweek*, January 9, 2021, https://www.newsweek.com/aclu-counsel-warns-unchecked-power-twitter-facebook-after-trump-suspension-1560248.

113 Nicas and Alba, "How Parler, a Chosen App of Trump Fans, Became a Test of Free Speech," *New York Times*, January 10, 2021, https://www.nytimes.com/2021/01/10/technology/parler-app-trump-free-speech.html.

114 "State of the First Amendment Survey," Freedom Forum Institute, June 27, 2019, https://www.freedomforum.org/content/uploads/2023/12/sofa_2019_report.pdf.

115 See Franks, "Reforming Section 230 and Platform Liability, Cyber Policy Recommendations for the New Administration," *Stanford Policy Center*, January 27, 2021, 3.

116 See, for example, Cat Zakrzewski and Rachel Lerman, "Trump Files Class Action Lawsuits Targeting Facebook, Twitter and Google's YouTube over 'Censorship' of Conservatives," *Washington Post*, July 7, 2021, https://www.washingtonpost.com/technology/2021/07/07/trump-lawsuit-social-media/.

117 Brian Fung, Ryan Nobles, and Kevin Liptak, "Trump Signs Executive Order Targeting Social Media Companies," *CNN*, May 28, 2020, https://www.cnn.com/2020/05/28/politics/trump-twitter-social-media-executive-order/index.html.

118 See, for example, Zakrzewski, "Florida Governor Signs Bill Barring Social Media Companies from Blocking Political Candidates," *Washington Post*, May 24, 2021, https://www.washingtonpost.com/technology/2021/05/24/florida-gov-social-media-230/; John Villasenor, "Texas' New Social Media Law Is Blocked for Now, but That's Not the End of the Story," Brookings Institution, December 14, 2021, https://www.brookings.edu/blog/techtank/2021/12/14/texas-new-social-media-law-is-blocked-for-now-but-thats-not-the-end-of-the-story/.

119 *NetChoice, L.L.C. v. Paxton*, 49 F.4th 447–448 (5th Cir. 2022).

120 "Model Penal Code" at 2.02(2)(c), American Law Institute. *Black's Law Dictionary* defines *recklessness* as "conduct whereby the actor does not desire harmful consequence but . . . foresees the possibility and consciously takes the risk" or

"a state of mind in which a person does not care about the consequences of his or her actions," *Black's Law Dictionary*, 11th ed. (2019), s.v. "recklessness." *Ballentine's Law Dictionary* defines *recklessness* as "indifference to consequences; indifference to the safety and rights of others," *Ballentine's Law Dictionary*, 3rd. ed. (1969), s.v. "recklessness."

121 See Franks, "Moral Hazard on Stilts: Zeran's Legacy," Law.com, November 10, 2017, https://www.yahoo.com/news/moral-hazard-stilts-apos-zeran-083 033447.html?guccounter=1.

122 Communications Decency Act, 47 U.S. Code § 230 (a) (1995).

123 Communications Decency Act, 47 U.S. Code § 230 (a) (1995).

124 598 U. S. ____ (2023).

125 Michael L. Rustad and Thomas H. Koenig, "Taming the Tort Monster: The American Civil Justice System as a Battleground of Social Theory," *Brooklyn Law Review* 68, no. 1 (September 2002): 4.

126 John Robertson, "'For Our Own Good': Federal Preemption of State Tort Law," *William and Mary Environmental Law and Policy Institute* 20, no. 1 (October 1995): 169.

127 Cristian Farias, "Will the Supreme Court Blow Up the Internet?," *Vanity Fair*, February 22, 2023, https://www.vanityfair.com/news/2023/02/supreme-court -section-230-youtube-twitter-internet.

128 Dell Cameron, "Section 230 Is the Foundation of the Internet, So Why Do Republicans Want to Change It?," *Gizmodo*, March 29, 2019, https://gizmodo .com/section-230-is-the-foundation-of-the-internet-so-why-d-1833590565.

129 Eleni Kyriakides, "Sixth Circuit Reinforces Intent of Section 230, Reverses Ben-Gal Cheerleader Case," Center for Democracy and Technology, June 24, 2014, https://cdt.org/insights/sixth-circuit-reinforces-intent-of-section-230 -reverses-ben-gal-cheerleader-case/.

130 Elliot Harmon, "In Debate over Internet Speech Law, Pay Attention to Whose Voices Are Ignored," *The Hill*, August 29, 2019, https://thehill.com /opinion/technology/458227-in-debate-over-internet-speech-law-pay-attention -to-whose-voices-are/.

131 Communications Decency Act, 47 U.S. Code § 230 (a) (1995).

132 See, for example, *Jane Doe No. 1 v. Backpage.com, LLC*, 817 F.3d 12 (1st Cir. 2016).

133 See, for example, *Daniel v. Armslist, LLC*, 2019 WI 47, 386 Wis. 2d 449 N.W.2d 710, *cert. denied*, no. 19-153, 2019 WL 6257416 (U.S. Nov. 25, 2019).

134 Matt Laslo, "The Fight Over Section 230—and the Internet as We Know It," *Wired*, August 13, 2019, https://www.wired.com/story/fight-over-section-230 -internet-as-we-know-it/.

135 See, for example, *Oberdorf v. Amazon.com, Inc.*, 295 F. Supp. 3d 496 (M.D. Pa. 2017), *affirmed in part, vacated in part*, 930 F.3d 136 (3d Cir. 2019), *vacated en banc*, 936 F.3d 182 (3d Cir. 2019).

136 Alexis Kramer, "Armslist Online Gun Sale Case Won't Get Supreme Court Review," *Bloomberg Law*, November 25, 2019, https://news.bloomberglaw .com/tech-and-telecom-law/armslist-mass-shooting-case-wont-get-supreme -court-review.

137   "New Book Details How California Prosecutors Took Down Sex Trafficking Site Backpage," *Morning Edition*, National Public Radio, January 12, 2022, https://www.npr.org/2022/01/12/1072372496/new-book-details-how-cali fornia-prosecutors-took-down-sex-trafficking-site-backp.

138   Michael L. Rustad and Thomas H. Koenig, "Rebooting Cybertort Law," *Washington Law Review* 80 (2005): 382.

139   *Chambers v. Baltimore & Ohio Railroad Co.*, 207 U.S. 142, 28 S. Ct. 34, 52 L. Ed. 143 (1907).

140   John C. P. Goldberg and Benjamin C. Zipursky, *Recognizing Wrongs* (United Kingdom: Harvard University Press, 2020), 9.

141   Douglas A. Kysar, "The Public Life of Private Law: Tort Law as a Risk Regulation Mechanism," *European Journal of Risk Regulation* 9, no. 1 (2018): 48–50.

142   Rustad and Koenig, "Rebooting Cybertort Law," 382.

143   Citron and Franks, "Cyber Civil Rights."

144   Citron, "Cyber Civil Rights," *Boston University Law Review* (February 2009), https://scholarship.law.bu.edu/faculty_scholarship/617.

145   Jonathon Penney, "Whose Speech Is Chilled by Surveillance?," *Slate*, July 7, 2017, https://slate.com/technology/2017/07/women-young-people-experience -the-chilling-effects-of-surveillance-at-higher-rates.html; Caitlin Ring Carlson and Haley Witt, "Online Harassment of U.S. Women Journalists and Its Impact on Press Freedom," *First Monday* 25 (November 11, 2020), https://first monday.org/ojs/index.php/fm/article/download/11071/9995; Lucina Di Meco and Saskia Brechenmacher, "Tackling Online Abuse and Disinformation Targeting Women in Politics," Carnegie Endowment for International Peace, November 30, 2020, https://carnegieendowment.org/2020/11/30/tack ling-online-abuse-and-disinformation-targeting-women-in-politics-pub -83331.

Chapter 5: The Promise of Fearless Speech

1   Annette Dumbach and Jud Newborn, *Sophie Scholl and the White Rose* (London: Oneworld, 2018), 190–191.

2   Dumbach and Newborn, *Sophie Scholl*, 198.

3   Frank McDonogh, *Sophie Scholl: The Real Story of the Woman Who Defied Hitler* (Cheltenham: History Press, 2009).

4   Kathryn J. Atwood and Muriel Phillips Engelman, *Women Heroes of World War II: 32 Stories of Espionage, Sabotage, Resistance, and Rescue* (Chicago: Chicago Review Press, 2019).

5   "Sophie Scholl and the White Rose," White Rose International, https://white roseinternational.com/sophie-scholl-and-the-white-rose/.

6   A previous version of this chapter appeared in Mary Anne Franks, "Fearless Speech," *First Amendment Law Review* 17 (2019): 294."

7   Jonathan Simon, "Parrhesiastic Accountability: Investigatory Commissions and Executive Power in an Age of Terror," *Yale Law Journal* 114, no. 6 (April 2005): 1421–1422.

8 Teresa M. Bejan, "The Two Clashing Meanings of 'Free Speech,'" *Atlantic*, December 2, 2017, https://www.theatlantic.com/politics/archive/2017/12/two-concepts-of-freedom-of-speech/546791/.

9 Dana Fields, *Frankness, Greek Culture, and the Roman Empire* (New York: Routledge, 2021), 9.

10 Keith Werhan, "The Classical Athenian Ancestry of American Freedom of Speech," *Supreme Court Review* 1 (2008): 293–347.

11 Michel Foucault, "The Meaning and Evolution of the Word 'Parrhesia': Discourse & Truth, Problematization of Parrhesia," lecture series, University of California at Berkeley, October–November 1983, https://foucault.info/parrhesia/foucault.DT1.wordParrhesia.en/.

12 Foucault, "The Meaning [of] Parrhesia."

13 Jonathan Simon, "Fearless Speech in the Killing State: The Power of Capital Crime Victim Speech," *North Carolina Law Review* 82, no. 4 (May 2004): 1395–1396.

14 Foucault, "The Meaning [of] Parrhesia."

15 Foucault, "The Meaning [of] Parrhesia."

16 Simon, "Fearless Speech," 1391.

17 Foucault, "The Meaning [of] Parrhesia."

18 Foucault, "The Meaning [of] Parrhesia."

19 Foucault, "The Meaning [of] Parrhesia." (Emphasis added.)

20 Fields, *Frankness*, 2.

21 Werhan, "The Classical Athenian Ancestry."

22 Fields, *Frankness*, 3.

23 Foucault, "The Meaning [of] Parrhesia."

24 Foucault, "The Meaning [of] Parrhesia."

25 Foucault, "The Meaning [of] Parrhesia."

26 Quoted in Michael Foucault, "Parrhesia in the Tragedies of Euripides: Discourse & Truth, Problematization of Parrhesia—Six Lectures Given by Michel Foucault at the University of California at Berkeley," October–November 1983, https://foucault.info/parrhesia/foucault.DT2.parrhesiaEuripides.en/.

27 Quoted in Foucault, "Parrhesia in the Tragedies of Euripides."

28 Foucault, "Parrhesia in the Tragedies of Euripides."

29 Simon, "Fearless Speech," 1401–1402.

30 Simon, "Parrhesiastic Accountability," 1451.

31 Simon, "Parrhesiastic Accountability," 1390–1391.

32 Emma Brown, "California Professor, Writer of Confidential Brett Kavanaugh Letter, Speaks Out about Her Allegation of Sexual Assault," *Washington Post*, September 16, 2018, https://www.washingtonpost.com/investigations/california-professor-writer-of-confidential-brett-kavanaugh-letter-speaks-out-about-her-allegation-of-sexual-assault/2018/09/16/46982194-b846-11e8-94eb-3bd52dfe917b_story.html.

33 Brown, "California Professor."

34 Brown, "California Professor."

35 Erin Durkin, "Christine Blasey Ford's Life 'Turned Upside Down' after Accusing Kavanaugh," *Guardian*, September 19, 2018, https://www.theguardian.com /us-news/2018/sep/19/christine-blasey-ford-brett-kavanaugh-sexual-assault -accuser-threats.

36 Aaron Blake, "Trump's 'Restraint' on Christine Blasey Ford Was Always Oversold," *Washington Post*, September 21, 2018, https://www.washingtonpost .com/politics/2018/09/21/trump-has-been-suggesting-that-christine-blasey -ford-is-liar-days/.

37 Sheryl Gay Stolberg and Nicholas Fandos, "Christine Blasey Ford Reaches Deal to Testify at Kavanaugh Hearing," *New York Times*, September 23, 2018, https://www.nytimes.com/2018/09/23/us/politics/brett-kavanaugh-christine -blasey-ford-testify.html.

38 Daisy Murray, "'Empowerment Through Empathy'—We Spoke to Tarana Burke, the Woman Who Really Started the 'Me Too Movement,'" *Elle*, October 23, 2017, https://www.elle.com/uk/life-and-culture/culture/news/a39429 /empowerment-through-empathy-tarana-burke-me-too/.

39 Jim Killackey, "Hill Wasn't Asked to Quit, OU Says Reactions to Resignation Mixed," *Oklahoman*, March 17, 1995, https://www.oklahoman.com/story /news/1995/03/17/hill-wasnt-asked-to-quit-ou-says-reactions-to-resignation -mixed/62397226007/.

40 "The Anita Hill Chair: A New Chapter in the Long Racial History of the University of Oklahoma College of Law," *Journal of Blacks in Higher Education* 11 (Spring 1996): 20–22.

41 Oprah Winfrey, "Golden Globes Acceptance Speech," January 7, 2018, Beverly Hills, CA, quoted in Yohana Desta, "Golden Globes 2018: Read Oprah's Entire Showstopping Acceptance Speech," *Vanity Fair*, January 7, 2018, https://www.vanityfair.com/hollywood/2018/01/golden-globes-2018-oprah -winfrey-cecil-b-demille-acceptance-speech.

Chapter 6: Profiles in Fearless Speech

1 Michel Foucault, *The Courage of Truth: The Government of Self and Others II: Lectures at the Collège de France 1983–1984*, ed. Frédéric Gros, trans. Graham Burchell (New York: Palgrave Macmillan, 2011), 10.

2 Foucault, *The Courage of Truth*, 9.

3 Foucault, *The Courage of Truth*, 11.

4 Catharine Sedgwick, *Bentley's Miscellany* 34 (1853): 418.

5 Sedgwick, *Bentley's Miscellany*, 418.

6 Sedgwick, *Bentley's Miscellany*.

7 Ben Z. Rose, *Mother of Freedom: Mum Bett and the Roots of Abolition* (Waverley, MA: TreeLine Press, 2009), Kindle, 31.

8 Mary Wilds, *Mumbet: The Life and Times of Elizabeth Freeman: The True Story of a Slave Who Won Her Freedom* (Greensboro, NC: Avisson Press, 1999), 49.

9   Jon Swan, "The Slave Who Sued For Freedom," *American Heritage* 41, no. 2 (March 1990).

10 Wilds, *Mumbet*, 49.

11 Swan, "The Slave Who Sued For Freedom."

12 Rose, *Mother of Freedom*, 42.

13 Swan, "The Slave Who Sued For Freedom."

14 Rose, *Mother of Freedom*, 46.

15 Rose, *Mother of Freedom*, 49–50.

16 "Jury Decides in Favor of Elizabeth 'Mum Bett' Freeman," Mass Moments, August 22, 1781, https://www.massmoments.org/moment-details/jury-decides -in-favor-of-elizabeth-mum-bett-freeman.html.

17 Rose, *Mother of Freedom*, 49–50.

18 Rose, *Mother of Freedom*, 55.

19 Rose, *Mother of Freedom*, 72.

20 Sedgwick, *Bentley's Miscellany*, 421.

21 Peter Kurth, *American Cassandra: The Life of Dorothy Thompson* (Lexington, KY: Plunkett Lake Press, 2012), Kindle, 128.

22 Kurth, *American Cassandra*, 244.

23 Kurth, *American Cassandra*, 237.

24 Alan Steinweis, "The Trials of Herschel Grynszpan: Anti-Jewish Policy and German Propaganda, 1938–1942," *German Studies Review* 31, no. 3 (October 2008): 472.

25 Kurth, *American Cassandra*, 416.

26 Kurth, *American Cassandra*, 418.

27 Kurth, *American Cassandra*, 419.

28 Clyde Haberman, "Today in History: The Father Coughlin Story," *PBS*, March 9, 2022, https://www.pbs.org/wnet/exploring-hate/2022/03/09/today -in-history-the-father-coughlin-story//.

29 "Father Coughlin Blames Jews for Nazi Violence," *History Unfolded, US Newspapers and the Holocaust*, https://newspapers.ushmm.org/events/father-coughlin -blames-jews-for-nazi-violence.

30 Kurth, *American Cassandra*, 422–423.

31 Kurth, *American Cassandra*, 422–423.

32 Kurth, *American Cassandra*, 424.

33 Sarah Kate Kramer, "When Nazis Took Manhattan," *Code Switch*, February 20, 2019, https://www.npr.org/sections/codeswitch/2019/02/20/695941323 /when-nazis-took-manhattan.

34 Dorothy Thompson, "Miss Thompson Issues Statement on Bund Rally," *New York Herald Tribune*, February 21, 1939, 3.

35 Thompson, "Statement."

36 Thompson, "Statement."

37 Thompson, "Statement."

38 *Bates v. State*, 210 Ark. 652, 658 (1946).

39 Daisy Bates, *The Long Shadow of Little Rock: A Memoir* (Fayetteville: University of Arkansas Press, 1986), 10.

40 Bates, *The Long Shadow of Little Rock*, 15.

41 Bates, *The Long Shadow of Little Rock*, 29.

42 Grif Stockley, "Arkansas State Press," Encyclopedia of Arkansas (Central Arkansas Library System), February 5, 2024, http://www.encyclopediaofarkansas.net/encyclopedia/entry-detail.aspx?search=1&entryID=592.

43 Bates, *The Long Shadow of Little Rock*, 4.

44 Bates, *The Long Shadow of Little Rock*, 61

45 *Bates v. City of Little Rock*, 361 U.S. 516, 520 (1960).

46 *Bates v. City of Little Rock*, 361 U.S. 516, 522–523 (1960).

47 Judith Bloom Fradin and Dennis B. Fradin, *The Power of One: Daisy Bates and the Little Rock Nine* (New York: Clarion Books, 2004), 84–85.

48 Bates, *The Long Shadow of Little Rock*, 171.

49 Bates, *The Long Shadow of Little Rock*, 174.

50 Bates, *The Long Shadow of Little Rock*, 175.

51 Bates, *The Long Shadow of Little Rock*, 155.

52 Bates, *The Long Shadow of Little Rock*, 178.

53 Willard B. Gatewood Jr., Foreword to Bates, *The Long Shadow of Little Rock*, xii.

54 Carolyn Calloway-Thomas and Thurmon Garner, "Daisy Bates and the Little Rock School Crisis: Forging the Way," in "The Voices of African American Women in the Civil Rights Movement," special issue, *Journal of Black Studies* 26, no. 5 (May 1996): 616–628.

55 Eleanor J. Bader, "'Yours in Freedom' Chronicles the Early, Dangerous Fight for Birth Control," *Progressive*, December 21, 2023, https://progressive.org/latest/yours-in-freedom-chronicles-the-fight-for-birth-control-bader-20231221/.

56 John Killilea, "Time Runs Out for William Baird," *Harvard Crimson*, October 23, 1967, https://www.thecrimson.com/article/1967/10/23/time-runs-out-for-william-baird/. Bill Baird, "The Politics of God, Government, and Sex: A Thirty-One-Year Crusade," *St. Louis University Public Law Review* 13, no. 139 (1993): 158. Nick Kolev, "50 Years Later: Revisiting the Moment in BU History That Helped Shape the Abortion Rights Battle," *BU Today*, July 11, 2022, https://www.bu.edu/articles/2022/activist-bill-baird-abortion-rights-bu-lecture/.

57 Killilea, "Time Runs Out for William Baird."

58 Lindsey Gruson, "Abortion-Rights' Scorned Prophet," *New York Times*, April 14, 1993, https://www.nytimes.com/1993/04/14/nyregion/abortion-rights-scorned-prophet-hated-both-sides-bill-baird-raises-hackles-not.html.

59 Eleanor J. Bader and Patricia Baird-Windle, *Targets of Hatred* (New York: Palgrave Macmillan Trade, 2001), 26.

60 Bader and Baird-Windle, *Targets of Hatred*, 35.

61 *Eisenstadt v. Baird*, 405 U.S. 438, 453 (1972).

62 *Eisenstadt v. Baird*, 405 U.S. 438, 455 (1972).

63 *Eisenstadt v. Baird*, 405 U.S. 438, 459–460 (1972).

64 *Eisenstadt v. Baird*, 405 U.S. 438, 457–58 (1972).

65 Baird, "The Politics of God, Government, and Sex," 140.

66 Baird, "The Politics of God, Government, and Sex," 142.

67 Gruson, "Abortion-Rights' Scorned Prophet."

68 Myra MacPherson, "The Forgotten Father of the Abortion Rights Movement," *New Republic*, October 7, 2019, https://newrepublic.com/article/155240/for gotten-father-abortion-rights-movement.

69 MacPherson, "The Forgotten Father of the Abortion Rights Movement."

70 Gruson, "Abortion-Rights' Scorned Prophet."

71 Shawn G. Kennedy, "Head of Burned Abortion Clinic Trades Charges With Opponent," *New York Times*, February 17, 1979, https://www.nytimes.com /1979/02/17/archives/head-of-burned-abortion-clinic-trades-charges-with -opponent.html.

72 MacPherson, "The Forgotten Father of the Abortion Rights Movement."

73 "VFA Celebrates, Honors and Thanks Bill Baird, Abortion Rights Activist," Veteran Feminists of America, https://www.veteranfeministsofamerica.org /legacy/Bill_Baird.htm.

74 Eleanor J. Bader, "Reproductive Rights Pioneer Sheds Light on His Battle Against Anti-Abortion Extremists," *Ms. Magazine*, June 18, 2022, https://ms magazine.com/2022/06/18/bill-baird-anti-abortion-extremism-dobbs-roe -v-wade.

75 Baird, "The Politics of God, Government, and Sex," 165.

76 MacPherson, "The Forgotten Father of the Abortion Rights Movement."

77 Baird, "The Politics of God, Government, and Sex," 180.

78 Lu Hsiu-Lien and Ashley Esarey, *My Fight for a New Taiwan: One Woman's Journey from Prison to Power* (Seattle: University of Washington Press, 2014), Kindle, 116.

79 Hsiu-Lien and Esarey, *My Fight for a New Taiwan*, 117.

80 Hsiu-Lien and Esarey, *My Fight for a New Taiwan*, 155.

81 Hsiu-Lien and Esarey, *My Fight for a New Taiwan*, 52.

82 Hsiu-Lien and Esarey, *My Fight for a New Taiwan*, 53.

83 Hsiu-Lien and Esarey, *My Fight for a New Taiwan*, 52–53.

84 Hsiu-Lien and Esarey, *My Fight for a New Taiwan*, 54.

85 Hsiu-Lien and Esarey, *My Fight for a New Taiwan*, 54.

86 Hsiu-Lien and Esarey, *My Fight for a New Taiwan*, 55.

87 Hsiu-Lien and Esarey, *My Fight for a New Taiwan*, 64.

88 Hsiu-Lien and Esarey, *My Fight for a New Taiwan*, 64.

89 Hsiu-Lien and Esarey, *My Fight for a New Taiwan*, 67.

90 Farah Stockman, "How a Harvard Rivalry Changed Taiwan," *Boston Globe*, July 3, 2012, https://www.bostonglobe.com/opinion/2012/07/03/how-harvard-rivalry-changed-taiwan/FVBW05iJno6fTa8HkzpgHM/story.html.

91 Stockman, "How a Harvard Rivalry Changed Taiwan."

92 Hsiu-Lien and Esarey, *My Fight for a New Taiwan*, ix.

93 Hsiu-Lien and Esarey, *My Fight for a New Taiwan*, 162.

94 Hsiu-Lien and Esarey, *My Fight for a New Taiwan*, 261.

95 "Russian Journalist Who Made Anti-War Protest on TV Describes Escape to France," *Moscow Times*, February 10, 2023, https://www.themoscowtimes.com/2023/02/10/russian-journalist-who-made-anti-war-protest-on-tv-describes-escape-to-france-a80202.

96 Zoya Sheftlovich, "The Mysterious Case of Marina O.," *Politico*, May 1, 2022, https://www.politico.com/news/magazine/2022/05/01/the-mysterious-case-of-marina-o-00029150.

97 Vitaliy Shevchenko, "Ukraine War: Protester Exposes Cracks in Kremlin's War Message," *BBC News*, March 15, 2022, https://www.bbc.com/news/world-europe-60749064.

98 Sheftlovich, "The Mysterious Case of Marina O."

99 "Anti-War Protester Fined After Disrupting Russian News Program," *Radio Free Europe/Radio Liberty's Russian Service*, March 15, 2022, https://www.rferl.org/a/russia-antiwar-protester-state-television/31753824.html.

100 "Russian State TV Editor Interrupts Live News Broadcast with Anti-war Message," *Meduza*, March 14, 2022, https://amp.meduza.io/en/short/2022/03/14/russian-state-tv-editor-interrupts-live-news-broadcast-with-anti-war-message.

101 "Marina Ovsyannikova: Russian Journalist Tells of 14-Hour Interrogation," *BBC News*, March 15, 2022, https://www.bbc.com/news/world-europe-60749279.

102 "Responsibility for War Crimes of the Russian Military Is Inevitable—Address by the President of Ukraine," March 15, 2022, https://www.president.gov.ua/en/news/vidpovidalnist-za-voyenni-zlochini-dlya-rosijskih-vijskovih-73561.

103 "Anti-War Protester Fined After Disrupting Russian News Program."

104 Agence France-Presse in Moscow, "Russian Journalist Who Staged TV Protest over Ukraine Invasion Briefly Detained," *Guardian*, July 17, 2022, https://www.theguardian.com/world/2022/jul/18/russian-journalist-who-staged-tv-protest-over-ukraine-invasion-arrested-again.

105 "Russian Journalist Who Famously Protested Ukraine War on Live TV Sentenced for Second Protest," *Radio Free Europe/Radio Liberty's Russian Service*, October 4, 2023, https://www.rferl.org/a/russia-ovsyannikova-protest-sentenced-tv-journalist-ukraine-war/32622546.html.

106 Lucy Williamson, "Marina Ovsyannikova: Anti-war Russian Journalist Recounts Dramatic Escape," *BBC News*, February 10, 2023, https://www.bbc.com/news/world-europe-64604233. "Marina Ovsyannikova's Extraordinary

Flight from Moscow with RSF's Help," *Reporters Without Borders*, https://rsf
.org/en/marina-ovsyannikova-s-extraordinary-flight-moscow-rsf-s-help.

107   Anna Chernova and Katherina Krebs, "Russian Journalist Who Protested
       War on Live TV Says Moscow Stripped Her of Custody of Daughter," *CNN*,
       October 26, 2023, https://www.cnn.com/2023/10/27/media/russian-journal
       ist-custody-war-protest/index.html.

108   Tucker Reals, "Alexey Navalny's Message to the World 'If They Decide to Kill
       Me,' and What His Wife Wants People to Do Now," CBS, February. 17,
       2024. https://www.cbsnews.com/news/alexey-navalny-message-if-they-
       decide-to-kill-me-wife-yulia-message-today/.

109   Andrew Osborn and Filipp Lebedev, "Navalny Was Close to Being Freed in
       Prisoner Swap between Russia and West," Reuters, February 26, 2024, https://
       www.reuters.com/world/europe/navalny-was-close-being-freed-prisoner
       -swap-says-ally-2024-02-26/.

110   "This Will Lead to Our Country's Collapse," *Meduza*, March 16, 2022, https://
       meduza.io/en/feature/2022/03/16/this-will-lead-to-our-country-s-collapse.

111   George Zornick, "6 Minutes and 20 Seconds That Could Change the World,"
       Nation, March 24, 2018, https://www.thenation.com/article/archive/6-minutes
       -and-20-seconds-that-could-change-the-world/.

112   Emma González, "Speech at March for Our Lives Rally," March 24, 2018,
       https://awpc.cattcenter.iastate.edu/2018/09/26/march-for-our-lives-rally
       -march-24-2018/.

113   González, "Speech at March."

114   Frances Robles, "Where Are the Parkland Activists Today?," *New York Times*,
       July 18, 2022, https://www.nytimes.com/2022/07/18/us/x-gonzalez-parkland
       -activists-sam-fuentes.html.

115   Alexa Schapiro, "Parkland Shooting in Their Eyes," *Los Angeles Times*, High
       School Insider, March 18, 2018, https://highschool.latimes.com/champs
       -charter-high-school-of-the-arts/parkland-shooting-in-their-eyes/.

116   Schapiro, "Parkland Shooting in Their Eyes."

117   CNN staff, "Florida Student Emma Gonzalez to Lawmakers and Gun Advo-
       cates: 'We Call BS,'" CNN, February 17, 2008. https://www.cnn.com/2018
       /02/17/us/florida-student-emma-gonzalez-speech/index.html.

118   X González, "Parkland Survivor X González on Why This Generation Needs
       Gun Control," *Teen Vogue*, March 23, 2018, https://www.teenvogue.com/story
       /emma-gonzalez-parkland-gun-control-cover.

119   González, "Parkland Survivor X González on Why This Generation Needs
       Gun Control."

120   Hayley Miller, "Parkland Survivors Meet with Chicago Students to Tackle
       Gun Violence 'Beyond Gated Communities,'" Huffington Post, March 4,
       2018, https://www.huffpost.com/entry/parkland-students-chicago-gun-viole
       nce_n_5a9c17b4e4b0479c025377c9.

121   Angie Drobnic Holan and Amy Sherman, "PolitiFact's Lie of the Year:
       Online Smear Machine Tries to Take Down Parkland Students," Politifact,

December 11, 2018, https://www.politifact.com/article/2018/dec/11/politifacts -lie-year-parkland-student-conspiracies/.

122 Gianluca Mezzofiore, "No, Emma Gonzalez Did Not Tear Up a Photo of the Constitution," *CNN*, March 26, 2018, https://www.cnn.com/2018/03/26/us /emma-gonzalez-photo-doctored-trnd/index.html.

123 X González, "The Education of X González," *Cut*, January 3, 2023, https:// www.thecut.com/article/x-gonzalez-parkland-shooting-activist-essay.html.

124 González, "The Education of X González."

125 González, "The Education of X González."

126 González, "The Education of X González."

127 Emma González, "Parkland Student Emma González Opens Up About Her Fight for Gun Control," *Harpers Bazaar*, February 26, 2018, https://www .harpersbazaar.com/culture/politics/a18715714/protesting-nra-gun-control -true-story/.

Chapter 7: Fostering Fearless Speech

1 Pulin B. Nayak, "A K Dasgupta on Gandhi and the Economies of Austerity," *Economic and Political Weekly* 52, no. 50 (December 2017): 40–45, https:// www.jstor.org/stable/45132598.

2 Mohandas Gandhi, "The Gandhi Talisman," in *Mohandas Gandhi: Essential Writings*, ed. John Dear (Maryknoll, NY: Orbis Books, 2002), 190–191.

3 Coalition for the Abolition of Prostitution, "Last Girl First," accessed on April 25, 2024, https://www.cap-international.org/campaigns/the-last-girl-first/

4 Sarah Azaransky, "Jane Crow: Pauli Murray's Intersections and Antidiscrimi-nation Law," *Journal of Feminist Studies in Religion* 29, no. 1 (2013): 157.

5 Kimberlé Crenshaw, "Demarginalizing the Intersection of Race and Sex: A Black Feminist Critique of Antidiscrimination Doctrine, Feminist Theory and Antiracist Politics," *University of Chicago Legal Forum* 1989, no. 1 (1989): 149.

6 John Rawls, *A Theory of Justice: Revised Edition* (Cambridge: Harvard University Press, 1999), 266.

7 Matthew 25:40–45 (New International Version).

8 Martha Albertson Fineman, "The Vulnerable Subject: Anchoring Equality in the Human Condition," *Yale Journal of Law & Feminism* 20, no. 1 (May 2008): 11.

9 Martha Albertson Fineman, "The Vulnerable Subject and the Responsive State," *Emory Law Journal* 60, no. 2 (October 2010): 268–269.

10 Fineman, "The Vulnerable Subject: Responsive State," 269.

11 Fineman, "The Vulnerable Subject: Anchoring Equality," 15.

12 Crenshaw, "Demarginalizing," 167.

13 Angela Glover Blackwell, "The Curb-Cut Effect," *Stanford Social Innovation Review* (Winter 2017): 28, 30, https://ssir.org/articles/entry/the_curb_cut_effect.

14 Blackwell, "The Curb-Cut Effect," 28.

15 Blackwell, "The Curb-Cut Effect," 28.

16 Astra Taylor, *The People's Platform: Taking Back Power and Culture in the Digital Age* (New York: Henry Holt, 2014), 139.

17 I published a version of these suggestions in Franks, "Reforming Section 230 and Platform Liability," *Cyber Policy Recommendations for the New Administration, Stanford Cyber Policy Center,* January 27, 2021, https://fsi-live.s3.us-west -1.amazonaws.com/s3fs-public/cpc-reforming_230_mf_v2.pdf.

18 See Mary Anne Franks and Ari Ezra Waldman, "Sex, Lies, and Videotape: Deep Fakes and Free Speech Delusions," *Maryland Law Review* 78 (2019): 892.

19 *Packingham v. North Carolina*, 137 S. Ct. 1730, 1737 (2017).

20 Nancy Fraser, "Rethinking the Public Sphere: A Contribution to the Critique of Actually Existing Democracy," *Social Text* 25/26 (1990): 57.

21 Fraser, "Rethinking the Public Sphere," 57.

22 See Jürgen Habermas, *The Structural Transformation of the Public Sphere: An Inquiry into a Category of Bourgeois Society,* trans. Thomas Burger (Cambridge: MIT Press, 1991), 36.

23 Douglas Kellner, "Habermas and the Public Sphere," in *Re-Imagining Public Space: The Frankfurt School in the 21st Century,* eds. Diana Boros and James M. Glass (New York: Palgrave Macmillan, 2014), 24.

24 Fraser, "Rethinking the Public Sphere," 62.

25 Fraser, "Rethinking the Public Sphere," 66.

26 Fraser, "Rethinking the Public Sphere," 66.

27 Fraser, "Rethinking the Public Sphere," 67.

28 Jane Mansbridge, "The Long Life of Nancy Fraser's 'Rethinking the Public Sphere,'" in *Feminism, Capitalism, and Critique,* eds. Banu Bargu and Chiara Bottici (New York: Palgrave Macmillan, 2017), 106 (internal citations omitted).

29 Mansbridge, "The Long Life of Nancy Fraser's 'Rethinking the Public Sphere,'" 106.

30 See Franks, "The Miseducation of Free Speech," *Virginia Law Review* 105 (2019): 220–221.

31 *Wieman v. Updegraff*, 344 U.S. 183, 196 (1952).

32 Dena Goodman, *The Republic of Letters: A Cultural History of the French Enlightenment* (Ithaca, NY: Cornell University Press, 1994), 13–14.

33 Evelyn Gordon Bodek, "Salonières and Bluestockings: Educated Obsolescence and Germinating Feminism," *Feminist Studies* 3 (1976): 185.

34 Steven Kale, "Women's Intellectual Agency in the History of Eighteenth- and Nineteenth-Century French Salons," in *Political Ideas of Enlightenment Women,* eds. Lisa Curtis-Wendlandt, Paul Gibbard, and Karen Green (London: Ashgate Publishing Limited, 2013).

35 Justine Kolata, "A Renaissance of Salon Culture," *Public Sphere,* https://perma .cc/6C7X-JPLJ.

36 "About," MetaFilter, accessed February 27, 2024, https://www.metafilter.com /about.mefi.

37 "AskMeFi," MetaFilter, accessed February 27, 2024, https://ask.metafilter.com.

38 See Hannah Pileggi, Briana B. Morrison, and Amy Bruckman, "Deliberate Barriers to User Participation on MetaFilter," *DigitalCommons@UNO* (2014): 2, https://digitalcommons.unomaha.edu/cgi/viewcontent.cgi?article=1063&c ontext=compscifacpub.

39 Pileggi et. al., "Deliberate Barriers," 1.

40 Pileggi et. al., "Deliberate Barriers," 1.

41 Adam Fisher, "50 Best Websites 2009: MetaFilter," *Time*, August 24, 2009, https://content.time.com/time/specials/packages/article/0,28804,1918031_1 918016_1917970,00.html.

42 Matthew Ingram, "If a High-Quality Site Like Metafilter Can Be Crushed by Google, What Hope Do Other Sites Have?," *Gigaom*, May 22, 2014, https:// www.benton.org/headlines/if-high-quality-site-metafilter-can-be-crushed -google-what-hope-do-other-sites-have.

43 Caitlin Dewey, "Metafilter's Downfall Is the Perfect Metaphor for the Way We Internet Now," *Washington Post*, May 22, 2014, https://www.washington post.com/news/the-intersect/wp/2014/05/22/metafilters-downfall-is-the -perfect-metaphor-for-the-way-we-internet-now.

44 John Lewis, "Together, You Can Redeem the Soul of Our Nation," *New York Times*, July 30, 2021, https://www.nytimes.com/2020/07/30/opinion/john-lewis -civil-rights-america.html.

45 Cyndi Suarez, "White Supremacy and the Fight for the Public Square," *Nonprofit Quarterly*, August 23, 2017, https://nonprofitquarterly.org/white-suprem acy-fight-public-square/.

46 See Franks, "Beyond the Public Square: Imagining Internet Democracy," *Yale Law Journal Forum* 131 (2021): 427.

Conclusion: "I Choose My Own Way to Burn"

1 Sam Whiting, "Memories Fire Playwright's 'Magic,'" *SF Gate*, March 23, 1999, https://www.sfgate.com/performance/article/Memories-Fire-Playwright -s-Magic-Story-traces-2940665.php.

2 Heath Harrison, "75 Years Later, a Legacy of Bravery," *Ironton Tribune*, February 17, 2018, https://www.irontontribune.com/2018/02/17/75-years-later-a -legacy-of-bravery/.

3 Lillian Garrett-Groag, *The White Rose* (New York: Dramatists Play Service, 1993), 62.

4 Garrett-Groag, *The White Rose*, 62.

5 *Terminiello v. City of Chicago*, 337 U.S. 1, 4 (1949)

6 *Terminiello v. City of Chicago*, 337 U.S. 1, 35 (1949).

7 *Terminiello v. City of Chicago*, 337 U.S. 1, 35 (1949).

8 *Terminiello v. City of Chicago*, 337 U.S. 1, 35 (1949).

9   Megan Specia, "'The Power of Life and Death Is in the Tongue,' Senate Chaplain Says in a Powerful Prayer Calling for Unity," *New York Times*, January 7, 2021, https://www.nytimes.com/2021/01/07/us/politics/senate-chaplain-prayer-capitol.html.

Epilogue

1   Andrew Cain, "Virginia's Tribute to Barbara Johns a Step Closer to Statuary Hall," *Richard Times-Dispatch*, August 15, 2023, https://richmond.com/news/state-regional/government-politics/virginias-tribute-to-barbara-johns-a-step-closer-to-statuary-hall/article_0a11b3e2-3ac9-11ee-91e3-479425c6486a.html.

2   Joe Bubar, "The 16-Year-Old Who Fought Segregation," *New York Times UpFront*, April 22, 2019, https://upfront.scholastic.com/issues/2018-19/042219/the-16-year-old-who-fought-segregation.html?language=english #1120L.

3   Bubar, "The 16-Year-Old."

4   Larry Bleiberg, "Barbara Johns: The US' Forgotten Civil Rights Hero," BBC, December 12, 2022, https://www.bbc.com/travel/article/20221211-barbara-johns-the-us-forgotten-civil-rights-hero.

5   Bleiberg, "Barbara Johns."

6   Bleiberg, "Barbara Johns."

7   Bleiberg, "Barbara Johns."

8   Jonathan Simon, *Fearless Speech in the Killing State: The Power of Capital Crime Victim Speech*, 82 N.C. L. Rev. 1377, 1400–01 (2004).

Index

defamation, 14, 38, 51, 56, 63, 161, 176

Depp, Johnny, 37–41, 45, 51

DeSantis, Ron, 62–63, 67, 75

desegregation, 17, 47

Dewey, Caitlin, 172–173

disinformation, 88, 109, 147–148, 163

District of Columbia v. Heller, 90

Dixon, Thomas, Jr., 20

Dobbs v. Jackson Women's Health, 54–55

domestic violence, 32, 37–41, 45, 51, 144

Donegan, Moira, 40–41, 45

Douglas, David, 95

Douglas, William O., 138, 177

doxing, 2, 59, 64, 81, 86, 95, 97, 121, 163

Duncan, Kyle, 71

Dworkin, Andrea, 44, 48, 59

Easterbrook, Frank, 49–50

Eckford, Elizabeth, 135

Eisenstadt v. Baird, 138

Electronic Frontier Foundation, 82

Elliot, Stephen, 41

El Paso mass shooting, 84

Equal Protection Clause, 66

Eshoo, Anna, 119

Espionage Act of 1917, 9

Estes, Adam Clark, 86

Euripedes, 117–119

extremism
online, 82, 84–86, 96–98, 102, 105, 107
right-wing, 85–86
violent, 32, 85

Facebook, 80, 81, 82–85, 86–88, 91, 93, 96–98, 101

false equivalence, 26, 73–74, 163–164

Falwell, Jerry, 42, 43

Faubus, Orval, 135

fearless speech
college curriculum and, 163–164
curb-cut effect and, 156–157
"last girl first" principle and, 154–156
law school curriculum and, 164–166
parrhesia, 12, 111–119, 121, 125
public square models and, 166–173
reckless speech versus, 11–12, 112–116
technology law reform and, 158–163
See also Baird, William; Bates, Daisy; Freeman, Elizabeth "Bet"; González, X; Lu Hsiu-lien, Annette; Ovsyannikova, Marina; Thompson, Dorothy

February 28 massacre (Taiwan), 141

Federal Trade Commission (FTC), 81, 158

Feinstein, Dianne, 119

Felton, Rebecca, 8

Feminine Mystique, The (Friedan), 46

feminism, 42, 47–48, 45–51, 56, 59, 141–143, 155, 170

Fields, Dana, 112, 115, 116

"fighting words" doctrine, 51–52, 57

Fight of the Century, 23–25

Fine, Randy, 67

Fineman, Martha, 155–156

Finley, Lucinda, 57

Floyd, George, 179

Flynt, Larry, 42–44, 58

Ford, Christine Blasey, 119–122, 124

Foreman, Amanda, 35

Foucault, Michel, 113–114, 116–118

Foundation for Individual Rights and Expression (FIRE), 55, 62, 72–73

Fourteenth Amendment, 55, 66

Dr. Mary Anne Franks is a nationally and internationally recognized expert on the intersection of civil rights, free speech, and technology. She is the Eugene L. and Barbara A. Bernard Professor in Intellectual Property, Technology, and Civil Rights Law at George Washington University School of Law. Her other areas of expertise include Second Amendment law, criminal law and procedure, and family law. She is the President and Legislative and Tech Policy Director of the Cyber Civil Rights Initiative and an Affiliate Fellow of the Yale Law School Information Society Project.

She is author of *The Cult of the Constitution: Our Deadly Devotion to Guns and Free Speech* (Stanford University Press, 2019), which won a 2020 Independent Publisher Book Award Gold Medal and received the 2020 Association of American Publishers PROSE Excellence Award in Social Sciences.

Dr. Franks holds a JD from Harvard Law School as well as a doctorate and a master's degree from Oxford University, where she studied as a Rhodes Scholar. She previously taught at the University of Chicago Law School as a Bigelow Fellow and Lecturer in Law and at Harvard University as a lecturer in social studies and philosophy. She is originally from Pine Bluff, Arkansas.